THE OTHER HALF

THE
OTHER
HALF

The Life of Jacob Riis
and the World of
Immigrant America

TOM BUK-SWIENTY

Translated from the Danish by Annette Buk-Swienty

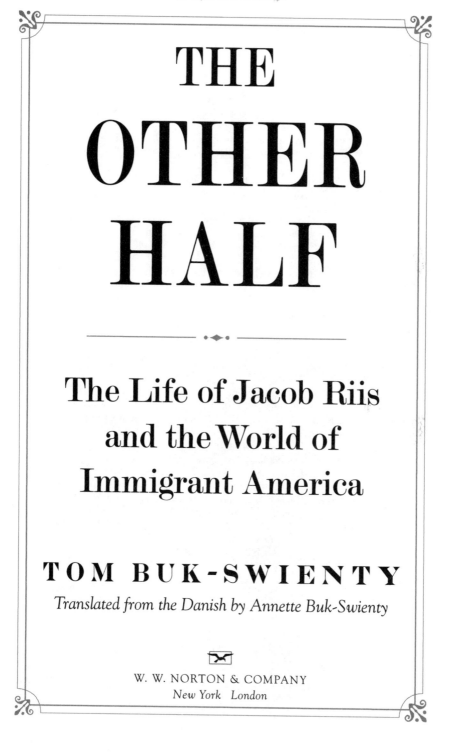

W. W. NORTON & COMPANY
New York   London

For information about permission to reproduce selections from this book,
write to Permissions, W. W. Norton & Company, Inc.,
500 Fifth Avenue, New York, NY 10110

For information about special discounts for bulk purchases, please contact
W. W. Norton Special Sales at specialsales@wwnorton.com or 800-233-4830

Manufacturing by RR Donnelley, Harrisonburg, VA
Book design by Dana Sloan
Production manager: Andrew Marasia

Library of Congress Cataloging-in-Publication Data

Buk-Swienty, Tom, 1966–
[Ideelle amerikaner. English]
The other half : the life of Jacob Riis and the world of immigrant America /
Tom Buk-Swienty ; translated from the Danish by Annette Buk-Swienty.
p. cm.
Includes bibliographical references and index.
ISBN 978-0-393-06023-2 (hardcover)
1. Riis, Jacob A. (Jacob August), 1849–1914. 2. Immigrants—New York (State)—
New York—Biography. 3. Danish Americans—New York (State)—New York—Biography.
4. Social reformers—New York (State)—New York—Biography. 5. Journalists—New York
(State)—New York—Biography. 6. Investigative reporting—New York (State)—New York.
7. New York (N.Y.)—Biography. I. Title.
CT275.R6B85 2008
974.7'043092—dc22
[B]
2008022853

W. W. Norton & Company, Inc.
500 Fifth Avenue, New York, N.Y. 10110
www.wwnorton.com

W. W. Norton & Company Ltd.
Castle House, 75/76 Wells Street, London W1T 3QT

1 2 3 4 5 6 7 8 9 0

For Annette, Alex, and Sasha,
in memory of our American years

❧ CONTENTS ❧

PART ONE:
RESTLESSNESS

PART TWO:
RIIS AND THE OTHER HALF

❦ LIST OF ILLUSTRATIONS ❦

JACOB A. RIIS, REFORMER, DEAD

Social Worker Who Was Roosevelt's "Ideal American" Succumbs to Heart Disease.

CLEARED MULBERRY BEND

Made a Name and a Career as a Police Reporter—Author of Several Books.

BARRE, Mass., May 26.—Jacob A. Riis, author, reformer, and social worker, once characterized by Theodore Roosevelt as New York's most useful citizen, died this afternoon at his Summer home here. Mr. Riis's end was peaceful. For a day or more he had been only half conscious most of the time. Although oblivious to what was going on about him, he occasionally rallied sufficiently to recognize his wife and his son, Edward, who were at his bedside. His life ended while he appeared to be sleeping.

Chronic myocarditis or degeneration of heart walls was the cause of death. For many years Mr. Riis had been subject to heart disease, but it was not until a year ago that his condition caused any concern. About two months ago he suffered a breakdown while on a lecture tour in the South, and was removed to a sanitarium at Battle Creek, Mich., where he remained for more than a month. He arrived here on May 10, but his trip proved such a strain upon his weakened heart that he collapsed in an automobile when almost in sight of his Summer home. This collapse was followed by a brief rally, and then a steady decline began.

Arrangements for the funeral, which is to be held here on Thursday, have not been completed.

━ PREFACE ━

THE FIRST TIME I heard about Jacob A. Riis, I was a Danish exchange student at the University of California at Santa Barbara. It was 1989, and I was taking an American history course on the Gilded Age and the Progressive Era, approximately covering the years from 1870 to 1914. It was during this latter part of the nineteenth century, in response to the ever-increasing divide between rich and poor, that America's first large-scale social reform movement took hold. The professor spoke at length about a Danish American journalist, one Jacob Riis, who had been one of the first muckrakers, well before that term entered the vernacular, and had written a groundbreaking book about the deplorable living conditions in New York City's tenements called *How the Other Half Lives*. It was stressed repeatedly that Riis's book, with its vivid descriptions and revolutionary photographs of abject poverty, significantly influenced the nascent reform movement.

I became perplexed. Had a Danish American really influenced American social history? My curiosity was whetted. Who *was* he? Even though I was a history major, I had never heard about this fellow Dane, who immigrated to the United States in 1870 at the age of twenty-one. I later discovered that he was relatively unknown in Denmark. Eager to learn more about my famous countryman, I went to the university library, where I found an old, worn copy of *How the Other Half Lives*, and I grew even more fascinated.

Several years went by, however, before I got a chance to study him in earnest. Five years later, in the mid-1990s, I had become the American bureau chief for a Danish newsmagazine, and was living in New York. One day my editor called me from Copenhagen and asked me to write a review of an exhibition of Jacob Riis photos at the Museum of the City of New York.

Even though I am reluctant to admit it, I was not hugely impressed that day by Riis's original photographs. Somehow I felt I had seen those images, or similar ones, so many times before. And, of course, I had. We are indeed constantly being bombarded with images of human misery and suffering to the point where we have become almost immune to their implicit cry for help.

Still, Riis and his work remained with me as I walked toward Penn Station to take the train home. I stopped at a bookstore and bought a huge and beautifully illustrated volume called *Jacob A. Riis: Photographer & Citizen*, featuring Riis's photos, a book that included a biographical chapter by Alexander Alland Sr. As darkness fell and the train began its gentle, rocking motion, I opened Alland's book and immersed myself in Riis's world. I studied the photographs closely and suddenly understood what an extraordinarily original journalist and photographer Riis was. His photos, I realized, must have been quite arresting at the time, as they on closer examination still are today.

Looking at the immigrant faces staring at you, you feel transported to a bygone era. The photographs inevitably reify their subjects' hopes and dreams, their trials and tribulations; and the very fabric of the city in both its glory and its abject distress springs to life, one's visceral response a tribute to Riis's prodigious photographic talent.

What really affected me, however, was Alland's chapter on Riis's life. I could hardly believe what I read; his story was almost incredible. It was there on that train ride home that I decided I would one day write the full story of Jacob Augustus Riis.

If an author had sat down to write Riis's story as fiction, he would undoubtedly have been criticized for stretching the truth. As if plucked from a variant Horatio Alger novel, his is the story of a poor young Dane from the isolated yet picturesque medieval town of Ribe who immigrates to the United States in 1870 because of a broken heart, nearly starves during his first months there, and is so despondent that he nearly dies. He then goes on to live what can only be described as the proverbial American dream: He starts at the bottom, struggles mightily, and then makes a living as an iron salesman. Once again, though, he loses all; then by chance he gets a job as a low-paid journalist and, in a few years, becomes a star police reporter and, finally, the author of a resounding best seller and classic, *How the Other Half Lives*. At the same time he practically invents modern photojournalism, is knighted by the Danish king, and becomes a close friend of Theodore Roosevelt. Together they fight police corruption and work to eradicate the worst slums in New York City, their herculean efforts succeeding beyond anyone's expectations.

Initially, the more adventurous aspects of Riis's life inspired me to write his biography, but as I delved deeper into his life and work, I found not only a fascinating story but also a message that has great reasonance today. It is apparent that Riis significantly influenced America's self-perception at the onset of the twentieth century. Not only did his reform work make a perceptible difference in the lives of thousands of immigrants, but his work as a photographer is widely perceived by photohistorians as revolutionary. At a time when the new barons of Wall Street force us to recall the robber barons of the Gilded Age, poverty both in America and in Europe remains an ugly reminder that all is not well. Riis forced Americans to confront the squalor of immigrant conditions, and he demanded that these immigrants not be treated as second- or third-class citizens. Both Denmark and America are faced with similar quandaries now, as they both struggle to treat today's immigrants as equal human beings.

Furthermore, Riis's personal struggle should remain of great interest to us now. Nothing ever came easy to him, and his tenacity is both admirable and inspiring. In fact, Riis never gave up. Even when all appeared hopeless, he did not falter. It is the central focus of this book to follow Riis's journey from boyhood, through the hardships of his early years, to middle age, when he reaches the pinnacle of his career as a reformer and journalist. *The Other Half* thus examines the values he brought with him from Denmark, and what motivated him to become a reformer and writer. I will, in other words, attempt to chronicle the rise of Riis, the poor young immigrant, who became Riis, the famous American muckraker.

                                                —Tom Buk-Swienty
                                                Ribe, Denmark
                                                March 2008

⇒ THE OTHER HALF ⇐

—————— • ◆ • ——————

"The Ideal American"

WORCESTER TRAIN STATION, MASSACHUSETTS, SUNDAY, May 10, 1914. It was 1:47 AM, and a train had just arrived. Four people got off, stepping slowly onto the platform and into the pitch-black New England night. One of them, Jacob Riis, an elderly gentleman with gray hair, leaned heavily on his three companions. He could barely walk, and if it had not been so dark, one would have seen how pale Riis was—the etched lines in his face and the wispy quality of his mustache. One would have also noticed his suit, which, after weeks of illness, had become several sizes too big and seemed almost to engulf him.

It had been more than two months since he had collapsed in New Orleans while on a lecture tour of the South. It was his heart—not surprisingly. Fourteen years earlier, he had been diagnosed with chronic myocarditis, inflammation of the heart muscle, and his doctors had told him to cut down on his work load, quit journalism, and, if possible, discontinue his lecture tours. If he did not, they had warned, he would not live long.

Yet even though he sometimes felt too weak to cross the street, he had not heeded their advice. He had rarely taken time off to rest and relax and had been used to working long hours ever since he was a young man. Still, it was not merely inflexible work habits that kept him on the lecture circuit: He needed the money. In 1912, he had left New York for a small farm in Massachusetts reminiscent, he hoped, of his boyhood home in Denmark, where he planned to retire and enjoy the remaining part of his life in peace. But the agricultural life produced little remuneration, and at sixty-five, he had set out on a major lecture tour, traveling the length and breadth of the country.

He was still a highly sought-after lecturer, receiving sizable fees. His lectures and slide shows depicting the lives of "the other half"—those people who were marginalized to the underbelly of society—could still move and shock audiences. He was considered one of the most influential social reformers in the United States and enjoyed considerable celebrity. With the Progressive Era in full swing, civic virtues were suddenly taken seriously, and most people agreed that an ideal citizen was someone who took active responsibility for the welfare of his fellow man and fought for social change.

Touring the country, however, quickly proved to be too much for Riis. The irrepressible zeal that had fueled him in his early years—when he faced the greatest hurdles—now failed him, and he could not overcome his advancing age and weak heart, a family illness that afflicted him as well as many of his close relatives.

In letters to his family, he often acknowledged his foolish decision to travel extensively and the deleterious effect it had on his health. But his tone was always somewhat flippant, as if he believed he could elude death by trivializing his condition. He did have reason to believe in his own transcendence, for he was a man who had accomplished the impossible more than once. He had started out poor, hopelessly and unrequitedly in love with a betrothed Danish woman. Yet he succeeded in getting everything he had ever wanted; remarkably, he managed to become an influential figure in his adopted country. Of course, as he implied in the title of his popular 1901 autobiography, *The Making of an American*, he was as influenced by America as he himself influenced the nation.

※

FOLLOWING HIS COLLAPSE in New Orleans on March 7, Riis was taken north to the Battle Creek Sanatorium in Michigan, where he had stayed previously when he had felt too weak to work. This time his doctors ordered complete bed rest, and so, for the following weeks, he focused on rest and his condition improved. The *New York Times*, which had kept its readership abreast of his condition, reported that he was out of danger. Only a few weeks later, however, the same publication reported that he was "in a more serious condition than is generally known" and that he was "devoting his energies to a battle for life." His doctors were pessimistic and again stressed the need for complete bed rest.

❈

THE THREE COMPANIONS assisting Riis off the train in Worcester were his nurse, his youngest son, and his wife, a tall, elegant woman. They had traveled from Massachusetts to Michigan to accompany him on his journey home. They all realized it was a risky undertaking. The journey would be exhausting for him, and the toughest, albeit shortest, stretch still lay ahead once he reached Worcester. An automobile waited for them at the station for the drive to Pine Brook Farm, on Hubbardston Road, in the hilly countryside near the village of Barre a couple of hours west. Their automobile had poor suspension, making the trip on the bumpy roads grueling. In fact, the ride was so rough that all four soon realized it was too much. They should have stuck to their original plan and let Riis stay overnight at the local hospital in Worcester before attempting the arduous journey to the farm. When they reached Coldbrook, a few miles from Pine Brook Farm and Harwood's Crossing, his condition had worsened considerably, and they tried to find accommodations. Fortunately, the Eagle Inn lay just down the road. The local medical officer, Walter S. Bates, tended to Riis. His condition improved overnight, and on the morning of May 11 he was moved to his farm.

He had long insisted that what he needed was simply to be home at Pine Brook. He was convinced his health would improve in this bucolic setting, where he could hear the murmuring of the creek and the chirping of the birds; where his fishing rod awaited him; where he could inhale the sweet scent of grass and spring. His doctors at Battle Creek had reluctantly agreed to discharge him, realizing it would take a miracle to cure him.

At first, the farm did appear to be a miracle cure. Shortly after his arrival, the *New York Times* reported that he was improving. The local weekly, the *Worcester Gazette*, was almost jubilant: "We are pleased to inform our readers that [he] is resting comfortably at his home, Pine Brook Farm. His condition has greatly improved since he returned to Barre, and it is hoped that he will be able to be out within a short time."

✳

No one found it strange that Riis and his family had such optimistic expectations for his recovery. It was after all spring: The blooming of the trees and flowers combined with the fresh, crisp air convinced his family that Riis would see new life yet again.

Once, many years ago, he had given gifts of spring flowers to the poor, believing that they spread joy and hope. The idea of giving flowers had come to him one morning when he had watched his own children picking flowers in the meadow by his house in Richmond Hill, then a newly settled hamlet. Clara, Katie, and John had begged him to bring these flowers to the poor on Mulberry Street, where he worked as a police reporter. Laden with daisies, he left for his office, at 301 Mulberry Street. Running on the street were the ragamuffin bands of barefooted children whom he had once described as "dirty, little, ragged savages, most of whom would dodge a kind, helping hand, thinking it meant a blow." When they saw him that morning, the "savages" nearly tore the flowers from his arms, and, within seconds, their tears, in the vernacular of muckraking journalism, had turned into smiles. Riis, who had spent most of the past ten years in the slums, was so moved by their reaction that, as he recalled in his memoirs, he sat down on the curb and wept. It was a cathartic moment for him, leading to an epiphany that would change his life and alter the American understanding of what it is to live in poverty.

If something so simple as flowers could inspire such deep emotion, Riis concluded it must be possible to battle the disease of the slums, which was eating the city from within. Astonishingly, close to a million of the city's 1.5 million residents were living in ramshackle tenements. In 1888 Riis took up the fight to educate the populace on the state of slums and combat the urban decay through informed and committed support, following up two years later with the publication of *How the Other Half Lives*. His readership was spellbound by the lively description of tenement life and the engrossing narratives of the tenement dwellers. Reviewers hailed the book as a classic almost the moment it was published, in December 1890.

❀

THE IDEAS PRESENTED in *How the Other Half Lives* were greatly influenced by a group of determined Progressive pioneer-reformers. They had worked tirelessly for the implementation of social reforms in the 1870s and 1880s, during which time the United States received 30,000–60,000 impoverished immigrants every month. As the reformers pointed out, the country was being transformed by industrialization, and they stressed that without far-reaching social change, the United States would quickly become a fertile breeding ground for revolutionary and anarchic movements.

Riis was neither the first nor, perhaps, the most original reformer, but he became unique because of his novel approach to delivering the Progressive message. He understood far better than anyone else the importance of using the press as a weapon in the battle against poverty. It was his own press campaigns that cast him in the role of muckraker. His success was in large part due to the original use of photographs, whose stark power had become evident to Riis when he had worked as an advertiser using lantern slides. Using this so-called magic lantern, a progenitor of the modern slide projector, and *Blitzlichtpulver*, or flash powder, to capture the grim interiors of the slums, Riis's shows were nothing short of sensational.

Given Riis's star reporter status, his views on the slums carried great weight and his political influence grew quickly. With the publication of *How the Other Half Lives*, he became a recognizable public figure, constantly consulted as an expert on the slums. Following the path of many celebrities of the Gilded Age, he became a topic of interest himself. In October of 1903, the *New York World* ran two interviews by Riis—one with New York's mayor, Seth Low, and the other with opposing mayoral candidate George B. McClellan Jr. The interviews were significant not because of the politicians' remarks but rather because Riis personally had conducted them. One headline, from October 18, 1903, focused on Riis, the sensation, not McClellan, the candidate: "How Jacob Riis Interviewed Candidate McClellan." The headline, of course, played on the title of *How the Other Half Lives*.

Riis's newfound status, his tireless efforts to improve the slums, which among other things involved being on many boards and committees, seemed a natural precursor to a political career, and he was often urged to enter politics and run for mayor of New York, but Riis was not interested. He preferred his role as an independent social critic, a role that, in the latter part of his career, became quite lucrative. When *The Battle with the Slum*, a sequel to *How the Other Half Lives*, was published in 1902, the *Chicago Tribune* bought the copyright. Excerpts from the book ran daily as front-page articles from March 25 to April 8, Riis's byline set in large print, with each piece earning him a staggering one thousand dollars.

A celebrity not only in America, Riis was recognized for his social justice crusades in his native Denmark. Danish papers praised him for his efforts, and the king of Denmark, Christian IX, knighted him in 1900. Riis was made Knight of the Order of Dannebrog, and at home in Richmond Hill, his neighbors affectionately started calling him Sir Jacob.

THESE TRIUMPHS, achieved two and three decades previously, seemed distant as Riis attempted a recovery at the farm outside Barre, his eldest son, George Edward Valdemar, or Ed, as he was called, at his side.

Ed returned to his home in Brooklyn with the feeling that there might still be hope for his father. Riis had offered his son a glass of spring water from a pitcher on his bedside table. The elder Riis appreciated the water's "magnificent" taste and purity, according to Ed's recollection. Riis was capable of speaking only in a raspy whisper, but he summoned his strength to admonish his son, advising him to remain true to himself. Ed tried hard to find the gruff and feisty father he knew so well but saw only tenderness and love in the face of the aged man. This conversation would be their last.

The infusion of energy that Riis enjoyed after coming home to the farm quickly dissipated. "'Slowly sinking' was the report today regarding the condition of Jacob A. Riis. . . . Mr. Riis's physician expressed the belief that he could live only a short time," the *New York Times* recorded on May 24. Even though Riis remained alive, telegrams and letters of sympathy poured in from all over the country, the influx representing readers who wanted to honor him. In a letter to the editor of the *New York Times*, a reader advocated naming a park in the tenement districts after Riis.

> *In common with other New York papers, you have recently spoken of Mulberry Bend Park. The remarkable man to whom all credit for that park is due may live but a short time. Thousands of his admirers would be gratified if the name "Jacob A. Riis Park" were given to it at the earliest possible moment.*

"Jacob Riis Is Dying," a *New York Times* headline proclaimed the following day. The subheading read: "Marked Turn for the Worse—May Live for a Few Days at Most." Shortly after his return to Brooklyn, Ed saw these dire stories and immediately decided to return to Massachusetts. He arrived in Barre the following day at 10:00 AM. One of Riis's farmhands, in town to get some horses shod, offered to take Ed back with him as soon as he had completed his errands, but intuition urged the son to go immediately. In fact, Ed came to believe that God, rather than intuition, was speaking to him. Walking at a brisk pace, Ed hiked the three miles to the farm, hoping that he would not be too late. It was unseasonably hot, and as he half-ran, half-walked down the winding dirt roads, he was reminded of the tragic day in May 1886 when his baby brother Stephen had died, only five months old. When Ed reached the farm, his father was in a coma. He had difficulty breathing, his head hanging down at an odd angle.

Riis's family remained at his side, breaking only for lunch, which was interrupted by the nurse's bell. They all understood what that meant. Fifteen minutes later Jacob A. Riis died from complications of heart disease.

His death was front-page news in papers across the country. A heartrending homage to Riis in the *Worcester Gazette* was typical: "We Loved

Him," the headline read, and the article continued, "when he chose to make our Worcester County his home and claimed citizenship with us, we loved him all the more, and now this city joins the rest of the country in lamenting the departure from this world of that eminent American, Jacob Riis."

❊

WASHINGTON, D.C., Union Station, May 28, 1914, 5:26 PM. Former President Theodore Roosevelt had just arrived by train. It was there, in Union Station, that Roosevelt first heard the news. Shocked, he ran to the station's telegraph office and wired his condolences to Riis's widow. His telegram was the first one to reach the farm.

> Mrs. Jacob A. Riis, Barre, Mass.:
> I am grieved more than I can express. I feel as if I had lost my own brother. Jake's friendship has meant more for me than I can ever say.

Roosevelt had on many previous occasions expressed his admiration and love for Riis. From the moment the two men met in 1890, they felt like comrades-in-arms. *How the Other Half Lives* had deeply moved the then thirty-one-year-old former New York congressman, who saw Riis as an ally in the battle against rampant police corruption in New York City. After reading the book, Roosevelt had gone directly to Riis's office on Mulberry Street. Although Riis was not there, Roosevelt left him a succinct note: "Read your book, and have come to help."

❊

SEVERAL YEARS LATER, when, in 1895, Roosevelt had accepted the appointment as police commissioner, Riis became his mentor and his guide to the slums, leading Roosevelt on nightly expeditions, showing him how "the other half," a staggering two-thirds of the city's population, lived. The sights Riis explored shocked the upper-class Roosevelt. The horrid conditions, previously unfathomable to Roosevelt, would influence him throughout his political career, shaping his distinctive brand of Progressivism.

Roosevelt, who was rapidly accruing political clout, became an unusually powerful ally for Riis. Together they pressured the city into tearing down the worst tenements; they brought about the closing of the lodging houses run by the corrupt and brutal police, the shelter of last resort for the poorest, often homeless men.

In subsequent years, Riis and his family were frequent guests at Roosevelt's White House and exchanged hundreds of letters. When Roosevelt, for example, stepped down as police commissioner in 1897, he wrote to Riis that he was the most "distinguished man I ever knew." After he became president, Roosevelt repeatedly hailed Riis as a model citizen, calling him "New York's most useful citizen" and "the ideal American." Riis had, according to Roosevelt, been instrumental in creating a better, more equitable America by exposing the atrocious conditions under which the other half lived.

The story, then, of how a young man, a poor carpenter from a small, isolated medieval town in Denmark who left his homeland because of a disastrous romance, only to become one of the most well-known and most admired reformers in the United States—in fact, "the ideal American," in the words of a great president—is the subject of this book.

PART ONE

◆

Restlessness

1

The Old Town

A FEW MILES INLAND from the capricious North Sea, under a wide-open sky, surrounded by acres of marshland, is the small town of Ribe. For centuries, people have simply called it the Old Town—situated in the southwest corner of Denmark, it is, in fact, the country's oldest. The Danish poet Jørgen Bukdahl wrote of Ribe in 1921: "as if fallen off history's wagon, she has stayed behind and fallen asleep; letting time pass her by, leaving her only with her dreams—dreams of the fairy-tale kind that start with 'once upon a time.'"

In order to appreciate the scope of Jacob Riis's American odyssey and the thinking that inspired his reform work, one must explore his Danish background. Without the influence of his hometown, Riis's life and career might well have taken an entirely different direction.

Nestled in what is now known as the Ribe River Valley, Ribe was a prosperous Viking settlement as early as the seventh century. The Ribe River was wide and deep enough to accommodate the flat-bottomed long ships used by the Vikings, the riverbanks were steep, to prevent flooding at high tide, and the settlement lay far enough inland to be safe from pirate attacks. However, during the eighth century, religious wars raged across the marshland, the Christians eventually winning control of the town. Archbishop Ansgar, the legendary warrior of Hamburg-

Bremen, was granted permission by the Danish king to build a church in about 860.

A period of great prosperity followed. Ribe became one of Europe's ecclesiastical centers as well as a successful regional trading hub. Cattle, driven in from the north, grazed on the tidal meadows before being sold and shipped to Germany and the Netherlands. At its peak in the eleventh century, construction began on what would become one of Europe's preeminent cathedrals, made of imported tuff and sandstone from the Rhineland. Upon completion the monumental Byzantine-Norman structure boasted a magnificent tower, which on clear days could be seen from miles away.

With the growth of the city into a cultural center, the Danish king, Valdemar the Conqueror, decided to move his court to Ribe and make it the country's capital. He oversaw the construction of Riberhus Castle, and, according to legend, it was in Ribe that Valdemar's young wife, the much-adored Queen Dagmar, died in childbirth a few years later. The royal couple's fate seemed to foreshadow Ribe's own dark future.

Ribe's decline began during the Reformation in the sixteenth century and continued during the era of royal absolutism, with power increasingly concentrated in Copenhagen. The loss of influence perhaps explains the rise of the notorious Riberret, a harsh court of law that prevailed far into the seventeenth century. The punishment for theft typically was hanging. Beheading for even minor misdemeanors, such as peddling watered-down honey, was not unusual. "In the name of decency," read one law, "female thieves must be buried alive rather than hanged" —it was considered unseemly to have female corpses dangling from the gallows, allowing passersby to look up their skirts. The custom of burning witches was common practice until the mid-seventeenth century. The last woman burned at the stake was the local tailor's wife, Maren Splid, who met her death in November 1641.

A fire in 1580 burned Ribe to the ground, but the final blow, which reduced the town to nothing more than a dot on the map, came a generation later during the devastating Swedish wars. In 1644 Swedish troops invaded and set the town on fire. Several neighborhoods were consumed and Riberhus Castle looted and burned. The town was never to retain its prosperity or its grandeur. The modern deep-keeled merchant ships could not make it upriver to Ribe because of their structure and the sanding up of the river. The soil was too poor for agriculture, and farmers remained limited to sheep and cattle husbandry.

Time seemed to stop in Ribe—all modern development passed it by, perpetuating a culture of conservatism, antimodernism, and fatalism. "When a man's time is up, you die," was a typical saying in Ribe. Keeping technological progress at bay became a stubborn pastime: Long after most Danes had made the switch to pens, Ripensers, as inhabitants of Ribe are called, continued to write with feather quills. They preferred whale oil lanterns to coal oil, which was looked upon as a dangerous innovation. Matches were seen as radical, let alone the telegraph, which finally arrived in the late 1800s. Town criers continued to mark the hour longer in Ribe than in any other town in Denmark.

Ribe's permanence did have its charms. Walking down the cobblestoned streets on a spring or summer day, one heard the rhythmic splashing of the mill's water wheel; and the sweet scents carried in on the breeze from the soft, grassy meadows cushioning the winding river flooded the senses. Visitors were encouraged to "take an evening stroll on the Slotsbanke [castle grounds] and watch the sun set over the North Sea . . . the sky turn crimson, and the big red cathedral tower set aflame in the sun's afterglow." Even today, Ribe remains unscathed by modern development. No concrete construction breaks the picturesque rhythm of the beautifully restored old homes, clustered around the towering cathedral.

However, the romantic ambiance and idyllic scenery were no bulwark against wars and a harsh environment. No dikes had been built to protect the town, which made it exceedingly vulnerable during the annual flood season of January and February. Ripensers were well aware of their vulnerability but were also, as so often happens in isolation, able to turn their weaknesses into strengths. An exceptionally strong, close-knit community prevailed in the eighteenth century, with comfort sought in familiarity. In late summer, when it was time to cut the hay in the meadows, families met on the riverbanks with their picnic baskets. During the fall and winter months, the Social Club, instituted by the wealthiest families in town, organized get-togethers. At no other time of year was community sentiment more evident than at Christmas, celebrated over a period of two weeks, with preparations—killing the goose, baking, cooking, and decorating—begun long before. Besides the traditional lunches and dinner parties there were two grand balls. One was reserved for the children, who held hands and danced around the tree, singing carols, before receiving their gifts. The ball for adults was a spectacular formal event. Then, on Christmas Eve, church bells summoned Ripensers to service in the cathedral, lit by thousands of small, flickering candles placed around the immense nave.

The memory of Christmas stayed with the children of Ribe forever, its rituals helping to foster a nostalgic sense of place that far outweighed the town's limitations: an unbending mindset, smothering conservatism, and sheer isolation. "The town is small, but my memories of it are large," wrote the Danish author H. V. Clausen. "When I remember [Ribe], I am filled with a great sense of serenity and peace," wrote one Mathilde Cold in the late nineteenth century. Inevitably, the power of ritual shaped all Ripensers, but perhaps none more powerfully than those who fled the town's unchanging vista, for in fleeing they retained an image of Ribe that was as idealized—as firmly governed by sentiment and its expression—as their earliest impressions and memories.

✖

It was said of one boy, born May 3, 1849, in a small house that belonged to Ribe Cathedral Latin School, at 1 Skolegade, that he grew obsessed with the notion of transforming New York City in Ribe's image. The idea seemed preposterous—less for its inception, however, than for the degree to which he can be said to have succeeded.

2

The Early Years

J ACOB RIIS was born in the shadow of Ribe Cathedral. From the bedroom window of his parents, Niels Edvard and Caroline Riis, the cathedral tower loomed so large it looked as if it was about to topple onto their house. Despite their proximity to the church, it would take several months before their son was baptized: The year 1849 found the Old Town drawn into one of the bloodiest wars in the country's history, bringing life to a standstill.

Part of a small Danish-ruled enclave in the German duchy of Schleswig, Ribe was at the center of an ethnic powder keg, which ignited in 1848 when Schleswig-Holstein and Lauenburg declared secession from Denmark. When war broke out, the men of Ribe formed a defense committee, vowing to defend the town at all costs. A guard was organized and the streets were barricaded. The town's only heavy artillery, two old cannons normally used for ceremonial purposes, were positioned at the city gates, and two hundred pounds of gunpowder was hurriedly purchased from the only other Danish towns in the area, Kolding and Varde. An additional thousand pounds of gunpowder was ordered from Copenhagen and 150 guns from the Danish army, head-quartered on the island of Funen in the middle of the country. These weapons never made it to Ribe, and the town attempted to arm its residents with old muskets from the local rifle club. A considerable number, left unarmed, took up scythes and began an arduous training program, using these tools as weapons.

Ribe could not defend itself against the quickly advancing, highly disciplined, and well-equipped Prussian forces supporting the German rebels, and the townspeople were forced to surrender. The Prussians effortlessly pushed back the Danish army, which retreated to Funen and Zealand. Panic spread across the undefended peninsula of Jutland, and Ribe, without putting up a fight, was promptly occupied by two Prussian companies, which, according to the local newspaper, *Ribe Stiftstidende*, were quite "civilized."

Fortunately for Denmark, Great Britain and Russia did not support the rebel duchies, and in the late summer of 1848 they forced a truce favoring Danish interests. The Prussian soldiers withdrew to the southern parts of Schleswig. In April 1849, less than a month before Caroline Riis gave birth to her third child, Denmark broke the truce, and Ribe was again thrust into war. The town prepared itself for battle, and when on May 29 news came that Prussian dragoons were headed toward Ribe, the town's women and children were evacuated to the marshlands. One of the evacuees was Caroline Riis, holding in her arms her twenty-six-day-old infant boy, soon to be named Jacob Augustus.

Niels Edvard stayed behind. One of the difficult decisions he and the remaining townsmen considered was whether or not to open the town's floodgates, an action that might have thwarted or, at the very least, postponed an invasion.

Surely both Niels Edvard and Caroline deeply regretted their recent move to this remote and war-torn area of the country. Niels Edvard, 32, a small, bookish man, and Caroline, 26, had arrived only three years before, when he was offered a position at Ribe Latin School, also known as the Cathedral School. Neither was accustomed to small-town life, having both spent their first years in the vibrant port town of Elsinore, on Zealand, known to Shakespeare lovers as the setting for *Hamlet*. Both had lived in Copenhagen as young adults. The early years of their marriage were passed in Roskilde, then a sizable town in Zealand.

Ribe had neither the sophistication of Elsinore nor the gentle landscape of Zealand, with its small farms, forests, and rolling hills. The couple was completely unprepared for what awaited them in West Jutland: the stark marshland, the unending plains, and the self-contained inwardness of their new town. "The only thing that broke the sad monotony of sand and heather—which our eyes, accustomed to Zealand, found hard to get used to—were the small rivers meandering through the neat little meadows," wrote a traveler from Zealand of his trip to Ribe in 1820. When Caroline and Niels Edvard encountered the same landscape twenty-six years later, it had barely changed. For most people from Zealand, West Jutland felt like a foreign country. A young scholar from Zealand, who lived in Ribe in the 1850s, noted that the West Jutland dialect was so heavy he could barely understand what anyone was saying.

✳

It took Niels Edvard, Caroline, and their first-born child three days to reach Ribe from Roskilde. On the first day, they sailed across the Great Belt between Zealand and Funen. After a night's rest at a small inn, they continued by coach across Funen, another full day of travel. One more, albeit shorter, boat trip across the Little Belt between Funen and Jutland followed. Upon reaching Jutland, they found an inn for the night, and on the morning of the third day, they began the last and most exhausting stretch of their journey, crossing the width of the peninsula from the east coast town of Kolding to Ribe, on the west coast. The roads were miserable and known to be the worst in the country, frequently submerged in winter because of flooding, and when the winter darkness set in and the storms raged, travelers were known to disappear without a trace on the moors.

✳

The Riises arrived in Ribe in the summer of 1846 and had only a few years to settle in before they were drawn into the war. In the end, Ribe did not suffer any great losses. The men had decided against flooding the fields, which would have killed all their livestock, a huge loss for one of the country's poorest towns. Hence Ribe was occupied again, this time by the Schleswig-Holstein rebels, who were not as "civilized" as the Prussians. The occupation was brief. In 1850 Russia and Great Britain forced Prussia out of the war, and the Danish army was able to place the rebels on the defensive. The war moved farther south, and in Ribe life returned to normal.

※

THE RIIS FAMILY grew quickly in the years following the war. Caroline, who had already borne three children, went on to have ten more in quick succession, four of whom died shortly after birth. By the time he was ten, Jacob Riis had eight thriving siblings. Niels Edvard began numbering them: The sixth child was named Peter Vilhelm Sextus and the ninth, Carl Edvard Nonus. "He was talked out of calling the twelfth child Duodecimos, because it was felt the other children would nickname him 'dozen.' How I avoided being called Tertius, I don't know. But he probably had not foreseen that so many more would follow," Riis wrote later in his memoirs.

In addition to himself, his siblings, and his parents, the family included Emma Reinsholm, the orphaned daughter of Niels Edvard's older sister Augusta Christine. Only Emma, Jacob, and a sister twelve years his junior, Sophie Hedvig, lived into adulthood. Most of the other children died of tuberculosis.

Riis was particularly close to Emma, and the two exchanged many letters after his departure for the United States. Their correspondence is among the best primary sources we have of Riis's adult life. His relationship with his older brothers Peter Ditlev and Sophus Charles was both fraught and typical. Riis, four years younger than Peter Ditlev and two years younger than Sophus, had a difficult time accepting his inferior rank in the family. He disliked not being able to assume a leadership role and hated being bossed around, a character trait that carried over into adulthood. In between fights and arguments, however, the boys reconciled and enjoyed the emotional benefits that often accrue to siblings in a large family. The household included at least one maid, who came in from Mandø, a sandy speck of an island a few miles off the coast. Servants were a must for a family of the Riises' standing, regardless of income.

❈

DURING THE 1850s, the Cathedral School, a modest but handsome
red brick building—the only baroque structure in Ribe—became too
small to house the increasing number of students and teachers. In 1856
the school moved to a new location a few streets south of the cathedral.
The teachers and their families were required to seek new lodgings as
well. Riis's father rented a small two-story red brick building on narrow,
overcrowded Sortebrødregade.

The family's new home was owned by a local grocer, J. H. Quedens,
who lived and had his store in a neighboring house. Quedens, once a
thriving businessman, had become wizened and old by the time the
Riises moved in, though in retrospect, it seemed to Jacob that Quedens
had always looked ancient. A kind and mild-mannered man, he was not
insistent on getting the rent on time. Money was always scarce, despite
Niels Edvard's position as a senior teacher. To make ends meet, he sometimes worked as an editor for the *Ribe Stiftstidende*. Since he was fluent in several languages, he also held the unique position as the town's
bottle-message reader. When a bottle with a message washed ashore, it
was Niels Edvard who, for a modest payment, read and translated it. Far
from being a rare occurrence, this throwback to another time, with its
whiff of piracy, happened often, at least in Riis's telling.

As a child, Riis responded to the family's frequent periods of acute
poverty with humor and gusto. The year he and his siblings went without winter coats, he devised a gambit to avoid embarrassment: "I tried to
organize a Spartan Society among my schoolmates, the cornerstone of
which was contempt of overcoats as plain mollycoddling," he wrote in
The Old Town. "As a means of attracting the boys there were secret pass-
words and an initiation that had to be worked at dusk in the moat by the
Castle Hill and was supposed to be very grewsome [*sic*]. It took a while,
until the mothers put a stop to it. I believe one of them who had read
Aesop's fable about the fox that had lost its tail and tried to persuade the
other foxes that it was the latest fashion, saw through my dodge."

Another winter, the Riis children wore identical green winter coats
when Niels Edvard managed to procure a large roll of green woolen fab-

ric at a reduced price. "We looked like frogs," Riis recalled, "but at least
we weren't cold." The fact that the family never starved may in part
account for Riis's insouciance. While there was not meat on the table
every day, there were always enough potatoes and mush to make a child
feel full and satisfied. The mush was served in one large bowl placed in
the center of the dining room table so that they all could reach it with
their spoons. A popular Danish dessert was sometimes served as dinner:
"I defy anyone to find a summer dish that compares with 'Rødgrød and
Fløde,' which was just currant juice and corn-starch with cream," Riis
later wrote.

Occasionally, the children were given spending money. One
Christmas, Riis, who was twelve or thirteen, received a whole mark.
Walking past Rag Hall, Ribe's poorhouse, he decided on impulse to
donate his money to one of the resident families. The mess in front
of the establishment and the unkempt, dirty-faced children were so
distasteful to him that he knocked on a door and promised a stunned
father that if he washed his children and dressed them in clean clothes,
the mark would be his.

Riis was fearless, forthright, and confident, with a social conscience
and eagerness to help set things right that awakened early. These values were instilled in him by Caroline, who believed in helping people
in need.

Riis noted repeatedly that because Ribe was so small and isolated from the rest of the country, people generally looked out for one
another, setting aside class distinctions. In truth, the social divide in
Ribe was negligible compared to other Danish towns. There was a small
upper class made up of government officials: the mayor, a district doctor, the county medical officer, the bishop, a prefect, a customs inspector, a postmaster, the councilor, and the district revenue officer. The
ministers and teachers at the Cathedral School, as well as a few landowners, merchants, and businessmen, were also considered upper class,
but apart from a handful of the most successful businessmen—a fac-
tory owner, Balthazar Giørtz; the pharmacist, Frederik H. von Støcken;
and a few merchants—there were no truly wealthy people. The salary
paid to government officials was low, most making little more than the

resident farmers, fishermen, milliners, butchers, smiths, millers, and wheelwrights.

The handful of wealthy Ripensers did not make up a socially viable class on their own. When, in 1798, they founded the Social Club—Klubben—it was open to all. According to its mission statement, the club was to "amuse with conversation, music, balls and theater." These "amusements," which always drew a big crowd, took place once a week, often accompanied by generous amounts of alcohol. The town's affluent also regularly opened their homes, especially during the dark and oppressive winter months, when the need for human warmth and comfort was pronounced.

That Ripensers provided for one another was evident in the Ribe County budget. In 1856 the town spent a total of 18,804 Danish kroner (the equivalent of 2,000 U.S. dollars); of this 3,200 was spent on relief for the poor, an amount that far exceeded the public payroll. Ribe's progressive welfare system included its so-called work establishment, which ensured work for the unemployed. The very poor also had places to go when they were hungry. In addition to a number of private charities, a public soup kitchen fed approximately twenty of the town's poorest on a daily basis.

※

THE SUGGESTION that Riis abhorred filth and grime is supported by stories of the furious energy he put into cleaning the sewer in front of his home on Sortebrødregade, a primitive, rat-infested open gutter. Riis was known to shovel out rats' nests for hours. It was, of course, a hopeless battle, but he never gave up, and his efforts earned him the nickname Jacob the Delver.

The hardworking boy, obsessively cleaning gutters, was innately restless. Even as an adult, he could not sit still for long. Riis loved outdoor activities and was a keen observer of nature and animal life. The starling was his favorite bird, and his first building project was a wooden birdcage. When his father took the cage down years after Riis had left home, he found an inscription on the back: "This box is for starlings, but, by the great horn spoon, not for sparrows."

Riis was intrigued by the stork, the town's symbol since the 1800s. He also loved watching the elegant swallows swoop down to catch insects and, like most of his friends, enjoyed hunting and fishing. He shot sparrows with his own shotgun, and on days he and his friends managed to shoot several birds, they built a fire and roasted and ate their catch. The first larger animal Riis shot was a duck. When it fell into the river without his noticing where it had landed, he waded in to retrieve it. The bird seemed to have vanished, and Riis was about to give up when he spotted it. He splashed his way across the river, grabbed the bird by the neck, and proudly carried it through town to his house, where he ceremoniously handed it to the maid. However, the animal apparently had merely fainted from fright, and it was left to the maid to slaughter it.

Although he claimed in his memoirs to have caught trout and pike in the nearby Ribe and Kongeåen rivers, it is tempting to question his ability to catch any fish:

> Drop your bait there, right at the edge of the rushes, so—a swirl and a sudden tightening of the line! Let him run, and take out your watch. Eight minutes to the dot and he is off again. That is when he turns the bait around in his mouth and swallows it, having lain by waiting for signs of treachery. Now, pull him in. Here he is!

Most details of his childhood derive from his two memoirs, *The Old Town* and *The Making of an American*. Riis was a storyteller who admittedly did not shy away from exaggeration. In *The Old Town*, he describes Ribe's police force as consisting of two night watchmen and a church usher with a wooden leg. In fact, Ribe had 28 police officers, according to local archives. Whether any sported a wooden leg is uncertain.

While such invention may simply be seen as creative writing, Riis's glorification of Ribe was rooted in more than happy childhood memories. When he published *The Making of an American* and *The Old Town*, he was already famous for his efforts to improve the conditions of the New York City slums and well known for his argument that overcrowded cities ruined people's health, whereas a healthy environment improved not only their health but their minds. Riis sought to paint as quaint a portrait of Ribe as possible, downplaying and romanticizing its drawbacks.

One of the most conspicuous examples of his embellishments was his description of Ribe's often deadly floods: "We boys caught fish in the streets of the town, while red tiles flew from the roofs all about us, and we enjoyed ourselves hugely." The floods were intense and frightening, with a recorded history of fatalities stretching back hundreds of years. In 1634, the greater part of southern Jutland, including Ribe, flooded, and 1,100 to 1,200 people were killed. The fear of another colossal storm was ever-present. A young woman, Petrea Müller, wrote of one storm, "The two-foot-high waves crashing into our living room—our death seemed imminent, and this terrifying condition lasted for five hours. No man in sight to come to our rescue. The only sound we heard from the streets was the foaming waves thrashing." Her diary entry dates from 1833. "It was a terrible storm, and the full moon shed light on this horrible sight."

✳

ONE TRAGIC EVENT that Riis chose not to embellish or gloss over occurred on a summer day in 1860 near the house on Sortebrødregade. Kølholt Slippe was a narrow, six-foot-wide alley between the Riis home and a neighboring house. The children loved to play in the murky alley after a hard rain, when the sound of gushing water filled the air, but, as Riis discovered at the age of eleven, it wielded a strong and destructive power.

Kølholt Slippe led down to the Ribe River. Even today it exerts its pull, although a fence barricades the alley. On July 6, 1860, there was no fence, and Riis's nine-year-old brother, Theodore, fell into the water and went under. A neighbor shouted with prophetic fatalism: "He has departed!" Eight days later, searchers found Theodore's nearly decomposed body. Caroline Riis never recovered from the loss. Though she mourned the death of each of her children, Theodore's seemed particularly hard to bear. For years she kept his chair at the dining room table, often looking mournfully at it during dinner.

For the children, the tragedy took its place among the other events of their lives, and they began playing in the alley again. They were so accustomed to losing siblings, "it became but a shadow," wrote Emma Reinsholm many years later. However, Riis's heartbreaking version of the event in *The Old Town*, a book written to pay homage to Ribe, bears out how saddened and shocked the eleven-year-old was by Theodore's dramatic death.

Other sources confirm how difficult it was for the family to overcome the untimely deaths of ten of their children. In an interview in 2003, Angla Kuhlman, a grandchild of Sofie Hedvig Riis, said, "Every time my great-grandmother would look at her kids, her eyes would tear up because it pained her to think of the ones she had lost." In a letter to his doctor outlining his medical history, Riis made reference to his childhood home as "a poisoned old house." A chronological list of the children's deaths is testament to the sheer persistence and regularity of this particular form of sorrow in the household: 1853, Johan, five days old; 1857, Augusta Matilda, fifteen days old; 1860, Theodore Emil, nine years old; 1860, a stillborn; 1869, Henry Emil, five years old; 1870, Charlotte Emilie, fifteen years old; 1874, Sofus Charles, twenty-seven years old; 1875, Peter Ditlev, thirty years old; 1879, Carl Edvard Nonus, twenty years old; 1880, Theodore Frederic, nineteen years old.

As a reformer Riis was particularly interested in children's needs. He knew only too well how quickly even a young life could be extinguished, and it formed the basis of his conviction that, as a human race, the least we can do is to ensure our children a healthy upbringing.

※

RIIS'S INCLINATION to romanticize his childhood helps explain his father's relative absence from the memoirs. Niels Edvard was exceedingly hard on his children, a tough disciplinarian both at school and at home. A small, sinewy man who had worked hard to climb the social ladder and perhaps to cover up the insecurities commonly associated with upward mobility, he became controlling, uncompromising, and fastidious. According to school historian Bjørn Kornerup, he "was known to be an unbending grammatical nitpicker, who lacked a deeper understanding of ancient culture." The elder Riis was so inflexible "it harmed the school's reputation, and [he] was passed over for school principal in 1874."

Niels Edvard was not born into poverty. His grandfather, Niels Johansen Riis, was a country lawyer in the small Zealand town of Slangerup, and his parents, Ditlev Godthard and Charlotte Claudine Riis, were prosperous farmers. In 1812 they bought a house in Elsinore for the considerable sum of 9,369 kroner. Their wealth, however, could not change their social status. Because Ditlev and Charlotte made their money from farming and distilling and selling schnapps, they were forever trapped in the lower echelons of society.

Both longed to move up in society. Charlotte's father, Adrian Werleigh, also a lawyer, had brought his daughter up to succeed. She was "a small, elegant woman, who, even though she served her grandchildren schnapps when they came visiting, was quite refined and would often recite poetry," wrote Emma Reinsholm. The couple had great aspirations for their four children, hoping they would surpass their parents in education and social standing. Niels Edvard, their third child, was born on March 18, 1817. He showed an aptitude for learning, and his parents did everything they could to support him in his studies, even building him a small study in the back yard.

He fulfilled his parents' expectations, graduating in 1833 from grammar school with honors and attending a high school for the gifted in Elsinore, Den Lærde Skole. In 1838 he was accepted at the University of Copenhagen, where he majored in classical philology. As was the custom for students of limited means, he lived in a room at Regensen, a dormitory in downtown Copenhagen.

Ditlev did not live to witness his son's entry into high school, dying in 1832. "One morning he came in from the fields very sick with chest pains. Charlotte advised he try sleeping on the other side. . . . He immediately felt better. But when she asked him how he was feeling the next morning, he didn't answer. He was dead." He had a weak heart, a condition that was to become a family curse. Charlotte saw her son start at university but died four years before his graduation, in May 1844.

Immediately following graduation, having mastered Latin, Greek, and the principal European languages, Niels Edvard was hired as a teacher at a grammar school in Roskilde, where his students soon learned to fear him. His gaze behind his oval glasses was direct, his expression stern, and a smile never seemed to cross his thin face. In private he could be gentle and affectionate, even sentimental. He wrote songs for family parties and enjoyed writing romantic short stories, with titles like "Clement's Love" and "Only a Telegram." Once he even permitted himself an emotional public outburst: On arriving in Copenhagen in the late 1830s, he on one occasion told his students, he had felt so utterly alone in the world that he had collapsed on his suitcases and cried. However, such moments were rare. As an adult he always wore a mask of brusque seriousness and seemed unable to forgive the smallest infractions.

He was obsessed with his children's education—he wanted them to excel in their studies and attend university and had especially high expectations of Riis. "Of all my sons, Jacob is the smartest," he was fre-quently heard to say. Still, though Riis was an intelligent and bookish child, he was a great disappointment to his father.

An avid reader, Riis learned English at an early age and ran through Charles Dickens, whose paper *All Year Round* was delivered to the house; other favorites were James Fenimore Cooper and Hans Christian Andersen. All three greatly influenced Riis: Andersen and Dickens were, in entirely different ways, writers who sharpened Riis's social con-science, whereas Cooper's romanticized frontier novels planted in Riis a dream of America, which he envisioned as a vast wilderness inhabited by noble, bloodthirsty savages and a handful of civilized white pioneers. Riis's fondness for stories led to his first job on a newspaper. During the periods when Niels Edvard worked as an editor for the *Ribe Stiftstidende*, Riis assisted him. As Riis explained to Emma: "I helped Father read-ing proofs and I brought the paper back and forth from the office to our house. It was my first job in the news business, and even though it was insignificant and quite boring, I much preferred it to homework."

Working together at the paper did not bring father and son any closer. Riis detested his father's off-putting manner and rebelled against him at every turn. Doing poorly at school was undoubtedly his most effective act of disobedience. Riis's school years were from the begin-ning a failure. On his first day the maid had to drag him kicking and screaming to the schoolhouse. By way of punishment and to give him a chance to cool off, Riis was thrown into a pigsty next to the schoolhouse. According to Cathedral School records, Riis constantly got into trouble. On September 11, 1861, his behavior was so unacceptable that a Mr. Trugaard "found it wise to send him out of the class room." He regularly forgot his books and pencils and failed to complete his homework. In the school year 1862–63, Riis ranked only eighth in a class of nine students, or disciples, as they were called. His poor performance resulted in his having to repeat fourth grade, a humiliation for his father. Repeating the grade did nothing to improve Riis's academic standing; by the end of that year, he ranked seventh out of seven disciples.

The school's Disciplinary Provisions, though hardly more draconian than most, ensured the failure of a rambunctious boy like Riis, of course, even before he had crossed the threshold of the building:

> *Disciples must arrive promptly: in the morning at five minutes to eight, in the afternoon [after lunch] at exactly 2:00 PM. Everyone must take his seat immediately after entering the class room and remain quiet. There must be no running or talking in class, which must at all times be calm and orderly. . . . During recess there must be no unseemly shouting or ruckus in the hallways. Violations of the school rules will be punished in accordance with the nature of the misdemeanor. For serious violations the disciple will receive corporal punishment or be suspended.*

Beyond the rules, the long hours were intolerable. Riis had almost forty hours of school per week, starting in the first grade. In fourth grade he had nine Latin lessons, five Greek. He hated both subjects. There were only two lessons per week in Danish and geography, which he loved.

Niels Edvard was incensed by his son's poor performance and spanked him when he came home with bad report cards. Corporal punishment thus became an integral part of Riis's childhood, as it was for many children. Riis eventually came to believe that spanking was good for him and for children in general. It was a belief he maintained into adulthood and put into practice as a father. "It is merely harking back to personal experience that I sometimes think a boy is just pining for a whipping and won't be happy till he gets it," he wrote in *The Old Town*.

Although the harsh punishments may have been cathartic for Riis, they failed to achieve their objective. His behavior did not improve; on the contrary, it became worse. It was a vicious circle, and Niels Edvard only alienated his son, making him as stubborn and inflexible as he was himself. Once, in adulthood, Emma asked Riis why he had not tried harder in school. "I do not know what devil possessed me and made me always disappoint him," Riis answered. In a letter to Riis's daughter, written a few years after his death, Emma reflected upon Riis's poor behavior in school. "I think his father Niels Edvard was strict and at times too strict."

The correspondence between father and son in the years after Riis moved to the United States illustrates that Niels Edvard remained strict and difficult to please. In almost every letter to his son there is criticism or condescension. Newly appointed editor of the *South Brooklyn News*, Riis immediately dispatched copies of the paper to Denmark. Niels Edvard's only response was that he learned nothing new from the publication. When Riis had become a best-selling author, the old teacher, still wielding a red pen, found cause, now grudgingly, to criticize: "I've only found two misprints," he wrote in reaction to *How the Other Half Lives*.

❋

RIIS'S RELATIONSHIP with his mother was exceptionally close. He loved her deeply, and Caroline, as she did all her children, loved Riis unconditionally.

Born in 1823, Caroline Bendsine Lundholm was the daughter of Peter Vilhelm and Sophie Hedvig Lundholm. Peter Vilhelm, known as P. V., managed the powder magazines at Kronborg Castle. Caroline was born there and spent her first years playing within its massive walls, a gentle girl with large, kind eyes and a round face. During the greater part of the Napoleonic Wars the Lundholms lived at the castle, which played a strategic role in Denmark's defense. The country's alliance with France became a costly affair, ultimately leading to national bankruptcy in 1813. The powder magazines were closed in 1828, and, with six children, P. V. and Sophie bought a bakery in Elsinore. It prospered, but only for a time.

The family moved to Copenhagen, hoping for better luck, but a miserable existence awaited them there, and they lived out the rest of their lives in abject poverty. Still, they somehow managed to send their daughter to Schmidt's finishing school, where she trained to become a governess. That she was able to graduate was as remarkable as her eventual marriage to a man with a university degree. In all likelihood, it was the intense struggle for upward mobility that formed the basis of the attraction between Caroline and Niels Edvard.

※

DESPITE HUMBLE ORIGINS and great misfortune, the Riises and the Lundholms had managed to make a better life for their children. Both families believed in the value of education and went to great lengths to ensure that their offspring could attend the best schools. As parents, Caroline and Niels Edvard's efforts to carry on this tradition failed when it came to Jacob. With ill-disguised irritation on his father's part and with loving concern on his mother's, Riis's parents were forced to acknowledge that he was an incurable dreamer.

3

Heartache

I N THE DECADES following the Napoleonic Wars, Denmark slowly got back on its feet. In 1850 the country emerged victorious from the First Schleswig War, and economic boom times followed, an upswing that brought industrialization to Ribe. An iron foundry, employing seventeen people, was built in 1848 by H. von Støcken, whose pharmacy had prospered. A salt works, a lime kiln, and several dye works followed within the next decade.

The most successful of the new generation of industrialists was Balthasar Giørtz, who had taken over his father's textile mill in 1858. When the mill opened for production in 1850, it had twenty-one steam-powered weaving machines, imported from England. By the time it was passed on to Giørtz, the number of machines had climbed to eighty, there were sixty-five employees, and it was by far the largest business in town. By Ribe standards Giørtz, with an annual income of about 6,000 Danish kroner, was a phenomenally wealthy man. In 1863, he began construction of a spectacular brick mansion in the center of town. Designed by the nationally renowned architect Lauritz Albert Winstrup and built in the Dutch renaissance style, with light sandstone frescoes, its resemblance to King Christian IV's Rosenborg Castle in Copenhagen and to his country seat, Frederiksborg Castle in northern Zealand, earned it the name The Castle.

The mansion, set on a small hill, had gently sloped gardens that extended down to the Ribe River. The crown jewel of the grounds was an ornate gazebo. Across the river, from the second floor of their modest dwelling on Sortebrødregade, Riis had a clear view of The Castle. In the years to come he would spend countless hours gazing longingly at the imposing structure.

When The Castle was completed, in 1864, Giørtz decided he was ready to expand the mill. Among those who worked on the addition was the fifteen-year-old Riis, who had dropped out of school and decided to take up a vocational training position. Niels Edvard, resigned to the fact that Riis was unfit for school, accepted his son's decision to apprentice as a carpenter.

✳

AROUND THE TIME Riis left school, the Second Schleswig War broke out. As before, control of the duchies of Schleswig-Holstein was at issue. This second war left Denmark devastated, the size of the kingdom reduced by a third. Jutland was rendered defenseless early in the war when the ill-equipped and vastly outnumbered Danish troops were forced to retreat from their positions along the Dannevirke, a fortification line running the width of the peninsula, to a flank position at Dybbøl, on the east coast of southern Jutland. Panic spread, and Ribe once again considered barricading the town in an attempt to defend itself. As everyone knew, it was a hopeless endeavor, and nothing came of these heroic plans.

On April 18, 1864, the Danish forces at Dybbøl suffered a crushing defeat, and soon German forces entered Ribe. "[German troops] ravaged [the town of] Møgeltønder before they came to Ribe with demands that the town pay them 50,000 kroner, a demand with which our local authorities refused to comply," the Ribe Stiftstidende reported. "In response the enemy soldiers arrested ten of the town's most outstanding citizens." They were quickly released, however, and the Danish flag was raised. A few days later the German troops left, but they returned with reinforcements—350 soldiers. According to the *Stiftstidende*, "An enemy soldier and officer's servant entered the house of farmer Otto Bederfen demanding a beer. Because he did not comply fast enough, he was shot through the head." The paper reported that the perpetrator had been captured and shot. In fact, he had only been thrown in detention, according to a disclaimer published two days later.

The Second Schleswig War scarred Denmark deeply, and Riis, a fervent patriot, never forgave the Germans. For Riis, perhaps the gravest insult was a Catholic Mass celebrated by German soldiers in Ribe Cathedral. The memory of this event remained with Riis for the rest of his life. Like many of his peers, he had longed to join the Danish army and fight for his country, but he had been forced to accept the fact that he was too young to enlist.

Still just fifteen, Riis was to experience within the space of several months both the ravages of war and the pain of first love when he became completely besotted with Elisabeth Dorothea Nielsen, known in Ribe as Elisabeth Giørtz. Only twelve years old when Riis fell in love with her, Elisabeth was ravishing, with golden curls, a beguiling smile, and, according to all who knew her, a cheerful, imperturbable nature. She was also the foster child of Balthasar Giørtz, Riis's employer.

※

BORN IN THE JUTLAND town of Herning on June 5, 1852, to a solicitor, Niels Christian Nielsen, and Elisabeth Titusine von Beissenhertz, the young girl was only three when her utterly incompatible parents obtained a divorce, highly irregular at the time. Elisabeth never saw her father again. His life spiraled out of control and he died years later impoverished, blind, and alone. Elisabeth was taken in by her aunt, Clara Giørtz, Balthasar's wife. To spare the child grief, Clara withheld from her the truth about her parents, their divorce, and her adoption into the Giørtz family. Instead, Elisabeth was made to believe that her father had died young without leaving his wife and daughter enough to get by, necessitating her adoption. Elisabeth never questioned the validity of the story, and for the rest of her life, when asked about her adoption, she would explain how her father's death had forced her mother to give her up. Her mother had actually managed quite well. For many years she was the manager of a school in Kolding. The reasons for her choosing to leave her daughter with her sister are a mystery. Notwithstanding Elisabeth's start in life, "I am so happy, I don't know what to do," she would often say to Clara, whom she called Mother. The Giørtzes, who had been unable to have children of their own, adored Elisabeth, whose beauty and charm impressed everyone she met. The object of many boyhood infatuations, she exuded a confidence that was just shy of audacity. The first time Riis saw her, he was taking a lunch break at her father's new mill. Riis would later come to view this encounter as one of the pivotal moments in his life, and he chose to open *The Making of an American* with a poetic recollection of the meeting:

> *On the outskirts of the ancient town of Ribe . . . a wooden bridge spanned the Nibs River when I was a boy—a frail structure, with twin arches like the humps of a dromedary, for boats to go under. Upon it my story begins. The bridge is long since gone. The grass-grown lane that knew our romping feet leads nowhere now. But in my memory it is all as it was that day nearly forty years ago, and it is always summer there. The bees are droning among the forget-me-nots that grow along the shore, and the swans arch their necks in the limpid stream. The clatter of the mill-wheel down at the dam comes up with a drowsy hum; the sweet smells of meadow and field are in the air.*
>
> *On the bridge a boy and a girl have met. He whistles a tune, boy-fashion, with worsted jacket slung across his arm, on his way home from the carpenter shop to his midday meal. When she has passed, he stands looking after her, all the music gone out of him. At the other end of the bridge she turns with the feeling that he is looking, and, when she sees that he is, goes on with a little toss of her pretty head. As she stands one brief moment there with the roguish look, she is to stand in his heart forever—a sweet girlish figure, in a jacket of gray, black embroidered, with schoolbooks and pretty bronzed boots . . .*

It was love at first sight for Riis, and he felt as if his life as he had known it vanished forever. From the moment he saw Elisabeth on that bridge, all his thoughts were focused on her. He daydreamed about marrying her, his every action geared toward making his dream come true.

The next time Riis saw Elisabeth, he was wielding an ax, and she was balancing on a beam a few feet away. Her presence made him so nervous that he sliced his shin with the tool. The third time he saw her, he accidentally chopped off the tip of his forefinger. A doctor was able to reattach it, but the finger remained stiff and unbendable for the rest of Riis's life. On their fourth meeting, he fell off a scaffold and twisted his arm.

Though Riis was always painfully aware of Elisabeth, she never seemed to notice him. To her he was nothing more than a worker in her father's employ, and despite the relative egalitarianism of Ribe, she could not consider him in any other way; she was, after all, the daughter of the richest man in town. Had he been strikingly handsome, perhaps he would have stood a chance. Despite Riis's beautiful, bright blue eyes, he was not considered handsome in his youth. Nor was he physically prepossessing, with his 5'3" frame and slight build. Yet Riis pursued Elisabeth. He began by taking classes at her dance school. As the oldest boy, he had the privilege of choosing his partner first, and, of course, he always chose Elisabeth. Riis was a terribly clumsy dancer, and his attentions only exasperated her. His frustration led to an uncontrolled outburst at the year-end ball. Custom dictated that the young dance students had the floor until midnight, at which point the adults took over. A couple of minutes before midnight, an eager Balthasar Giørtz stepped onto the floor, and Riis ordered him to wait his turn. Giørtz stood his ground in the face of the young man's impudence, and Riis, enraged, struck Giørtz. He was as shocked as anyone by his own behavior: ". . . how I could do such a thing is beyond me, except on the principle laid down by Mr. Dooley that when a man is in love, he is looking for a fight all around." The incident may well have been what prompted Riis to decide to start his apprenticeship as a carpenter in Copenhagen.

�֍

HE ARRIVED in Copenhagen on May 1, 1865, a year after Denmark's humiliating defeat by the Germans in the Second Schleswig War. Masses of Danish refugees from Schleswig had descended upon the city, and a 10 percent unemployment rate and overcrowding had given rise to enormous problems. With 170,000 inhabitants, Copenhagen was the most densely populated city in Scandinavia, but it still had the services of only a small town. Fearing attacks on the city, the military had deferred plans of expansion beyond the city ramparts until the 1850s.

By day large streams of people navigated the narrow, crooked streets, and at night the poorest squeezed into tiny apartments, many living in slumlike conditions. As the population continued to grow at an explosive rate, rents skyrocketed, and increasing numbers of families were forced to cram into smaller and smaller spaces. Congestion and primitive sewage produced a cholera epidemic in 1853, which killed 5,000. Only then did the king and his generals finally decide, in the late 1850s, that expanding the city beyond its walls was imperative. When Riis arrived in the mid-1860s, however, most of Copenhagen was still within the medieval city ramparts. Amid burgeoning industrialization, an ever-increasing number of smokestacks broke the skyline of green copper roofs, church steeples, and neoclassic buildings, but the city still seemed undecided about what kind of place it wanted to be, a small town or a metropolis. Artisan shops and schnapps distilleries abounded, the latter lending a distinct country feel. Pulp left over from distillation could be used as cow fodder, and, loath to let it go to waste, the distilleries typically kept cattle, the creatures' chronic inebriation a source of homegrown humor.

Riis was surprisingly quiet about the years he spent in Copenhagen. There is no mention of the slums or the homeless; instead he talked about his stay in the same lighthearted, almost folkloric tone he used to describe his childhood and school years in Ribe. According to his memoirs, three days after his arrival in Copenhagen, he chanced unknowingly on King Christian IX, with whom he struck up a conversation. The encounter took place at the Charlottenborg Art Gallery, which Riis was visiting with his brother Sophus Charles, a medical student in Copenhagen. Riis had wandered off alone into a restricted area when a distinguished man in an elegant blue tailored coat offered to escort him back to the main part of the museum. Riis told him about his plans for the future, his schooling, and his father, the senior teacher, whom he felt sure the gentleman knew by name. When Riis was safely back in the main part of the gallery and had rejoined his brother, he told him of his conversation, pointing the man out. Sophus Charles exclaimed: "You don't mean to say he was your guide? Why, that was the King, boy!" Another time, Riis and a few friends met and harassed an elderly Hans Christian Andersen, out for an evening stroll. They kept circling the famous writer and, each time they passed, took off their hats and bade him good evening. It was dusk, so Andersen did not notice that he repeatedly was greeted by and shook hands with the same young men: ". . . we [went] away gleefully chuckling and withal secretly ashamed of ourselves. He was in such an evident delight at our homage."

Perhaps Copenhagen did not make a great impression on Riis because his stay there was temporary, he was not thrilled about his work, and the city was not particularly welcoming to strangers. Riis was also still obsessed with Elisabeth, the brawl between him and Giørtz and his subsequent exile having done nothing to cool his feelings for her.

Shortly after Riis had settled in Copenhagen, Elisabeth visited the city with her father. Riis called on them at their hotel. He brought gloves, intending to "forget" them so he had an excuse to visit again. Giørtz returned the gloves by courier.

Riis soon got another opportunity to court his beloved. In 1867 Elisabeth was sent to Copenhagen to attend a finishing school owned by the formidable Nathalie Zahle. She was escorted to school every day by her cousin, Christian Middelboe, a lieutenant in the navy. "A real sailor," Elisabeth wrote to her friend Christine Bendtsen, whose father served as principal of the Cathedral School, the position for which Niels Edvard Riis had been passed over, "who looks great in uniform, and whom I really like a great deal." Riis was jealous and spied on the couple, following them at close range. Eventually, he found the courage to ask Middelboe about the relationship between him and Elisabeth. Although Middelboe assured Riis that he and Elisabeth were just friends, Riis suffered anxiety over each of Elisabeth's flirtations. Elisabeth wrote to a friend of Frederik Moe, a minister's son from Ribe, with whom she had fallen in love, "He is the person dearest to my heart, and you will understand just how much I miss him."

Her love for Moe, however, did not last long and seems never to have been of much consequence to her, as were few things or people in her privileged existence. She moved in a rarefied circle in Copenhagen, had a select group of friends, and looked with interest upon the young men she met at the many parties she attended. Bernhard, a friend of Christian Middelboe's, was "quite adorable and [has] a lovely singing voice." The chatty, carefree tone of her letters shows a young woman happily immersed in her busy social life. "You wouldn't believe the number of parties and events I attend here, when I come home, we must shake up the old place and have parties both at my house and in Puggaard Street," she wrote Christine Bendtsen.

❋

WHILE RIIS spent his time working, Elisabeth took classes in French, German, English, history, biology, and music. She was an accomplished pianist. French conversation was one of her most demanding subjects. Her teacher, Mademoiselle Janoski, from Poland, did not speak any Danish, "so, we really have to work hard in her classes," wrote Elisabeth.

A conscientious student, she always did her homework and managed to make a favorable impression on Nathalie Zahle. In her evaluation of Elisabeth, Zahle wrote: "[she] has always shown a great interest in her classes and worked with increasing diligence. Her fluency in foreign languages is satisfactory, English especially. In history and Danish essay writing, however, her skills are affected by her youth and lack of prior guidance." Zahle concluded by saying, "with her open mind and charming personality, she has been a delightful student to work with, and we [at the school] will always remember her with pleasure."

In her letters home, Elisabeth mentioned many names, old and new, but never Riis, who was simply of no interest to her. Yet he continued to admire and court her, sending her flowers when she was sick—which she promptly discarded to avoid her friends' teasing. Her rebuffs only made her more attractive to him: "She is among the prettiest girls in Copenhagen, which is full of pretty girls." His obsession was so intense that he once interrupted a theater performance because one of the actresses—about to be attacked in the play—bore an uncanny resemblance to Elisabeth. In the audience were King Christian IX and the king of Greece. When Riis leapt out of his seat and onto the stage to save the young woman, he was thrown out of the theater.

Elisabeth finished her schooling in May 1869 and returned to Ribe. Five months later Riis concluded his apprenticeship as a carpenter and hurried home. It was now or never, he decided: Now twenty, he would propose to the seventeen-year-old Elisabeth. It was obviously an absurd plan, but at least he had the sense not to approach her in person. He also knew that the doors to The Castle were closed to him. Instead he declared his intentions in a letter, which his mother delivered on October 17, 1869, to Clara Giørtz, who in turn gave it to Elisabeth with these words: "I don't have to tell you that your father and I will not agree to this marriage until Jacob can provide properly for a family."

※

THE DAY MARKED a turning point for Riis, and for many years he believed it to be one of the most consequential in his life. He waited alone, at home, for Elisabeth's reply, pacing up and down the small rooms of the house on Sortebrødregade, lying down on his bed, then getting up again and continuing his pacing. It was as if time had stopped or slowed down. Each tick of the clock, as he wrote one year later, "bruised my heart." He knew she was reading his letter, or maybe she had already read it and dispatched one of the servants with her answer: "It was a terrible time for me. I thought it would never end."

When Elisabeth's response arrived, it was late afternoon and already dark. The messenger handed him a sealed envelope, which he took with trembling hands. Among the thoughts that rushed through his mind, he later wrote, was that her hand had, moments before, touched this paper: "Letter in hand, kissing it, I knelt and prayed. Oh, how I prayed I would read the answer I so desired in that letter."

When he opened the letter a surge of fatigue swept over him. Elisabeth's neat handwriting, he wrote, crushed all his hopes and dreams for the future. She had been moved by his beautiful words, she told him; she had even been moved to tears. But she was never in doubt of her answer—and she was completely honest with him. "Jacob," she wrote, "I will never be able to love you."

For almost five years he had been convincing himself that it was only a matter of time before she would fall in love with him. He had been sure that, once he completed his apprenticeship and got a job, she would say yes. Knowing that he would one day share his life with Elisabeth had been his sole motivation for finishing his vocational training. Incredibly, he was not prepared for rejection.

Riis's parents, too, were devastated. The sympathy displayed even by Niels Edvard, who had admonished his son to give up his hopeless dreams of Elisabeth time and again, was heartfelt and profound.

Riis spent a grim winter in Ribe. Though they could ill afford it, his parents allowed their unemployed son to live at home. With Ribe still suffering economic hardship in the wake of Denmark's lost war, Riis found himself unable to get work. Caroline and Niels Edvard looked on helplessly as he sank into depression. The death of his sister Charlotte Emilie, from consumption, added to the family's heartache. Riis spent much of his time at the local tavern, lamenting his fate to anyone willing to listen. Luckily, he had many caring friends: Making friends had always been easy for him, as people were naturally drawn to his high energy. In the spring, as the days grew lighter, Riis's determination and drive began to resurface, as did his innate restlessness—the restlessness that had made it impossible for him to sit still in school—and the undaunted drive that had given him the resilience to pursue the indifferent Elisabeth for five years.

※

THERE WAS a mantel clock in the house on Sortebrødregade, made in Waterbury, Connecticut. As a boy Riis had often looked at it and wondered what kind of place Waterbury, Connecticut, was. As the April sun shone upon the frozen ground, he came up with a magnificent plan: America. His position in Ribe untenable now even to him, he would go to America.

4

--- • ◆ • ---

"A Terrible
Homesickness"

THOUGH RIIS'S DECISION to emigrate was primarily motivated by his desire to distance himself from Elisabeth, he was also
inspired by the times. The mid- to late nineteenth century saw the largest wave of immigration in world history, as hundreds of thousands of
starving Irishmen fled the potato famine of 1845 for the United States,
followed a few years later by German farmers and skilled workers.
Although the majority were forced by circumstances to abandon their
homelands and embark on the strenuous voyage to America, where an
uncertain future awaited, others, not unlike Riis, were stirred by restlessness and a love of adventure.

By 1860, the United States received about a hundred thousand
immigrants every year. There was a slight lull during the Civil War, but
as soon as the last shot was fired at Appomattox, a new stream of immigrants, increasingly from Scandinavia, began pouring in.

Immigration laws placed no restrictions on the number of European
settlers, and in 1862 Congress passed the Homestead Act, which offered
160 acres in return for a promise to farm the land for a minimum of
five years. The idea was to populate the West and transform the United
States into a vast farming empire. The country, however, was moving in
an entirely different direction, becoming a more urban and industrial-

ized nation. The majority of immigrants did not set up homesteads but looked for work in the industrial East, where manpower was in great demand.

The railroad industry in particular needed laborers. Tracks were laid with astonishing speed; a network of 35,000 miles was in place by the onset of the Civil War. After the war, hundreds of new private railroad companies shot up, backed by as many new banks, and soon even the smallest towns were connected by rail. By 1869, Americans could take the train from coast to coast.

Other industries kept pace. At shipyards, steamships were built at almost assembly-line speed, and at urban factories, locomotives and railroad cars were produced in large numbers to meet the increasing demands of the expanding rail system. The growing number of larger and larger factories required enormous resources, chief among them iron ore. The mining industry flourished, mines scarring the landscapes of West Virginia, Pennsylvania, Montana, and Colorado.

Coal, coke, gas, and petroleum were needed to fuel the new industries, and there was big money to be made in the fuel industry. In 1870, the year Riis arrived in New York, a young businessman named John D. Rockefeller saw the financial potential and founded American Standard Oil. Another young man, J. P. Morgan, joined forces with a bank in Philadelphia. Within a decade, the phenomenal success of Rockefeller, Morgan, and a Scottish immigrant named Andrew Carnegie, already a force in the steel industry, spawned a generation of robber barons whose exploits soon overshadowed those of Cornelius "Commodore" Vanderbilt, Jim Fisk, Jay Gould, Jay Cooke, and George W. Pullman, industrialists who had reigned supreme when Riis first set foot on American soil. The United States had leapt into the era Mark Twain and Warner Dudley called, with great sarcasm, the Gilded Age, a time of social Darwinism in which gigantic fortunes were made by a handful of men while millions merely subsisted. It was during this period that the term *big business* was coined.

Even immigration became big business. Newspaper advertisements and glossy brochures, produced and disseminated by the U.S. government and by private firms such as railroad companies, land speculators, and shipping companies, promised Europeans great riches in the New World. Almost every local paper, including the *Ribe Stiftstidende*, published large notices advertising irresistibly cheap fares to America. Port cities overflowed with emigration offices; and, not content to wait for recruits, emigration officers fanned out across the continent, actively hoping to sway those who hadn't yet made up their minds. The years 1871–1880 saw the arrival of 2,812,191 immigrants, and during the following decade that number almost doubled, with the fresh arrival of 5,246,613, including a million Germans and two million Eastern European Jews.

The insatiable appetite for manpower in the United States came just as Europe, too, was experiencing sweeping industrial change. Mechanization cost hundreds of thousands of farmworkers their jobs, and they fled to the cities in hopes of finding employment. The influx of workers, coupled with a population explosion in Europe, meant that even the great number of new industries could not employ all those seeking work. The disparity between the number of those seeking work and those providing employment created a significant push-factor, driving a huge number of unemployed Europeans to emigrate.

More than 50 million Europeans immigrated to America from 1870 to 1920. Among their number were 800,000 Norwegians, 1.2 million Swedes, and approximately 500,000 Danes. While the number of Danish immigrants may seem relatively small compared to that of other Scandinavian countries, it constituted a considerable population drain since, during this period, Denmark had only 2 million inhabitants.

※

IT WAS HARDLY the Danish population drain that worried Riis, when, on May 1, the day of his departure, he stole away to wait below Elisabeth's window, on Sct. Nikolaigade, just before dawn, hoping to catch one last glimpse of her. Elisabeth was sound asleep; nor did she come later. Some of the Giørtzes' servants had noticed Riis standing outside in the dark, and told Elisabeth. Riis wrote later that she had shrugged and said, "He never asked me to come and say farewell, did he?" Riis's father also did not see him off. Niels Edvard, against Riis's emigration plans from the start, stayed at home in protest. As Riis boarded the stagecoach for Copenhagen in the early morning, only his mother was there to hug him good-bye. Among his belongings was a lock of Elisabeth's hair and her photograph, given to him by Clara Giørtz, who pitied the forlorn suitor.

Riis was determined to shake off his gloom, as he wrote friends from Copenhagen on May 4. He explained that he was trying to pull himself together and look ahead: "I must desist this downtrodden behavior and cheer up!" It proved harder than he had expected. He wrote that, without the strand of Elisabeth's hair and her photograph, it would have been difficult for him to get through his first months in the United States. These items became his "dearest possession." Indeed, they were practically his only possessions. Apart from a few items of clothing, all he had were 40 American dollars given to him as a farewell present by friends.

❈

"THE FIRST THING anyone who is considering immigrating to America should do before making a final decision," recommends an 1871 Danish handbook, Conditions in America, "is to familiarize oneself with all things pertaining to the actual journey first, and next, to learn as much as possible about the conditions of the country; based on such research, one should consider carefully the advantages and disadvantages . . ." If the immigrant does not do his homework, the handbook cautions, he will simply encounter in the New World "exactly what he is attempting to flee from, namely want and misery."

Riis had not consulted an immigration guide. His image of America was based almost exclusively on James Fenimore Cooper's Leatherstocking Tales. In a vast wilderness inhabited by American Indians, courageous trappers, reckless frontiersmen, and herds of buffalo, "It is probably a good idea," he wrote half-jokingly, "to carry 2 guns in each pant and coat pocket and then one in each vest pocket and a couple of small bayonets or some minor weapons in my boots. Yes, and just for good measure, it might be a good idea to have a small knife or two between your teeth. Then you'd really be armed 'to the teeth.' " Upon arriving in Copenhagen, he had tried to book passage on the *Rising Star*, which sailed directly to New York on May 11, carrying 1,300 passengers. The ship was full, and Riis had to wait several days to embark. On Friday, May 13, he started on the first leg of his journey, sailing to Glasgow, where he was to board the Anchor Line's steamship *Iowa* bound for New York.

The *Iowa* was a medium-sized, 2,000-ton ship that could carry 540 third-class passengers and 80 first-class passengers with cabin accommodations. On this particular passage, the ship carried four Danes, including Riis, 111 Scotsmen, over 200 Irishmen, 20 Britons, a few Poles, and a few hundred Swedes. Riis, who had never before traveled outside Denmark, must have been overwhelmed by the diversity of people on board. He was by no means an unworldly man, however; fluent in German, he had grown up near the German border and was aware of the existence of other cultures. Unlike most European immigrants, he also spoke English fairly well. Riis traveled third class, like his fellow Danes, and the four of them became close friends. He also befriended a broad-shouldered German named Bernhard Adler.

Like many eager to secure permanent residency in the United States, Riis had contrived a new identity for himself in Copenhagen when he filed the obligatory departure papers with the Danish police. The twenty-one-year-old carpenter Jacob A. Riis described himself as a twenty-five-year-old farmer. Aboard the *Iowa*, he reinvented himself yet again, registering himself as a miner when he reached New York, as did his new Danish friends. Denmark did not have a mining industry, but Riis and his friends had heard that miners were in great demand in the New World. Similarly, Riis's farmer identity was most likely a fabrication based on information about America's efforts to cultivate the West. However, Riis's desire to create a new identity for himself was probably also motivated by a need to distance himself from Elisabeth. "I was tired of hammer and saw. They were insolubly linked to my dream of Elisabeth, which by then was shattered," he wrote in his memoirs.

Riis's voyage on the *Iowa* was relatively uneventful compared to the ordeal immigrants crossing on sailboats only a decade earlier had experienced. Sailboat voyages took about six weeks and were often plagued by

deadly epidemics. By 1870, more than 95 percent of transatlantic journeys were made by steamship and typically took only two weeks. The
food in third class, however, had not improved much. After a particularly nasty meal, Riis and Adler complained to the ship's captain, David
Ovenstone, presenting him with the foul-smelling food. Before Riis,
selected as spokesman, could present their case, Adler threw his tray
of food at the captain's head. He was immediately placed in the brig.
Upon his release, he complained incessantly about his treatment for the
remainder of the trip, threatening repeatedly to contact the German
Consulate in New York. His threats went unheeded.

After slight delays due to storms and fog, the *Iowa* reached the
Hudson River the night of Sunday, June 5, 1870—Whitsunday—and
dropped anchor at New York's Castle Garden, an immigration station
and former fort (in what is now Battery Park) on Manhattan's south-
western tip. The first few days of June had been damp and rainy, and it
was still muggy and gray when the *Iowa* docked, according to the *New
York Tribune*. Riis, however, remembered the day differently: "It was a
beautiful spring morning," he noted in his memoirs.

The ship was quarantined Sunday, so the passengers had plenty of
time to absorb from a distance the huge metropolis before them, stretching as far as the eye could see. Riis was dumbfounded; never had he imagined New York and its surroundings to be so vibrant. While the New
York of 1870 was already taller than most European cities, with buildings up to seven stories high, the majority of buildings were between five
and six floors, and tapered church steeples and rounded domes dominated the skyline. Riis had a good view of the 180-foot spire of Trinity
Church, whose golden cross shone brightly. A neo-Gothic building
on the corner of Broadway and Wall Street, it was the tallest structure
downtown, though to Riis it paled in comparison to the cathedral in
Ribe. It was New York's size that struck Riis, its 60,000 to 70,000 buildings standing in tight rows, from downtown, with its narrow, winding,
chaotic streets, to the more fashionable broad avenues uptown, from
Union Square to the grand mansions near Central Park.

New York in 1870 had almost one million inhabitants. From 1860
to 1890, the number of inhabitants doubled and the physical size of

the city quintupled. Walking the streets of late-nineteenth-century Manhattan, the sheer volume of people would be enough to overwhelm even a present-day New Yorker. From the *Iowa*, looking east, Riis could make out Brooklyn, which, with its 400,000 inhabitants, was in itself a large city—the third largest in the United States. In the west, Riis could see Jersey City, New Jersey; with its 20,000 inhabitants, it looked more like the towns Riis was familiar with at home. South was Staten Island—green, dotted with small villages. A calmer world unfolded on the Jersey shore along the Hudson River, where urban landscapes gave way to vast areas of woodland, and to the north Riis could glimpse the village of Manhattanville near Spuyten Duyvil Creek.

To Riis, as to most visitors, it was the degree of industrialization, the population density, and the volume of activity both in the streets and on the river that made the biggest impression. More than 100 wharves jutted out from Manhattan's southern tip, and the intricate ropework of thousands of ships' masts rose into the air. Steamships, schooners, and, of course, the barges, rowboats, and ferries shuttling between Manhattan, Staten Island, Brooklyn, and Jersey City crowded the river. What had been a small Dutch marketplace in the 1600s, bound on the north by a military defense wall—Wall Street—had become during the 1800s the country's economic locomotive. Nowhere in the United States was the concentration of capital, the number of businesses and factories, as great. Fifty-six of the nation's banks were headquartered in New York, controlling a combined capital of $106 million. According to the 1871 *Frank Leslie's Illustrated Family Almanac*, the total real estate value of New York City was $1,800,000,000. In Manhattan alone, it was $1,500,000,000.

❋

EVEN THOUGH the United States was still in many respects a frontier nation, New York had none of the Fenimore Cooper flavor Riis was expecting. Out west, the Plains Indians were still embroiled in a fight to save their land, and it had been only two years since the Sioux had succeeded in enforcing the Laramie Treaty, which, at least on paper, ensured their control over large parts of the Dakota Territory. Lieutenant

Colonel George Armstrong Custer's last stand at Little Bighorn would not take place for another six years. The 1870s saw many bloody encounters between whites and Indians in the West that became front-page stories on the East Coast. When Riis was finally able to leave the notoriously filthy Immigration Station at Castle Garden on Monday, January 6, 1870, the lead news story was about an attack on a post office in Hays City, Kansas. "Two Soldiers Killed and a Sergeant Wounded— Savages on the Warpath," proclaimed the banner headline in the *New York Times*. Such attention to the violence of the West in the press may explain why Riis felt compelled to spend half his modest fortune on a big pistol. "We [in Denmark] discerned no difference between the east and the west coast. [We believed that] herds of buffalo thundered down Broadway," Riis wrote in his memoirs.

One of the busiest streets in the world and the city's main artery, running from the southern tip of New York to Union Square, Broadway was lined with banks, investment firms, warehouses, businesses, theaters, hotels, and restaurants. Wagon, carriage, cart, and omnibus traffic was so dense that, twice daily, when traffic was at its heaviest, authorities had to send out officers to intervene and allow frustrated pedestrians to cross. It was estimated that more than 15,000 vehicles passed through Broadway every day. New Yorkers often complained it could take up to two hours by bus to travel its length. In 1868, a hatter initiated the building of a pedestrian bridge over Broadway.

Despite great diversity in dress—half of the inhabitants in 1870 were born outside the United States—it was unheard of for anyone to hang a pistol from his neck, as Riis did. When a police officer spotted the con-spicuously armed Dane, he kindly asked him to put away his piece. For a brief period in 1865 Riis had been a member of a gun club, and he knew how to handle weapons. Nonetheless, he was relieved by the officer's request—carrying the gun had, in fact, never made him feel safe.

Riis wandered through the streets of Manhattan, soaking up the atmosphere of the city. He had not made any definite plans for the future; he had only a recommendation addressed to the Danish consul and one to Albert G. Goodman, a businessman and later bank director, who had once gone aground outside Ribe during a storm. Riis felt sure that one or both would feel obliged to help him get a job. However, the consul and Goodman were both traveling in Europe.

❋

ON HIS FIRST NIGHT Riis stayed at an immigrant hostel near Castle Garden and Battery Park, which at the time was a chaotic human bazaar. The army recruited volunteers with promises of lifelong pensions in return for five-year contracts, frequently requiring soldiers to fight in the Indian wars. Petty swindlers roamed, preying upon new arrivals. Employers offered free train tickets out of New York; in return the immigrant was bound to take any job he was offered once he reached his destination.

An agent organizing a team of workers for the mines in western Pennsylvania recruited Riis and Adler. Only a couple of days after their arrival, the two friends found themselves on a train to Pittsburgh. From there they continued north to hilly, lushly forested Brady's Bend on the Allegheny River. A number of immigrants had accepted the agent's tickets, but all of them, with the exception of Riis and Adler, had deserted in Pittsburgh. Riis and Adler, who were practically broke, had no choice but to stay on, even if the wages were miserable.

"Smoke, smoke, smoke—everywhere smoke! Smoke, with the noise of the steam-hammer, and the spouting flame of tall chimneys—that is all we perceive of the hill opposite the site of Fort Duquesne," wrote a journalist of Pittsburgh in 1868.

> *The entire space lying between the hills was filled with blackest smoke, from out of which the hidden chimneys sent forth tongues of flames, while from the depths of the abyss came up the noise of hundreds of steam-hammers. There would be moments when no flames were visible; but soon the wind would force the smoky curtains aside, and the whole black expanse would be dimly lighted with dull wreaths of fire.*

In Brady's Bend, Riis was hired to build cabins for the miners of the Great Western Iron Works. Though he would come to appreciate getting work above ground, the irony of being hired as a carpenter was not lost on him. The area around Brady's Bend was a thinly populated wilderness, but the town itself—at a bend in the river where the Sugar Creek Stream meets it—was lively and fast growing, with 700 houses, several schools, and Catholic and Lutheran churches. The Great Western Iron Works had opened for operation in Brady's Bend in 1839 and gone bankrupt in 1858. The company recovered, and by the time Riis was employed it was thriving. There were 1,500 employees, with an annual output of 111,000 tons of coal and 70,000 tons of ore.

The days were long and taxing for Riis, and at night he was seized by melancholy. The young dishwasher at his boardinghouse sang the same sad song every night: "The Letter That Never Came." Riis only had a few days off a month, which he spent exploring the surrounding countryside. The endless forests and such vast expanses of wilderness were completely foreign to him. One afternoon, he realized how far from home he was. "I climbed the hills only to find that there were bigger hills beyond—an endless sea of swelling billows of green without a clearing in it. . . . A horrible fit of homesickness came upon me," he wrote in his memoirs.

He immersed himself in his work, and in the evenings he concentrated on improving his English. He was tutored by a young girl named Julia, a shy miner's daughter who, unbeknownst to Riis, felt attracted to him. One evening Riis overheard her mother talking about how Julia had set her cap for him. Confused as to what this English phrase meant, Riis asked Julia. Embarrassed, she ran away.

After a few weeks Riis and Adler, who worked in the foundry, tried to break the monotony of their routines by getting assigned to the mines—a decision they came to regret. Equipped with helmets and oil lamps, they trudged into the deep darkness and were nearly killed by a rock falling from the ceiling in one of the narrow shafts. The quiet blackness of the mine was oppressive, and all they could think about was getting out. Their revulsion was compounded by a sudden and frightening encounter with a glassy-eyed mule, an animal neither had ever seen. After a day's work on their knees in the low shafts, they had filled only two cars, for which they were paid a few cents. One day was enough for both of them. They never attempted mining again.

※

ON JULY 19, 1870, news of the outbreak of the Franco-Prussian War aroused Riis's patriotism, and he became consumed with the idea of volunteering for the French army to avenge Denmark's defeat by Germany in 1864. He envisioned himself a war hero on the battlefields of France and daydreamed of returning triumphant to The Castle in Ribe, dressed in a fancy uniform with shoulder straps. Riis immediately quit his job and left Brady's Bend. He was paid the infinitesimal sum of $10.63 for more than a month's work and headed to Buffalo, New York. He hoped French immigrant nationalists would receive him with open arms and pay for him to return to New York City, where he would board a ship for France. He never doubted that volunteers were needed.

While it is undoubtedly true that Riis had a genuine desire to help with the war effort, a desire he vividly described both in letters and in his memoirs, the war also presented him with a welcome escape route home. He had already learned enough about the New World to know that acquiring wealth and status was not a certainty. In fact, he understood that there was a distinct possibility that he might end up in worse circumstances than he had left behind. Ironically, the myth that America was a wellspring of great opportunity was to a large degree created by the immigrants themselves. Ashamed to be living in poverty, they frequently chose to write their families back home rosy fictions. It was letters like these that prompted new waves of immigrants from Europe.

There were no Frenchmen raising a volunteer army in Buffalo, and the only Frenchman in town interested in Riis was a pawnbroker, who with great pleasure took possession of his suitcase and all its contents in exchange for a one-way ticket to New York City. There, one disappointment after another awaited Riis. He was received coolly by the Danish consul, though he did promise to take down Riis's name in case something came up. The reception at the French consulate was even cooler. Riis was curtly informed that there were no plans to form a volunteer army, and he was shown the door. Unable to afford the dollar-a-day rent for a boardinghouse, he had no idea where he would get his next meal.

The sun was setting, the darkness loomed, and the city suddenly seemed menacing and oppressive. There were people everywhere, yet he knew no one. What was he supposed to do? He had pawned everything, even his pistol, and had only the clothes on his back, a duffel bag with a pair of clean socks, and a linen coat. Overcome by a feeling of intense loneliness, he began walking aimlessly.

At midnight he passed a house on Clinton Place. Hearing voices and laughter, he stopped for a moment and listened. The people inside spoke French. He knocked on the door. A French club was holding its annual ball. The servant opening the door took one look at the scruffy Riis and tried to slam the door in his face, but Riis squeezed past him and got the attention of two elegantly dressed Frenchmen. They listened incredulously to his story, and he was shown the door. He continued on, wandering north up a deserted Third Avenue until he was outside the city limits. He kept walking until he could walk no more, until the stars began fading and daylight trickled through. Exhausted, he fell asleep in a milk wagon parked on the road. The milkman soon arrived and pulled him out, mercilessly dumping him in the nearest gutter. Bogged down by fatigue and hunger, Riis had no choice but to resume his journey. He tried to forget his aches and his pangs of hunger by jumping into the Hudson River, which, though momentarily refreshing, finally left him feeling only hungrier and more tired.

Riis trudged along for several hours without making stops. At noon he reached Fordham College. The gate to the college was open and he went in. Here, for the first time in his life, he met a Catholic monk, who approached him with an offer of food. Since childhood Riis had been taught that Catholics were corrupt—indeed, they verged on the subhuman, according to his Lutheran upbringing. The monk's kindness was so convincing, however, that Riis quickly revised his view—his ability to sever his religious moorings perhaps a first step toward assimilation.

After providing him with a meal, the monk gave the grateful young immigrant enough money to buy food for several days. With a full stomach and money in his pocket, Riis continued north, following the railroad tracks until he reached rural Mount Vernon, where he got a job as a cucumber picker, staying on for a few weeks. One day he heard that the daily newspaper the *Sun* had published an article announcing that the United States was outfitting a volunteer army in New York to fight on behalf of the French. Riis immediately left for New York and went straight to Printing House Square—Newspaper Row, where most of the city papers had their offices—across from City Hall. The *Sun* was housed in a beautiful neo-baroque building. Riis secured an audience with the editor in chief, Charles A. Dana, who informed Riis that he did not read every single article in his paper and that he knew nothing about a volunteer army. Looking at the unkempt young man with his high hopes and great ideals, Dana offered him a dollar. "There, go and get your breakfast; and better give up the war."

The unintentionally condescending remark infuriated Riis. Spit flying, he gave vent to his high-flying idealism: How could the editor believe that he was for sale like that? That he would give up the war for a dollar? He had certainly not come for a handout, he concluded with great fanfare, and stormed out of Dana's office. Riis was once again penniless, having already spent the little money he had earned picking cucumbers, so he pawned his boots to buy food. After his meal, he continued his aimless wandering, this time going south. He left Manhattan by ferry, sailing to Perth Amboy, New Jersey. He worked for a few days at a brickyard but hated it—most of the employees were German, and they celebrated each victory in the Franco-Prussian War. He was also to discover that the company could not afford to pay its workers.

Riis decided to leave and head west. He stopped in New Brunswick, where he spent the night in a cemetery near a Dutch Reformed Church. The following day he came to the village of Little Washington, where he took job at Pettit's Brickyard, earning $22 a month plus room and board. The work was monotonous, and Riis began daydreaming about Elisabeth. One day, at least according to his memoirs, his daydreaming got him into serious trouble. The ground was muddy, and Riis, who was responsible for a horse and wagon, should have placed boards across a mud-spattered patch for the horse to walk on. He had been too engrossed in his dreams of Elisabeth to pay attention, and suddenly the horse slipped and fell down a hill, landing on its back with all four legs sticking up in the air. The incensed owner came running out, but to

Riis's utter bafflement the man found the sight of the upended horse so funny that he forgot to admonish Riis, who had been sure the incident would cost him his job.

In the late summer of that year Riis heard another rumor about a volunteer army forming in New York. Once again he quit his job and headed for New York City. Turned away at the French Embassy, Riis refused to give up. At the harbor he searched for French ships, hoping to obtain passage to Europe. Finally he met the captain of a French ship, who agreed to take him on board as a stoker. He was delighted and ran back to get his belongings from a boardinghouse. By the time he returned, his heart soaring, the ship had sailed without him. All he could see was the stern disappearing on the horizon. "It was the last straw. I sat . . . and wept with mortification," Riis wrote in his memoirs. Yet again he had suffered a deep disappointment, but this time, he accepted the reality: The Franco-Prussian War was over for him. And America was, at least for now, his destiny.

5

The Fast March to Buffalo

FILLED WITH DESPAIR as he watched the French ship disappear, Riis surely also knew that he had more to worry about than this latest chimera. Fall had set in, which meant fewer jobs for day laborers. The harvesting was done, the last apples picked, and the construction industry slowed during the cold season. New York City was a gigantic job generator, but it seemed there were always more people seeking work than there was work to be had. Not only did tens of thousands of immigrants pass through Castle Garden every month during the 1870s, but thousands upon thousands of job-hungry Americans descended upon New York as well. Every fall produced multitudes of starving unemployed workers, without plan or purpose. Riis became one of them that winter.

"I joined the great army of tramps," he later wrote,

wandering about the streets in the daytime with the one aim of somehow stilling the hunger that gnawed at my vitals, and fighting at night with vagrant curs or outcasts as miserable as myself for the protection of some sheltering ash-bin doorway. . . . It was under such auspices that I made the acquaintance of Mulberry Bend and the rest of the slum, with which there was in the years to come to be a reckoning.

New York's wretched and overcrowded tenements left an indelible impression on Riis, made stronger by his own near-death experience in the city's worst slum: Five Points.

※

NEW YORK was a city of extremes, and the contrast between rich and poor engendered hyperbolic judgment and description. "Strangers coming to New York," wrote the popular travel-guide author and journalist J. D. McCabe in the early 1870s, "are struck by the fact that there are but two classes in the city—the poor and the rich. The middle class, which is so numerous in other cities, hardly exists at all here. The reason for this is plain to the initiated. Living in New York is so expensive that persons of moderate means reside in the suburbs, some of them as far as forty miles away in the country." In fact, as Mike Wallace and Edwin Burrows demonstrate convincingly in *Gotham* (1998), the large number of middle-class New Yorkers included doctors, lawyers, editors, professors, architects, landscapes, librarians, reporters, engineers and marketing directors, business managers, shop owners, nurses, dentists, ministers, entrepreneurs, realtors, artists, and teachers. Still, depictions such as McCabe's became something of a self-perpetuating myth. There were indeed magnificent riches in the city: luxurious hotels with up to 500 opulent suites and rooms; elegant restaurants; mammoth Wall Street banks; ostentatious mansions surrounding Union Square, Washington Square, Madison Square, and Gramercy Park. Pockets of wealth adjoined the slums, where more than half the city's population lived. Filthy, untended children roamed the dark and dirty alleys, which were lined with brothels—at least 500 existed in the city—and stale-beer dives. There were 7,000 bars in New York. As a reporter Riis investigated the church-to-bar ratio south of Fourteenth Street: It was 111 to 4,000.

The problem of the slums was partly one of geography. New York had since its establishment as a Dutch colony in the first half of the seventeenth century been populated by immigrants, but as the ever-increasing tides of newcomers began overflowing the well-established residential areas, where wealthier, older New York families lived, an exodus of the rich resulted, changing the demographics of the city.

The rich escaped uptown—then consisting of Fourteenth to Twentieth streets—abandoning their homes to landlords who converted them into multi-unit residential buildings. This transformation had taken place by the beginning of the nineteenth century. Landlords began demanding exorbitant sums for these apartments, a development that is commonly viewed as the beginning of New York's tenement era. As more and more people needed a place to live, the prices of the apartments rose, and landlords divided them into smaller and smaller units. Immigrant families were willing to pay almost their entire income for even the humblest of lodgings. Disused factories were converted into housing.

The most notorious of these early tenement houses was the Old Brewery, a dilapidated flophouse at the center of Five Points—where Mulberry, Worth, Park, Baxter, and Little Water streets intersected. Before 1852, when it was finally purchased by missionaries, the Old Brewery, designed to house a few hundred residents at most, accommodated more than a thousand people. As the Five Points Mission, it was to function as a church, school, and bathhouse, but Five Points—once an idyllic picnic spot, Bunker Hill, defined by five-acre Collect Pond—was by then beyond rehabilitation.

Widely known for its crime, decadence, and poverty, its storied history drew writers from all over the world. Charles Dickens wrote in 1842:

> This is the place: these narrow ways diverging to the right and left, and reeking everywhere with dirt and filth. Such lives as are led here, bear the same fruit here as elsewhere. The coarse and bloated faces at the doors have counterparts at home and all the wide world over. Debauchery has made the very houses prematurely old. See how the rotten beams are tumbling down, and how the patched and broken windows seem to scowl dimly, like eyes that have been hurt in drunken frays. Many of their pigs live here. Do they ever wonder why their masters walk upright in lieu of going on all-fours? and why they talk instead of grunting?

When the mansions along the wharves fell into disrepair in the 1840s, two-story wooden tenement houses were constructed, many so poorly engineered that they collapsed before completion. Of the finished buildings so many were lost to fire or rot that in 1867 the city prohibited the use of wood as a primary building material. Henceforth all new multiple-unit residential houses were built of stone. The stone buildings were called railroad tenements because of their structure. Typically five to six stories, they had long, narrow rows of small rooms, like the compartments in railroad cars. Built side by side, only the front rooms had windows that provided direct light and ventilation. Developers, eager to utilize every square inch of free space, squeezed additional houses into courtyards behind the original railroad tenements, the so-called rear tenements, further blocking fresh air and sunlight.

Only a few years before Riis's arrival, pigs and other farm animals were kept on the streets of New York, adding to the stench of the closely spaced tenements. By 1870 it was no longer legal to keep pigs, but chickens and goats still roamed, leaving their droppings, as did the tens of thousands of horses used to pull carriages and omnibuses. According to Board of Health estimates, 400 tons of horse manure were deposited every day. In the poorest neighborhoods, human effluvia seeped from privies into the streets, mixing during heavy rains with animal excrement and rotting trash to create a bacteria-infested soup.

Not until 1881 did New York have a Department of Sanitation, then called the Department of Street Cleaning, to oversee the collection of waste and disposal. Before, much confusion as to whether the police or the Board of Health was responsible for waste removal and trash cleanup had, in effect, turned the streets of New York, particularly the slums, into dumping grounds. Weeks went by before streets were swept and garbage collected and disposed of. Often the waste was simply dumped into the Hudson River.

In the winter of 1871, the *New York Times* ran an article describing what it was like to walk the slums:

> *A tour around the City will reward the most morbid adventurer with a surfeit of loathsome horrors. In the vicinity of the Five Points—the cesspool of the Metropolis—is a spectacle of nauseous rarity. . . . thousands of persons, accidentally or purposely dumped all their ashes, garbage, and household filth—in some instances diseased clothing or rags and straw—on the snow.*

The mass melted and mixed together and now extends in puddles or sloughs of rottenness, evolving rank, choking stenches, too nauseous for description. Hester-street, north of Rivington, is submerged in pools of slime, heaps of decaying filth, and a conglomeration of offal, ashes and dirt of all kinds. In Chrystie-street the store fronts, in some cases, were plastered with filth scattered from the railway sweepers. One doorway is thus elaborately frescoed with chicken's entrails, potato peelings and bits of straw. Marion-street has black and greasy mud monuments to street contractors, two feet in height. . . . Gansevoort-street stinks with most flagrant fumes; the distillations of dead horse, putrid dog, and stale manure, the pavement being in so wretched a condition in the vicinity of the Bleecker-street Railroad stables that all excressent [sic] matter collects, as in a sink.

Below street level existed a world even more appalling. In the large, damp basements of the tenements, which were increasingly being used for habitation, people both lived and died, the cellars doubling as burial grounds. Those who did not succumb to typhus and smallpox contracted tuberculosis, bronchitis, and rheumatism. Although by the late 1860s the use of basements for habitation was prohibited, health inspectors soon realized that few abided by the law. According to an 1873 study of Houston Street, 549 basements were inhabited, and at least 450 of these were so damp and airless that they posed a serious threat to the lives of the people who lived there.

It was into this world that Riis was pulled in the fall of 1870. Fifteen thousand tenements stretched from lower Manhattan to Fifty-ninth Street, with the infamous Hell's Kitchen commanding some two dozen blocks, from Thirty-fourth Street upward. About half a million people and their numerous animals lived in the slums. As the temperatures dropped, Riis's situation became increasingly desperate. He got soaked by rain, and freezing winds cut through his thin clothes. He refused to admit that he was finding it difficult to survive; he even burned his letters of recommendation. Most evenings he waited for food at the back door of Delmonico's, an exclusive restaurant at the corner of Chambers Street and Broadway. The French cook often gave him leftover bones and bread. Averse to begging, Riis told himself that the French owed him. Delmonico's menu featured Consommé Britannica, Purée à la Derby, Cassolettes de foie gras, and Chaudfroid de rouge-gorges à la Bohémienne. The socialites who frequented the restaurant were formally attired, and their elaborate clothing and the magnificent dining rooms' beautiful furnishings and Venetian leather wall coverings must have seemed a constant rebuke to Riis. After his meager meal, he began the fight with other tramps for a place to spend the night, sometimes ending up on the doorstep of Barnum's Clothing Store on Chapman Square, in the Five Points area. Police officers came by periodically and, with a blow of the nightstick, shouted, "Get up there!" or "Move on!"

Caught in the vicious circle of the homeless, Riis gradually began looking and smelling like the people he lived among. In the late fall of 1870 he had given up all hope of finding work, and on a particularly cold and rainy night, while walking on the North River wharf, he stopped and looked out over the city, lit by 19,000 flickering gas lights. Closing his eyes, he thought about Elisabeth in Ribe and of the small, cozy houses in the Old Town. When he opened his eyes, he looked into the cold river. Moving closer to the water's edge, he asked himself whether anyone at home would miss him if he jumped. A few seconds and it would all be over.

Riis later wrote that the thought of suicide was uppermost in his mind. It seemed to him that there was no other way out of his misery. With him that night was an abandoned dog. Had the dog not snuggled up to him when his thoughts were at their darkest, Riis might well have ended his life. The moment passed, and with his dog in tow, he started searching for a place to stay. At midnight the two companions reached Church Street, and Riis decided to seek shelter at the police station. In the winter, police stations doubled as homeless shelters, but they were considered the worst in the city, the rooms cold, and the beds mere planks. Still, they offered protection from the weather, and they were free. Pets were not allowed, and Riis had to leave his dog outside. At first he had tried to smuggle the animal in under his coat, but an officer caught him and put the dog out.

Riis got the last available "bed." The lodgers that night were mostly Irish and German tramps. Riis argued with one of the Germans, telling him how he felt about Prussia. A few hours later Riis woke with a start. Instinctively, he knew something was wrong. A gold locket he had worn since leaving Ribe, which contained the lock of Elisabeth's hair and the photo Clara Giørtz had given him, was missing. Riis received no help from the officer on duty but instead was ridiculed: "How should he, a tramp boy, have come by a gold locket?" The officer, a German immigrant who had overheard Riis speak ill of the Prussians, had Riis ejected. In an attempt to defend Riis, the dog attacked. A second officer came to assist, grabbing the dog and smashing his head against the curb, instantly killing him. A blind rage seized Riis, and he started hurling paving stones from the gutter. His fury seemed to give him superhuman strength. Reinforcements arrived, a brief battle ensued, and Riis was put on a ferry to New Jersey.

Riis had not imagined the world could be so callous. When he had read Dickens, the human depravity portrayed in the novels had been an abstraction to him. Now, as he sailed for New Jersey, he felt changed, having personally experienced such depravity. He had paid for his ticket with his last item of value: a silk handkerchief. He had no regrets about letting it go; all that mattered to him was to get as far away from the slums as possible.

Once on the Jersey side, Riis followed a set of railroad tracks. After a full day of walking he reached Newark and decided to continue south, toward Philadelphia. He was joined by a swarm of other unemployed, homeless men, heading south to warmer climates. Their companionship was agreeable to Riis during the day, but at night when he sought shelter, typically in abandoned barns, he felt distinctly uncomfortable bedding down with tramps. One night, he was awakened by a loud thunderclap. In a flash of lightning, a pale, wide-eyed face stared at him and a trembling voice asked, "Is anybody there?"

"For the first time," Riis noted in his memoirs, "I was glad to have a live tramp about. I really thought it was a ghost."

Riis's mainstay on the road was rotten apples, though occasionally he was given a home-cooked meal for doing odd jobs for farmers. He jumped on a cattle train one evening to Camden, New Jersey, where he was arrested for vagrancy. The arresting officer took heart and fed Riis, put him up for the night in a jail cell, saw to it that his shoes were shined, and gave him a little money. At last marginally presentable, Riis went to Philadelphia and, swallowing his pride, decided to look up the Danish consul and ask for help. The consul, Ferdinand Myhlertz, opened his home to him.

After two weeks of rest Riis felt fully restored and ready, even eager, to move on. He missed Elisabeth with such force it hurt, and the only way he could numb the pain was to keep moving. The consul sent him to a friend in Jamestown, New York, near Lake Erie. A group of Scandinavians had settled there, and Riis befriended the Romers, who lived in a spacious house in the small village of Dexterville, on the outskirts of Jamestown. A Danish family of four, they offered him room and board. The Romers were housing two other young Danes, Anthony Rønne and a man whose surname was Munk. The three boarders and the Romers' two sons, Nicholas and John, became friends, and for a while Riis found peace of mind.

According to the British journalist B. P. Barry, who visited in 1866, Jamestown, originally a Dutch colony, was a small slice of heaven in the foothills of the Allegheny Mountains, close to Chautauqua Lake, where the fish were plentiful. The town produced huge quantities of butter and cheese for New York City.

There were almost as many jobs in Jamestown as there were fish in the lake, though none paid well. There were three sawmills, a furniture shop, a piano manufacturer, two cotton mills, a gasworks, and two newspapers. Riis made cradles at $2.50 per dozen, then worked as a steamship repairman. Later he tried harvesting ice, and for a brief period he worked as a lumberjack.

He bought a used dress coat for a dollar and shared it with his roommate Rønne, the two taking turns going to weekly parties in Dexterville. Dancing, considered immoral, was forbidden; instead the partygoers engaged in what Riis called "energetic kissing games," which, he wrote later in his memoirs, were innocent.

❋

IN EARLY 1871 the Romer family moved to Buffalo. Rønne and Munk joined them, Riis staying on in Dexterville. He lived alone in the big house, which bordered a forest, supporting himself as a hunter and trapper, living like a Fenimore Cooper character. In town he could sell his muskrat skins for 25 cents apiece. It was a short-lived period. Exceedingly uncomfortable when he was alone, Riis continued to be haunted by the memory of Elisabeth. He could not sleep at night, and rose each day fatigued and depressed.

Riis needed to be around other people, and it was the exigency of loneliness, finally, that thrust him into a role for which he appeared at first to be entirely unprepared: Twice a week, he began lecturing publicly on astronomy and geology. He based his lectures on a book by the popular French scientist Louis Figuier, *The World before the Deluge*, which adhered to the teachings of evolution while also leaning heavily on the Bible. The deluge of the title, Figuier claimed, had actually been several floods: the Asian Flood, the Scandinavian Flood, and the Middle-European Flood. In another chapter, Figuier asserted that certain archaeological findings proved the existence of unicorns. Riis's audiences were mesmerized, and lecturing became a lucrative business for him. The ticket price was 10 cents; Riis was making $3 a night. He enjoyed lecturing, and it seems not to have occurred to him that a foreign dropout was not the most likely candidate for such a job. On the contrary, Riis found he had a natural talent for public speaking.

His success came to an abrupt halt one night when he was called upon to explain latitude and longitude and got his coordinates wrong. The mistake was noticed by a sea captain in the audience, who made a fool of Riis. His audience, suddenly full of disdain, walked out. Riis, mortified but not dispirited, began looking for a new job.

In May, he packed up, left the Romer residence, and headed for Buffalo. As he was walking along the shore of Chautauqua Lake, he tried to shoot a duck for lunch. He hit one, but it flew far out over the lake before it fell. Riis continued his journey on an empty stomach, not stopping again until dark, when, weak from exhaustion and hunger, he fell asleep in a barn near Westfield, a railroad and mill town on Lake Erie. He woke up the next day ravenous and, walking into town, rang the bell of a beautiful, well-kept house and offered to work for his breakfast. The owners, a doctor and his wife, hired him as a servant, teacher, and handyman. His chores included milking a temperamental cow, Octavia, cutting wood, carrying the old family dog into the basement during thunderstorms, and teaching the family's two children Homer. Being the son of a Latin and Greek scholar had its advantages.

Though the doctor assured him he could make him a rich man, Riis's restlessness led him to quit after only a few weeks. He knew he aspired to more but could not seem to pin down exactly what it was he wanted, and his inchoate longings and ambition troubled him deeply. Back on the road, however, Riis was soon distracted by hunger.

※

IN COONVILLE, a village in Cattaraugus County thirty miles south-west of Buffalo (now the township of Yorkshire), Riis got a job laying rail. He worked in a gang of twenty laborers, seventeen of whom were Irish. Though they teased him incessantly, calling him "the Dutchman," they could also see that he was unaccustomed to grueling physical labor, and covered for him whenever possible. As the summer progressed and the heat grew thicker, Riis was forced to acknowledge that the work was inordinately difficult for him, and he quit. At first he traipsed through the beautiful countryside of upstate New York living hand to mouth and sleeping, weather permitting, under open skies. At night, he would gaze up at the stars and dream about Elisabeth. On a Sunday morning in August, he heard about shipyard work in Buffalo. Without hesitation he set out, writing in his diary:

> The news changed my aimless wandering into a fast march towards Buffalo. I walked all that night and even though I had to make some stops to eat, I was in Buffalo by sundown the next day. I slept in a barn and by dawn I walked into Buffalo and headed directly to Evan's Shipyard. . . . I got a job immediately and began working as a ship's carpenter that afternoon. . . . it was fine work and paid $2.50 a day.

Riis loved the work and made many friends among the two hundred Irish and German workers. He noted in his diary, "when you worked mostly among Irish, you learned to appreciate the Germans much more."

Buffalo was at the threshold of its own golden age when Riis arrived. With 117,000 residents, it was fast becoming one of the most important commercial cities in the United States, having doubled its population during the decade 1850–1860, from 50,000 to 100,000. Relatively young, in early 1800 it had been nothing more than a trading post, with fewer than 500 residents, but with the completion of the Erie Canal in 1825, linking Lake Erie and the Hudson River, it began servicing East Coast, Northeast, and Midwest trade, in particular large-scale transport of grain. Traffic to and from Buffalo on the Erie Canal was as dense and active as that of a modern highway. In 1871, 5,000 ships and boats sailed daily between New York and Buffalo, and 60 million barrels of grain were shipped from Buffalo to New York every year. Buffalo grain elevators, which dominated the city's skyline, held a combined 200 million barrels of grain.

During the 1850s and 1860s the railway became as important a means of transportation as the canal, and Buffalo was soon among the cities in the world with the heaviest railroad traffic; within the city limits alone there were 600 miles of track. The city accordingly experienced an industrial boom. Along the shores of Lake Erie and the Niagara River, shipyards, iron foundries, and machine works sprang up. Immigrants crowded the city, the majority British and German immigrants, but with large enclaves of Irish, Scandinavian, French, Polish, Russian, and Chinese. Buffalo also had a fair number of black migrants from the South.

As the population grew, so did the city's infrastructure. Impressive brick banks, schools, courthouses and government buildings rose along avenues the width of large rivers. It must have seemed to Riis that there would be plenty of work here, but he quickly understood that even a city as vibrant and flourishing as Buffalo was vulnerable to market fluctuations. After five weeks at the shipyard, the ship he had been hired to work on was finished, and with its launching in Lake Erie, Riis found himself out of work again.

6

———— •◆• ————

"My Lovely Dream"

D URING HIS FIRST few years in the United States, Riis was a meticulous diarist. In three thin, leather-bound, pocket-sized notebooks, he recorded his thoughts in pencil after long, grueling work-days or on Sundays, the diaries demonstrating, from the first page, his natural gift for storytelling. Riis wrote unaffectedly about commonplace events, with the occasional dramaturgical flourish ("Oh, Jacob, Jacob"), the result both a captivating tale of his emotional ups and downs and a testament to the hardships endured by immigrants struggling to gain a foothold in America. Riis bought the first of these small notebooks in New York City. Unfortunately, it did not survive. Perhaps the nomadic Riis lost it; he may also have deliberately disposed of it to obliterate this record of his days as a tramp. As a reformer, Riis was surprisingly harsh in his criticism of vagabonds.

"Vol. II," clearly soaked by rain and handled repeatedly when Riis was sweaty and dirty, was purchased on Main Street in Buffalo on September 12, 1871; Riis was still in the first flush of euphoria at having secured steady work at Evan's Shipyard. It is a measure of his constantly changing fortunes that the first entry, less than three weeks later, sounds a dire note:

October 2, 1871: I turn to the first page of my new diary. Only God knows what these pages will say . . . oh, how I wish I also knew. My luck had changed for the better at least regarding work and money since I finished the last diary, but now I am again unemployed . . . and like last fall, I now face the coming winter with neither money nor job and owing a week's rent. God only knows what will become of me.

Two weeks later, his prospects had proven better than anticipated. His friends from Jamestown, Rønne and Munk, were back in Buffalo, and he had earned a little money working for a sawmill, the Union Planning Mill, though he quit after only two days.

[It] only paid $1.25 a day for planing doors, I quit immediately and now have a job with a carpenter, who pays me $1.75 a day. It is all rather miserable. I run three miles to and from work, I work outside in the raw cold weather and live in a shabby boardinghouse full of Germans. I live on William Street, the landlord is a German by the funny name of Paulsachel, who only charges $4 for good room and board, but there is a saloon in the house and always so much racket. I feel like selling my tools and heading so far south that the winter cold cannot reach me . . . but if I shall travel, it will have to be now, otherwise winter will come down on me, and work as a carpenter this winter I simply will not do!

Three days later Riis felt overcome by despair. It was October 17, two years to the day Elisabeth had rejected him. As he had done the previous year, Riis gave vent to his misery:

October Seventeenth! When, Jacob, will you forget that day and that evening? Here I am on the second anniversary of that day, the seventeenth of October, and like that night, the letter I was awaiting is open on the table before me, bearing traces of the tears I spilled, and in some places the letters are blurred. That was the night, remember, Jacob, when we paced the floor gasping for air as if some heavy burden was pressing in on our chest . . . and then when the letter finally arrived and you were alone with your God and your fate . . . what a terrible decision was there in your hand, which almost refused to do service and open the letter. . . . it seemed to me so cruel for you [God] to fill a heart with love and then use this, the most noble and holy of emotions, to strike me and cause such pain, the most painful of pains a man can suffer.

Harsh weather exacerbated his grief, the trees stark and menacing against a gray sky, the rain pouring down. Five days later, Riis continued to feel dejected: "I am so unhappy working for the house-carpenter. . . . Oh, God, how sad it is that I cannot settle down and be content. But I simply cannot." He dreamed of warmer climates, the Amazon River, South America: "When I set out, I will travel far south, and thus it seems my life in the U.S. has for the time being come to an end. I'm studying Spanish using an English language textbook, and Spanish is as easy as it is pretty." Convinced that his plans would come to fruition, he lamented the fact that he would have to leave Rønne and Munk. "It is with a heavy heart that I must say farewell to my two friends, it saddens me so I cannot find words to express it. . . . I shall probably never have friends like these again in this lifetime."

Riis's dreams of the Amazon were soon dashed: "Now I must interrupt all my travel plans. . . . This Wednesday I was fired because I insulted his [Riis's employer's] Catholic sensibilities by working yesterday, which was All Saints' Day, and also because he found me 'too damned independent.' " He was next hired—for the second time—by the Union Planing Mill, but again he did not stay long. Offered 15 cents a door, which Riis figured would amount to a daily rate of about $2 if he could plane 14 doors, he felt sure of his ability to reach such an ambitious quota. When his employer lowered the unit price, Riis worked even harder, eventually earning $2.50 a day. His employer in turn lowered the unit price further, and in time Riis would be forced to quit.

During this period he moved in with Rønne and Munk, and their companionship offered some consolation, but in late November Riis and Rønne had a serious fight. Riis immediately regretted his part in it: "Rønne's friendship is the only valuable thing I have in the world," he wrote in his journal. Though the two men reconciled, Riis's mood suffered.

*I have been sick almost all week and not been able to work much. But my
prospects at the shop are grim. I barely make half the pay I had hoped for and
expected. It is no wonder I feel so completely at my wit's end, and again I am
terribly melancholic. Melancholy has haunted me before. Dear God, if only
it were summer and warm outside rather than this desolate winter, which has
covered the ground with its hard, cold ice-cape.*

Christmas arrived, and for the second year in a row, "no letter
reached me in time from Denmark. I feel so blue." Riis, Rønne, and
Munk went to Niagara Falls, where they drank at every bar on Main
Street, staying out all night. "We were greatly entertained, but goodness
it was expensive, it cost $4." The following day, a letter and a parcel
arrived from Riis's mother. His brother had successfully completed the
first stage of medical school, an accomplishment that Riis, clearly jealous, referred to in his diary as the "damned graduation."

On New Year's Eve Riis took stock of 1871 in a journal entry, possibly alcohol-induced, headed: "So far!" His mother had implored him to
come back to the family. "I probably will not see my parents ever again,"
he replied to himself. "They might as well get used to the idea that I will
never come home to Denmark, I have no reason to come home, no one
to come home to." Anger and resentment gave way to a sense of foreboding. "It is the second New Year's Eve here, which will close the door
on a bygone year, only the Lord knows what is in store for me in the new
year. Please God, let it not be something terrible." His ravings about
Elisabeth—"She is my ideal. She is perfection"—occupied several para-
graphs before he reached an avuncular conclusion: "A happy New Year
to all. God save little Denmark."

While working at Evan's Shipyard, Riis had a political epiphany:

*The other day a communist came aboard at lunch time and served up his
political drivel. To the delight of everyone I challenged him and tore his arguments to pieces. Discouraged, he withdrew with his fine ideas and goals. If
ever again a bunch of communists will gather here in Buffalo, I think I will
take the stand and make a speech in English against these insane ideas, which*

I so hate. Though I think that people here are too educated to fall for such nonsense.

A notion of performing a public service had begun to form in Riis's mind, and with this ambition came an impatience with the here and now, and with carpentry. As he wrote on February 11, 1872, "This [trade] cannot be what I am meant to do; I don't think I say this because I am lazy, but rather because other powers stir within and want out—and I should use these powers in this country, where hiding one's light under a bushel is considered foolish." Riis's powers of adaptation were considerable. With each day spent in America, he grew more confident, and confidence brought grandiose plans for the future. "I definitely think," he wrote, "that the right place for me is the newsroom."

Considering the career choices the twenty-two-year-old Riis had thus far made, journalism remains a curious choice. Perhaps it was a desperate whim—an occupation that would get him out of the cold and away from the instability of day labor. But the work he had done as a boy for the *Ribe Stiftstidende* surely provided inspiration, and his love of writing is apparent in the diaries. Only a few words and sentences have been crossed out, and the writing process was therapeutic, as Riis acknowledged on March 5: "I write only for myself, the concentration of the process wards off my blues: the dark thoughts and feelings which overcome me when the worm of sad memories starts gnawing at my heart on lonely evenings."

Riis sent letters of inquiry to the *Ribe Stiftstidende*, offering his services as U.S. correspondent, and to *The Scandinavian*, a U.S.-based paper for Scandinavian immigrants. He also tried getting an apprenticeship at one of the two largest newspapers in Buffalo. According to his memoirs, he walked unannounced into the newsrooms of *The Courier* and *The Express* and asked for a job as a reporter. He wrote that the editor of *The Express*, recently co-owned by Mark Twain, asked him: "What are you?"

"Carpenter," Riis replied. The editor roared with laughter and dismissed him without further question.

To Riis's great disappointment, *The Scandinavian* and the *Ribe*

Stiftstidende also turned him down. He responded by turning his sights to missionary work "in a foreign, heathen country! A missionary of God's word, of Jesus Christ—the true light that enlightens." His passion soon rivaled the ardor he had expressed for journalism. "If we do not take part in the battle of the spirit, in its victory, each to his own ability, we are no better than animals . . . that is why I want to be a missionary." Even this noble calling was quickly silenced when Riis sardonically confided his new career goal: "From Missionary to Traveling Salesman."

❋

IN JAMESTOWN IN 1871, Riis had met a couple of Danes who had started a cabinetmaking business called Ipson, Bestrup & Co. The two men wanted to sell their furniture outside Buffalo and told Riis they needed a salesman. He seemed the perfect candidate for the job. The company did not make enough money to support a salesman at the time, however, and Riis had soon forgotten about them. By April 1872, Ipson, Bestrup & Co. could afford to hire him, and he accepted the job. He was offered $25 in travel expenses and a commission on sales. By April 12 he had reached Allegheny City, Pennsylvania:

> *I am 333 miles from Buffalo. I'm writing from a small, neat house, owned by a German, who, I believe, thinks me a fellow German, as he has given me a room decorated with a large "schwartz-rote-goldene" flag. I've been traveling for 12 days as a salesman for Ipson and just about spent my $25, however, during this time I have gotten orders for $2,400 so I assume it is all right.*

His sales record was in fact more than all right; it was astounding.

From Allegheny City Riis went to Youngstown, Ohio. The work made him think less often about Elisabeth. His communication skills blossomed, and his hunger for social contact was satisfied. His diary entries are filled with descriptions of the places he saw and the people he met. By the end of May he was back in Jamestown and ready to collect $450 in commission. To his utter dismay, instead his career as a salesman for Ipson, Bestrup & Co. came to an abrupt end. The inexperienced businessmen had forgotten to figure in production costs; once prices had been adjusted accordingly, profits proved much lower than expected. Riis, who had traveled hundreds of miles in the past month, was, according to his memoirs, paid a scant 75 cents. It is quite possible that, in the thirty years between the event and the writing of his auto-biography, Riis forgot the actual sum; still, he was obviously paid far less than he had been promised.

Surprisingly, the disappointment did not rattle Riis. Upon his return to Jamestown he had caught a glimpse of a girl named Mary Rawson, who

> looked just like—I saw it at once—Elisabeth when she was younger. Seeing her brought back all the memories of my love with great force, and I decided then and there to become a telegraph operator, so I could afford to go home and see her again—I will say no more here—God willing my secret dream will come to fruition. It came to me suddenly, but with God's help I will be able to realize this dream.

From then on, he referred in his diary to his plan of returning home and presenting himself to Elisabeth as a telegraph operator—then a prestigious job—as "my lovely dream."

❈

IT IS UNCLEAR what led Riis to believe he could win Elisabeth's heart and her parents' approval by becoming a telegraph operator. Most likely he was drawn to the field because it paid well and appealed to his imagi-nation. A certain number of operators were stationed in remote wilder-ness areas, making the job attractive to young, adventurous men. For Riis, who came from a technologically backward town, the work would have held considerable allure. Riis may also have reasoned that since he could not return to Denmark as a war hero, the next best thing would be to come home as a telegraph operator, wearing a dashing uniform—a "Knight of the Key," possessing skills few others understood.

The industry, which was expanding rapidly, was dominated by Western Union. By the mid-1870s Western Union had 8,000 offices and 12,000 employees worldwide, and its profits increased 400 percent

from 1870 to 1890, when it boasted 18,000 offices. Operators were typically unionized, well paid, and solidly middle class. Moving up in society
was one of Riis's goals; only as a respectable middle-class citizen could
he ever hope to win Elisabeth.

Riis first had to earn enough money to finance his training. In an
issue of *Harper's Weekly*, he saw an ad for a job that sounded promising:

CANVASSING AGENTS WANTED
Agents earn $100 a week
Myers M'F'G' Co., 104 John St., NY.

Myers sold irons door-to-door to homemakers and seamstresses, its
chief product the Myers Combined Flatiron & Smoothening Iron. Riis
applied for the job, and the company, which was in need of cheap labor,
hired him. He was to cover several counties in Pennsylvania and New
York state. Myers would send the irons ahead to appointed cities, where
Riis would collect and sell them, receiving a percentage of sales. He felt
optimistic about his prospects. Most women had more than one iron,
the most popular model a heavy mass of metal that was heated on the
stove. Two were often used simultaneously. Some flatirons were hollow, to
accommodate a hot brick or hot coals, though it took considerable expertise to operate these, as the ashes tended to fall out and soil the clothes.

Competition among iron manufacturers was fierce. Each company
had agents crisscrossing the country. Riis, determined to become a successful salesman, pushed himself to the limit. "Work, work, work, and
the rewards cannot escape me," he wrote in his diary. "I'm all business
now." He was constantly on the road, traveling throughout western
New York and Pennsylvania, and the hard work and long hours took a
toll. Once, during a particularly bad spell, he sent five dollars to a doctor in New York who had won national acclaim for his book *Nervous
Exhaustion*, asking his advice. The doctor seems not to have replied.

Riis confided in his diary:

*I'm not sleeping well at the moment, my sleep is erratic, and during the day
I'm not at my best. Bad dreams wake me up early in the morning after a*

restless night. I'm not at all up to the mark, but then how could I be with my irregular lifestyle. I rarely have time for dinner and when I do eat, I bolt down my food, leaving no time for proper digestion.

He promised himself that he would break his bad habits, but he realized it would be difficult: "It's knowing that I'm making money and thus getting closer to my lovely goal that drives me relentlessly, and these days I feel so sure I will reach my goal."

Now consumed by his desire to return to Denmark, he fumed in Dunkirk, near Lake Erie, "Dunkirk, Dunkirk! Dunkirk be damned and the other seven kirks for that matter too, if they are as miserable for trade as this spineless town, the miserable, smug, we-don't-need-anything Dunkirk!" Riis's fundamental optimism and unyielding focus made these inevitable failures bearable. "Somehow, I will sell these irons," Riis wrote as he was preparing to leave Dunkirk. "I took to my heels again and went post haste." He headed toward Pennsylvania, and sales picked up, success prompting him to bid on a horse at an auction. Caught up in the moment, he bid $19; the horse was valued at $20. He lost to a last-minute bidder. "Which was probably a good thing," he noted in his diary, "had I gotten the horse, I would have gone straight home and packed up a few things like my gun, a blanket and a couple of shirts and headed South, to a place where winter would never catch up with me. I probably could not have resisted the chance of an adventure, I would have been too tempted." Years later, in his memoirs, he claimed he had owned the horse for fifteen minutes, and that it was the longest quarter of an hour he had ever had to endure.

❀

SALES CONTINUED to improve during the early fall, and on October 17, his unhappy anniversary with Elisabeth, Riis did not completely fall apart. Noting that "my old trouble pains my heart on this the darkest day in the year," he added: "I will let it lie for now and open with hope the first page of my new diary."

Four days later, Riis even found himself able to relax and enjoy an afternoon off on the banks of the Ohio River near Rochester, Pennsylvania. His spirits were high:

The air is strangely ethereal and curiously opaque on Indian summer days like these. Close objects appear closer and clearer than they really are. It is as if one could distinguish and touch each individual leaf and branch on the other side of the river, while faraway objects, like the hills out yonder, fade into a dreamy mist. The feather light mist, it is called "a haze" here, envelops everything in a transparent veil and puts the beholder in a state of other-worldly detachment that is wonderfully seductive. It is so quiet, no winds rustle the leaves, resplendent in their glorious fall hues, from the deepest red to the darkest green. The forest is at its most spectacular and once seen not a sight to be forgotten. The tap-tap of the woodpecker on the hollow bark, the rustling of squirrels jumping from branch to branch and the occasional wispy thumps of walnuts and chestnuts are the only sounds that interrupt the peculiar, almost solemn silence. It is as if all of nature is resting after its busy summer—a silent reverie for the coming winter lord with his ice spears and chilling northern winds. All is quiet and expectant, so different from spring which is full of joyous sounds. Summer has completed its task, and the muffled sound of a lumberjack's ax in a faraway wood brings about an involuntary shudder: man and nature are in deep harmony with one another without realizing it, as it is often the case.

The last days of summer are unsurpassed. The air is never cleaner or clearer, the rays of the sun never warmer—not sultry like in mid-summer—the sky is translucent, nuts and chestnuts cover the ground and your feet in a rich brown blanket, and as far as the eye can see, there are apple trees, weighed down by their gloriously lustrous fruit—it is truly a magnificent view one has here on the banks of the Ohio River, probably no season anywhere else in the world can compare in hue and scope to our American fall; once you have experienced it, you will never forget it, it is like a fairy tale of colors. The picturesque villages on the river's bank, with their quaint, white-painted houses, look so sweet in the tranquil air, the slender church steeples appear to be reaching for the heavens, and the friendly farmhouses are settled snugly in the woods. If only one time I could show everyone at home a scene such as this. You become a better person just looking at it.

Riis was earning more money than he needed for day-to-day survival, and, for the first time in the three years since his arrival in the United

States, he was able to save. He celebrated Christmas and New Year's with Rønne and Munk, who, like him, had been traveling and were beginning to do well. On December 31, as he evaluated the past year and expressed his hopes for the future, now an annual custom, he wrote:

> A year has gone by, I have lost much and failed many times. Plans I have made and attempted have fallen apart. . . . I have been led down strange paths by the Lord, who in all His wisdom, has guided me to achieve my goals. What last New Year seemed impossible, now seems close at hand just like in Denmark a few years ago, and I no longer doubt that I will reach my goal. No! Nothing can stop me now . . . and next Christmas, I dare say, I will be able to offer my hand and loyal heart in exchange for the greatest happiness on earth.

Riis seemed to believe that if only his desire for Elisabeth was sufficiently passionate, if he wanted her badly enough and could support her financially, she would eventually acquiesce. He pasted a poem, cut out of a newspaper and entitled "Never Give Up!" in his diary, marking the page so that he could easily find and reread it.

It had not occurred to Riis that the object of his lovely dream might have other plans. Indeed, Elisabeth had fallen in love with a thirty-eight-year-old war hero. Charming, handsome, and worldly, Wilhelm Johan Raymond Baumann, born in Izehoe, Holstein, had fought bravely against the Germans in the war of 1864.

7

• ◆ •

"True Love Can Never Die"

F OR THE GREATER PART of the 1864 war against Germany, Danish forces were hidden behind a fortification line of ten earthworks
near Dybbøl and besieged by an army three times their size. Throughout
the early spring, shells and grenades rained down on the dugouts. Danish heavy artillery consisted mostly of outdated smoothbore muzzleload-
ers, preventing return fire. The army was virtually immobilized, awaiting
the inevitable moment of defeat.

Since the news from the front was so dismal and the list of casual-
ties so long, reporters concentrated on the notorious raiding party of
First Lieutenant Bent Christian Mogens Aarøe. The Flying Corps, as
they were known, was the only unit in the Danish army that conducted
offensive missions during the war.

In March the Danish War Department had sent a desperate appeal
to the General Staff calling for offensive action, essentially to bolster
public morale. The letter suggested a few surprise attacks to unnerve
the Germans. The General Staff needed every able-bodied soldier in
the trenches to defend the position at Dybbøl. However, in order to
appear accommodating, General Headquarters set up a small special
operations unit to attack German outposts and conduct minor spy missions. Its commander was Aarøe, who had gained distinction in the First

Schleswig War. He was promoted to captain and given responsibility for the newly formed unit, consisting of 200 volunteers, which he organized into a company of foot soldiers and a cavalry squadron. To lead the cavalry, he appointed thirty-year-old Second Lieutenant Wilhelm Johan Raymond Baumann, a trusted friend.

Baumann, like his father before him, had chosen the military life. At eighteen he became an army cadet, and only two years later he was promoted to second lieutenant of the cavalry. Tall and well built, with brown eyes and a well-groomed mustache, he was, according to another second lieutenant in Aarøe's unit, "handsome, strong and intelligent as well as an elegant and fearless horseman. He was also spirited and full of life." While The Flying Corps had no impact militarily, the unit was hailed as daring to stand up to the all-powerful enemy, and they became national heroes, Baumann in particular often mentioned for his courage.

❋

AARØE'S FORCES were based in Assens, a small port town on Funen. The unit had two steamboats and a supply vessel. Its grand scheme, carried out in stages of decidedly varying success, was to sail down the coast of southern Jutland, go ashore under cover of darkness, and overpower the German coast guard, taking them hostage. The surprise attacks would force the Germans to send soldiers from Dybbøl to the coast, weakening the position at Dybbøl.

It was a plan that never got off the ground, because the unit's nightly drives often ended in failure, with boats stuck in the muddy, shallow water or the fog so thick the missions had to be aborted. Even when the unit managed to sail without incident, the soldiers sometimes resisted going ashore—in one instance because the water was too cold. A few excursions were successful; one night the unit captured four Uhlans from Brandenburg.

The most dangerous drive took place April 18, the day the German forces finally stormed Dybbøl. Thirty miles northwest of Dybbøl, The Flying Corps exchanged heavy fire with the Germans, and two Danish soldiers were killed. Baumann led his cavalry in pursuit of the Uhlans and captured two of them singlehandedly. Later that same night Baumann and his cavalry rode toward the small village of Sønderballe, where they encountered a battalion of Prussian foot soldiers who far outnumbered them. Baumann whispered to his men to turn back while he, in a wild ploy, yelled: "Alles in Ordnung, ich bin euer Freund!"— Everything is okay, I am your friend. The Prussians were not deceived and fired at Baumann. His horse, struck in the thigh, brought him to safety before it collapsed and died. Baumann was awarded the Order of Chivalry. In July, at war's end, he was engaged as an orderly officer to the Minister of War, and three years later he became a teacher at the army's cavalry school. His name was known throughout the country. When, at a horse show in Slagelse, he was pegged as a favorite to win, the nation was riveted:

> The officers flew through the air at the start signal. Lieutenant Baumann was soon in the lead, making it through the entire obstacle course until the very last jump, where his horse suddenly buckled and fell to the ground. Baumann quickly got up and, with blood streaming down his face, mounted his horse again and despite his mishap managed to come in second place. And the people cheered as much for him as for the winner.

Shortly after the show Baumann became second in command at the border patrol in Jutland. His appointment made the front pages of the *Berlingske Tidende*, the Danish equivalent of the *New York Times*. It was a demanding position requiring Baumann to conduct daily and nightly patrols along the new German border. After the peace accord the border had been moved from the Eider River to the Kongeåen River, just north of Ribe. Baumann was provided an official residence in Ribe, which, given its location just south of the border, was in effect a Danish outpost in Germany.

❋

BAUMANN MOVED INTO his new home on Nørreportsgade, near The Castle, just as Elisabeth was returning from Copenhagen after graduation from Zahle's. She continued her carefree existence at home, going to parties and spending time with friends. The golden-haired beauty charmed everyone, especially the young men, but she never seemed to fall in love with any of them. In a letter to her friend Christine she explained that, while the young men were kind and sweet, they were also boring. She still professed to have feelings for the minister's son, Frederik Moe, referring to him as "the one I favor above all others here on earth." But her relationship with the young Moe, who could not afford to live as she did, remained quite innocent, and Moe was clearly never a serious contender. In 1872, in a letter to Christine, Elisabeth confided that she was looking for a man who "must be tall and handsome with snow-white teeth and dark, sparkling eyes."

A few weeks later, in the beginning of June, she met him. He was an officer of high rank, and he was to become a frequent guest at The Castle. To Christine, Elisabeth described Raymond Baumann as not quite handsome, but dashing and superbly funny. His first visit with her lasted three hours. Elisabeth had enjoyed herself immensely, she told Christine, also assuring her friend that she was looking forward to the imminent return to Ribe of Moe.

Whether Elisabeth ever thought about Moe again is unclear. Before the month was over, she had fallen for Baumann, who seemingly was everything the young men of Ribe were not: mature, charismatic, manly. He could ride, dance, ice skate, and play the piano. He was, Elisabeth noted, "so different." When one day he addressed her as "his sweet child" and told her that he loved her, she was overjoyed. One winter night the two went ice-skating. It got so late that Elisabeth's brother was sent out to find them. Everyone in Ribe heard about their rendezvous and knew that the war hero had fallen for the beautiful Miss Giørtz. Though Baumann was not wealthy, Elisabeth's parents enthusiastically gave their consent to the marriage. Wedding preparations began soon after their engagement. Elisabeth wrote, "Never did the sun shine brighter, never did the sound of the church bells sound lovelier or more welcoming." The entire town looked forward to a spectacular wedding, to be held in Ribe Cathedral in the summer of 1873.

❋

WHILE ELISABETH was planning her wedding, Riis reached the pinnacle of his career as an iron salesman. He worked for a new company, Mann & Wilson, and his employer had given him exclusive rights to several counties in western Pennsylvania as well as Blair, near Pittsburgh, and Allegheny City. Riis had been so successful that he was able to hire his own sub-agents in January 1873. By spring that year he had seven agents working for him and made 75 cents on every iron they sold.

As an employer Riis could be ruthless. Agents he considered lazy or incompetent were fired. "Two ladies, whom I hired to work Indiana County," lasted only two days: "I don't think women are suited for this kind of work, though one should have thought it would come naturally to them." The grueling work and stern management practices, however, paid off. For the first time in his life Riis's income warranted opening a savings account. "It is so much easier having an account, than slogging the money around in your pockets," he wrote with pride. When his balance hit $120, he dispatched a letter to his parents, eager to share his good fortune with them. "Everything is big in America, my dear," Caroline replied kindly. "You speak of dollars, we of kroner. Perhaps one day you will even be able to help your mother, and who knows maybe you will be able to make us all rich?"

Niels Edvard delivered the sort of uncompromising lesson Riis had come to expect: "To be in America and not be influenced by business and their relentless pursuit of money would, I think, be impossible . . . on the other hand, I don't think the Yankees will be able to change you and make you care only for the things that rust and which moths can destroy."

In March Riis was offered the Chicago area, which he reluctantly accepted. He feared that going to Chicago would put an end to his success and destroy his dreams of becoming a telegraph operator. "I have always had an instinctive prejudice against Chicago," he wrote in his diary.

During the first half of the 1870s Chicago, like New York and Buffalo, had grown quickly. Its 334,000 inhabitants made their money in the lucrative grain trade and the booming railroad industry and from the production of farm equipment and shoes, the shipping of lumber and cattle, and the stockyards.

Two years before Riis arrived, Chicago boasted a vibrant downtown resplendent with hotels, banks, office buildings, theaters, department stores, and mansions. Such innovations as iron frames and masonry walls had allowed architects to construct increasingly tall buildings. With the exception of its elegant downtown, however, Chicago was in most respects a typical boomtown, gritty and characterized by hasty construction. The majority of the city's 60,000 houses were rickety wooden structures, and even some of the fashionable downtown buildings were unstable, with single-layer brick façades given to sudden, disastrous collapse.

However, a tragedy of much greater scale befell the city on October 9, 1871, a date invoked forever after as one that defined Chicago. It had been an unusually dry summer, and the ensuing drought caused massive wildfires. Prairies and forests and neighborhoods throughout the Midwest were destroyed by fires. On October 8, a neighborhood in Chicago burned to the ground, and the city's exhausted firefighters barely managed to prevent the fire from spreading to the rest of the city. So commonplace was the threat of fire that Chicagoans had become inured to the sound of the fire alarm. When it rang at 9:00 PM on October 9, most scarcely noticed it. The fire, which quickly burst into an out-of-control inferno, started, according to legend, in a barn at 137 De Koven Street when a cow knocked over a kerosene lantern. Residents went to bed that night assuming that this fire, like all the others that had ravaged their city that summer, would be controlled and put out.

A dry wind blew in from the prairie, feeding the flames, and the fire leaped from house to house. In the intense heat of the summer night, it roared through the city with such force that stone and brick buildings were destroyed. Firefighters could do nothing but watch in terror as the fire, within the space of a few days, transformed the city into a smoldering ruin, leaving 100,000 people homeless and taking the lives of 300.

Reconstruction was painstaking, but, in the words of several historians, Chicago rose like a phoenix from its ashes. Larger, more spectacular buildings were erected and entire neighborhoods rose out of the rubble in record time. However, while much of the city had been rebuilt by the time Riis arrived in 1873, other areas still lay in ruin. Riis hated the noisy construction sites, and the ghostly ruins depressed him, as did the endless prairies outside the city and the unsettled weather. "Chicago is such an ugly city," he wrote.

Filthy beyond reckoning—you wade through mud so thick and sticky it makes a sound like a cork popping when you try to retrieve your foot from its clammy grip. The endless prairies are flat and desolate, and gale-force winds blow off hats and tear at coattails. The relentless winds blow in alternately from the south and the north, effecting the strangest weather conditions. For instance this past Tuesday, April 1st, we had a terrible blizzard, the kind you would never experience if you were in a city nestled between hills. The winds were so fierce, you could not walk against them even in the city. It was unbelievable, and then this past Thursday, it suddenly got very hot for two days, the sweltering heat was followed by a peculiar thunderstorm Saturday night. In fact, it has been a long time since I've seen discharges of electricity like the ones we saw last night. And the rain, it rained so hard, I thought it would wash the city clear off its foundation. Such weather is intolerable: one day you need a winter coat; the next, you might as well be naked, it's so hot.

Riis's general aversion to Chicago was compounded by his own mishaps in the city. First his two Chicago agents, who he thought were friends, robbed him and disappeared. His employer refused to pay for his train ticket, which had cost him dearly. Worst of all, Riis discovered that if there was one thing Chicagoans did not need, it was irons. "Everyone seems to have at least two irons already, and they all cheat and steal here," he noted with great bitterness in his diary. "It is a house of deceit."

Traveling through Pennsylvania on his way back to Pittsburgh, he hoped at least to sell off his remaining stock. He intended to hold his boss responsible for his ill-fated Chicago adventure. Despite his grievous setbacks Riis was still optimistic and intent on carrying out his plans of becoming a telegraph operator. In Pittsburgh, however, heartbreaking news awaited him in a letter from his parents. Caroline, who had been bedridden when she heard the news of Elisabeth's engagement, had been postponing the inevitable:

People started talking about a Lieutenant Raymond, who had fallen in love with Elisabeth. Now she is his girl. When I heard this, I wished for it not to be true, but my boy, these were not kind thoughts. And I thought, I don't know what is right and wrong. It could be that the Lord has made other plans for you.

Niels Edvard delivered the message in his customary brusque manner. "I will not attempt to hide the truth from you; the fantastic dream of the future you, in your wild imagination, have concocted, will never come true."

"All is hopeless," Riis wrote in his diary. He left Pittsburgh with no clear plan in mind. In Franklin, Pennsylvania, he had to make an extended stopover to rest and recover from illness and severe exhaustion. On May 18, 1873, after three weeks of bed rest, Riis wrote:

I will put aside all my lovely memories. Her portrait, which I have had enlarged and colored and expect to receive any day now, will be my only memory of my youth and of light and happiness. I will save it always. Oh, dear Lord! Good-bye, Elisabeth. Oh, Elisabeth! If only you had known and understood. But now it is all too late. God save you and protect you, my darling Elisabeth. My light. My source of happiness. May the Lord take you through life on a sunny path to his Kingdom, may he give you peace—a peace I will never find, never again. Oh, Elisabeth, my darling girl, I have loved you so.

Two weeks later he added, "In the name of our Lord Jesus Christ, Elisabeth, my darling girl, we will meet again in a place where no wedding vows can be given or taken—where true love can never die."

8

"The Still Centre of a Cyclone"

H OWEVER DEEP-FELT Riis's loss, the news of Elisabeth's engagement also liberated him. He no longer had to risk everything he had worked for in order to return to Denmark and propose to a woman who only short of a miracle would have accepted. On some level Riis must after all have been aware that the odds were against him and that, had Elisabeth rejected him again, he would have been subjected to excruciating humiliation.

Elisabeth's betrothal simplified his life in another way as well. The decision of whether or not to stay in America was made for him; there was nothing left for him in Denmark, and the challenges of remaining in the United States had long ceased to seem quite so daunting as they once had. The hard work of the past few years, even considering his numerous setbacks, had convinced him that he possessed the skills to survive, and he felt reasonably sure that he could continue to succeed.

Still, during the weeks that followed Riis experienced alternating waves of despair and anger. "How many liaisons had a man like Baumann had, do you think?" he asked his friend Malfriede Øgmundsen on June 6, 1873, in a letter sent to Ribe. "This person, this Baumann," he continued, ". . . used his raw male power to take Elisabeth and ruin her." Yet in the midst of his misery a new optimism and determination slowly awoke. As he himself wryly noted many years later, "One does not die of love at twenty-four." Riis had decided to begin a new chapter in his life, to start over and reinvent himself once again. Significantly, he also began writing parts of his diary in English, a strong indicator that he was determined to leave Denmark behind and become an American. The long, often maudlin, passages about Elisabeth that had filled its pages disappeared. Riis picked up his case of irons and traveled east, making sales on the way. He traveled through Pennsylvania and New Jersey as an agent for a Mr. Hewitt, and for a short while he even worked for Mann, his old boss, the two having resolved their differences. Riis had not abandoned his dream of becoming a telegraph operator; on the contrary, he worked harder than ever to save for his training. He imagined that, even though he no longer needed the job to woo Elisabeth, it would be a ticket to adventures out west.

By the end of July he was back in the New York City area. He took a room on Montgomery Street, in Jersey City, and began his training as a telegraph operator at Thompson's Business School, on Fourth Avenue, near Astor Place. He established a routine, selling irons in Jersey City in the morning and in the afternoons crossing the Hudson to take classes at Thompson's from 2:00 to 4:00. Buying himself a small telegraph machine, he practiced every night, sitting in his small room, for which he paid $7 a month. In September Riis resolved to end his career as an iron salesman and settle in Manhattan, renting rooms with a classmate, a man whose last name was Ellison, on Thirtieth Street. He applied for a job as a reporter and editor for the *Long Island City Review*, with typical candor walking right into the editorial offices of the paper and asking for the editor in chief. Riis was surprised to discover that he was the only applicant. The editor in chief, a Mr. Love, hired him to cover Hunters Point and Blisville, two neighborhoods in Long Island City. Riis was elated and threw himself into the job with great enthusiasm, enjoying his new status as a reporter until he learned that Love had no money for salaries.

It was fall, traditionally a difficult time of the year to find work, and the country was on the brink of one of its greatest financial crises, precipitated by the September 18, 1873, bankruptcy of the Philadelphia banking firm Jay Cooke & Company.

The panic of 1873, as it became known, sent hundreds of thousands into poverty. Unemployment rose to 14 percent in less than a year, and thousands of businesses were forced to close. After the Civil War, Jay Cooke & Company had provided capital for massive investment in the railroad industry. Eventually it became evident that the industry had been greatly overrated and that railroads had been built in a frenzy without sound financial planning. In the words of Cornelius Vanderbilt, rails had been laid from "nowhere to nowhere." The federal government, hundreds of railroad companies, and numerous minor investment banks were dependent on capital from Cooke's. It would take five years for the United States to recover from the crisis, which culminated in a series of violent strikes in 1877.

Riis was an early victim of the crisis. He had mistakenly assumed that he had been through the worst, convinced he had gained enough knowledge and experience to avoid vagrancy if ever faced with hard times again. But now he scrambled helplessly for food and shelter. As he had done three years earlier in similarly dismal circumstances, he acquired another stray dog, a Newfoundland puppy. Riis called him Bob.

For a time he held a low-paying job selling subscriptions door-to-door to Charles Dickens's novels for *Harper's Weekly*. One day in November, according to his memoirs, Riis was hawking Dickens's *Hard Times*. Sales had been poor, and he had not eaten for two days. He and Bob had gone all day without selling a single copy. In the evening he rested on the stairs of Cooper Union. A chef at a local restaurant had given Riis some bones for Bob, who was sleeping contentedly at Riis's feet.

But just as Riis believed his darkest hour had arrived, help came from an unexpected ally. A man climbed the stairs where he was sitting. Riis looked up and recognized Mr. Thompson, the founder of the business school. He looked surprised to see Riis in such miserable circumstances, and according to Riis the following exchange took place:

"Why, what are you doing here?" Thompson asked.

Riis told him of his unhappy situation and explained that he was trying to sell books to survive.

"Books!" he snorted. "I guess they won't make you rich. Now, how would you like to be a reporter, if you have got nothing better to do? The manager of a news agency down town asked me today to find him a bright young fellow whom he could break in. It isn't much—$10 a week to start with. But it is better than peddling books, I know."

He poked over the book in my hand and read the title. "Hard Times," he said, with a little laugh. "I guess so. What do you say?"

Though it seems almost too convenient that Riis was selling *Hard Times* that day, we know from his diaries that the two men did meet on the steps of Cooper Union and that the meeting changed the young immigrant's life. Riis's later views on poverty and the poor were greatly influenced by this experience. He became a strong advocate for helping even the most abject poor, because, as he argued, they could be of value to society if given a chance. All it required was for someone to break the cycle of poverty, as Thompson had done for him.

Thompson sent a letter of reference to the editor of the New York News Association, recommending Riis for the job. He also offered to take care of the puppy, since Riis would not be able to bring Bob to work. Riis was to bring the puppy to Thompson's house the next morning.

His first morning on the job, Riis woke at dawn, washed his face and hands as best he could in the dog's water bowl, smoothed his clothes, and headed off with Bob to Thompson's. After taking leave of his canine companion Riis walked, full of trepidation, downtown to 23 Park Row. The last time Riis had been on Newspaper Row, he had come in the hope that the editor of the *Sun* would help him enlist in the French army. It seemed a very long time ago.

His News York News Association boss looked suspiciously at him, Riis cutting a strange figure with his rumpled clothes and uncombed hair, but he decided to give him a chance. Riis was asked to cover a luncheon meeting between some of the city's dignitaries at Astor House, an elegant restaurant catering to the business community. Fortunately, Riis had reached the third-day stage of hunger, when the pangs begin to subside. He was at "the still centre of a cyclone," as he wrote, able to concentrate on the meeting and not on the great quantities of food being consumed. When the editor read his piece, he merely said, "You will do. Take that desk, and report at ten every morning."

❈

THE NEW YORK NEWS ASSOCIATION, which sold stories to both the morning and the evening papers, required that Riis work seven days a week from about ten in the morning until midnight. "The pay is not great, about $10 a week, and the work is tough especially because of the annoying evening work," an exhausted Riis noted in his diary. The job kept him so busy that, though he attempted to keep up with his course work at Thompson's, he hardly ever made it to class on time and eventually gave up his studies.

Riis covered general news with two other young reporters, "Doc" Lynch, from Bohemia, Germany, and Crafts, who had just moved to New York from Maine. The three ran from one end of Manhattan to the other, from Harlem to the Bowery, digging up stories about robberies, brawls, weddings, sensational events involving children, horses, or dogs, street life, even the weather, if unusual. The quantity of stories was far more important than their quality, and at times, as Riis admitted in his diary, but—and this is noteworthy—not in his memoirs, life as a general reporter meant fabricating stories. On November 29, Riis wrote:

> *This business is a strange one at times. Yesterday, on Thanksgiving, I wrote a sermon, which was in the papers today, supposedly held by Dr. Hepworth, a well-known and prominent member of the clergy. I was asked to write on this subject and knew what his sermon would involve, but had no opportunity to hear it and thus there was nothing else for me to do. He preached about the republic's responsibility towards Cuba. I think I must have assumed correctly in my version as I have hitherto not been contradicted.*

Articles rarely had bylines—only essays by well-known people were routinely signed. Reporters wrote anonymously, serving as clerks who simply gathered the news and put it together reasonably coherently. Because Riis kept a diary, it has been possible to trace the Hepworth piece, which was published by the *New York Tribune*, among other papers. Headlined "The War Cloud," it is the earliest article we know with certainty was written by Riis. The piece is rather garbled and unintelligible. To his editors, however, this was inconsequential.

> *The position we occupy today is a very instructive and a curious one, and we can congratulate ourselves upon one work that has been well done. Crime has now met its just desert [sic] and honesty and integrity are now receiving their rewards. God rules. The sleeping people have been aroused. Diogenes has blown his light in the presence of a New York justice. What will you do about it?*

Riis embraced his life as a reporter and recorded the ironies of this latest turn in his fortunes in his diaries. The job had its perks; he dined regularly at restaurants such as Delmonico's, at whose back door he had begged for food only a few years earlier. The job brought him back to the slums of Five Points and other dark corners of the city. Walking the streets, he was reminded of the police officer who had killed his first dog, and acknowledged feeling a terrible thirst for revenge. Adjusting to the New York News Association's grueling deadlines, Riis quickly showed a natural talent for journalism. When the New York News Association was approached by a couple of prominent Democratic politicians from South Brooklyn who were looking for someone to write their weekly neighborhood paper, its editors did not hesitate to recommend Riis—or the Dutchman, as they had begun to call him.

✳

ON MAY 20, 1874, Riis left the New York News Association to become a reporter for the small local weekly *South Brooklyn News*, located at Fifth Avenue and Ninth Street, only a few blocks from Riis's new lodging, near Prospect Park. He was offered $15 a week for writing all four pages of the publication. Soon he was promoted to editor, receiving a considerable raise to $25 a week. The owners of the paper offered to put him in charge of printing as well. Riis turned them down; he had too much work gathering, writing, and editing the news, and was kept busy from early morning until late at night, seven days a week. He enjoyed the all-consuming nature of his job, which kept his mind off Elisabeth and gave him a sense of purpose, something he had longed for the past four years. It seemed he had finally found his calling. "I think," he wrote in his diary, "that I must have a flair for journalism, at least I'm successful at everything I do. I have my own office and, all in all, life is great."

Riis clearly took pride in his achievement. In four years he had achieved a degree of fluency in English that enabled him to perform with confidence as a journalist. Thousand of immigrants who, like Riis, learned English acquired only rudimentary language skills. Riis's conviction that as the son of a senior teacher he belonged in the professional class seems to have driven him to excel. A diary entry dated August 22, 1874, is short and succinct: "Today my name was printed in the paper for the first time. I had demanded it!" He wrote that he was certain of future success through the force of "my own greatness." Years later, a more accomplished, humbler Riis crossed out these words and replaced them with "pure luck."

※

ONE EVENING SHORTLY before Christmas, Riis, twenty-five, stood on the deck of the Fulton Ferry, taking in the view of Manhattan. He had just put the paper to bed. The city lay before him, bathed in light from thousands of gas lamps. To Riis it seemed to stretch itself, luxuriant and lazy, from the southernmost tip to uptown. It was an exquisite evening. The night air was clear, and far above him, beyond the reach of the lamps, there were millions of stars. For the first time in his life, Riis saw a shooting star. A wild hope flared—a yearning he thought he had quelled. But there it was, as bright as the shooting star itself, which for a brief, miraculous moment brushed the sky with silvery dust before its quiet descent into darkness. Riis wished for the impossible: Elisabeth. His hope flickered only for a moment. He had stopped believing in magic and was now, in his own words, a hardened, self-assured young man who rarely smiled and had grown a serious goatee. The incident upset him anyway, because he had not realized that the old, impossible dream still had a strong hold.

og med En, hvis trofaste Kjærlighed vil aldrig vil svigte. – Svar mig paa det, dersom Du skriver til mig, saa er Du sød. – Du har jo seet Riis, hvad synes Du om ham? – Vær saa sød at skrive snart til mig, jeg længes efter at høre hvad Du tænker om mig, sig det kun ærligt og ligefremt som Du altid har talt til mig, Du min egen bedste Kirsten. Jeg skriver ikke til mere end et Par af mine allernærmeste Veninder, det gjør mig at skulle gjentage det Samme saa ofte. – Vor Correspondance er nok rent gaaet istaa, men jeg er vis paa Du har tænkt paa mig, ligesom mine Tanker mange, mange Gange have dvælet hos Dig; Du er jo næsten uadskillelig fra mine bedste Barndomsminder. – Jeg faaer aldrig en Veninde som Dig. –

9

A Second Proposal

WHILE RIIS stood on the Fulton Ferry in December 1874, a tragic turn of events in Elisabeth's life was in fact propelling her in his direction. The past spring, a few months before her wedding day, Raymond Baumann fell ill several times, his symptoms ranging from those of a simple cold to weakness necessitating brief periods of bed rest. With each recovery, the couple's fear that his sickness was serious eased. Then more bouts of fever and chills followed, and the coughing fits began.

Their summer wedding was postponed, and Baumann went to Copenhagen for a medical examination. His doctors' diagnosis confirmed the couple's worst fears: Baumann had tuberculosis. He was advised to leave Denmark for the warmer, drier climate of southern Europe, but his pay was insufficient to finance the journey. He applied for a leave of absence and financial aid and was granted a leave until June 10, 1874, but received only 100 kroner in compensation, hardly enough to cover even his travel expenses. Elisabeth's parents refused to help their future son-in-law, though they had been nothing short of enthusiastic about him when the couple were first betrothed. Still, Baumann found the means to pay for a prolonged stay at a sanatorium in Clarence, near Montreux, in Switzerland.

Soon after his departure Elisabeth's parents explained why they had refused to help with Baumann's expenses: They no longer wished for her to marry the lieutenant. Elisabeth was stunned. When she asked what had made them change their minds, the answer she received revealed a chilling lack of empathy for both the ailing Baumann and Elisabeth, given her feelings for him. Nevertheless, her parents were acting in her interest. Elisabeth's father argued that Baumann in all likelihood would not get well, and that if she stayed with him, she might have to spend years of her young life nursing him, perhaps even contracting the disease herself.

Elisabeth loved Baumann and was still convinced that he would recover. Her parents had been in touch with his doctors, however, and knew it was only a matter of time before he succumbed to the disease. Desperate to protect their daughter, they wrote to Baumann without Elisabeth's knowledge, begging him to let her go. It would not only be in Elisabeth's best interest but also in his, they pleaded, as he would be relieved of the duty of supporting a wife. Elisabeth herself was given an ultimatum: If she chose to stay with Baumannn, she would no longer be considered part of the family.

Elisabeth, who had enjoyed a secure childhood with her parents, could hardly fathom the choice she was being forced to make. Still, there was never any doubt in her mind, and without hesitation she chose Baumann. Her father, too proud to give in, immediately asked her to leave and never contact them again. Elisabeth moved in with Baumann's brother Arthur and his wife, Mariette, in Holte, on Zealand. She helped out with washing, cleaning, and cooking. It was a sad and difficult winter. Her fiancé was fatally ill, she lived with people she did not know well in an unfamiliar town, and her parents had washed their hands of her. "It is so strange," she wrote to Christine, "to live in a new house and know my dear old childhood home is forever closed to me. But he [my fiancé] is surely worth the sacrifice."

In the spring of 1874, Baumann's condition seemed to improve. In his letters from the sanatorium, he said he was planning to return in May. Throughout his stay he and Elisabeth had exchanged many long letters affirming their love for each other and carefully avoiding any mention of their underlying fear for his health. Baumann, however, did not return home in May as planned, instead staying until June. His doctors were adamant: He needed more rest and recuperation. The War Department did not look favorably on his request for an extended furlough, and in order to get it he had to accept a demotion and a transfer as well as a considerable salary reduction.

Despite their reduced circumstances, Elisabeth and Baumann's reunion was a happy one. "Even if we will have little to live on, I think we will be really happy together," Elisabeth wrote to Christine. Baumann, however, weakened from the long illness, soon suffered a relapse and was hospitalized in Copenhagen, so weak he could barely get out of bed. In order to be close to him Elisabeth moved in with his mother, who lived in Copenhagen. Every morning that fall Elisabeth went to the hospital. She never spoke about how ill he was, and shushed him whenever he began talking about dying. In a letter to Christine she acknowledged, "he is so, so tired." On November 3, a cold and damp morning, Elisabeth left the house as usual shortly after daybreak to go to the hospital. The nurses had gotten to know her and gave her special treatment. When she arrived soaked from the rain, they would take her shoes and stockings and dry them for her. In the afternoon they would serve her coffee, even though beverages were not allowed in the visitors' lounge. She found it peculiar, then, that the nurse in charge pretended neither to see nor hear her when she greeted her with a cheerful "Good morning" on the third. When she reached Baumann's room, she understood. He lay lifeless on his bed.

✳

ON CHRISTMAS EVE, 1874, Riis returned home from work exhausted. It had been another long day, after another long week, and he was worried about the paper's future. Its financial backers were not prepared to keep the relatively new publication running unless circulation quickly increased and it started turning a profit. The owners of the paper were, among others, Democratic Party bosses: a judge by the name of Delmar and T. V. Talmage, a former city council member. Riis described them in his diary as "tough guys on their own turf."

Like many newspapers at the time, the *South Brooklyn News* was a political party organ, its purpose primarily to gain as many Democratic voters in South Brooklyn as possible. If Riis did not achieve this goal, Talmage and Delmar had recently informed him, it would cost him his job. It was Riis's fourth Christmas in America, and he had many worries, made worse by physical exhaustion. In the past months he had spent all his energy on the paper, rarely taking time off to rest. This evening, when he came home, he found a thick envelope waiting from Denmark and tore it open. It had pained him that his Christmas letters from Denmark had so far arrived days or even weeks late. He had bitterly noted these delays in his diary, but this year was different, and Riis wrote: "Imagine, on this Christmas Eve the letter came in time."

Unfortunately, it initially seemed as if the letter, which was from his parents, brought nothing but sad news. There were four pages, written in his father's characteristic neat cursive.

> *My dear Jacob,*
>
> *Illness and sorrow have moved into our house, may we have the strength to bear it. A month ago we received a letter from Sophus [Riis's older brother, in medical school in Copenhagen], telling us he was so weak from exhaustion that his professor had told him to go home and rest. You can probably imagine how sad he was to go home, being that he was so close to graduating. He is here at home now, he spends most of his days resting on the sofa, but still seems to grow weaker every day, and as of late he cannot even read. His illness seems to be beyond the reach of any medicine. The end is near, nearer perhaps than we may know, at least that is how it looks to us. We are prepared, though. God's will be done. He is himself, however, still hopeful and does not let on that he may have to go ahead of us a little. He remains hopeful but can only take milk. He has trouble sleeping at night and seems just to doze. It is far harder to watch him suffer so than it will be to part with him, I think. He read your last letter with great interest and thinks of you often.*

Riis's favorite aunt, Aunt Bine, was bedridden as well on Sortebrødregade. "She, too, is presumably at death's door," his father wrote. "Aunt Bine is in the top bedroom, and Sophus is in our room." Riis's brother Peter Ditlev was also at home ill, though his case did not seem to be serious. "He has pains in his leg, and doctor Kjær says he must not strain it and that it will only get better if he rests," Niels Edvard wrote. Although much illness had befallen the house, "Your mother and I are well," he continued.

"It is a sad letter to receive on Christmas," Riis noted later in his diary. One piece of news overshadowed the rest, however. On the third page of Niels Edvard's letter, his father had written, "Lieutenant Baumann died on November 3 of tuberculosis." It was as if he had hoped his son would fail to take note of Baumann's death if he omitted any details. But of course it was momentous news to Riis. Though Niels Edvard had not mentioned Elisabeth, her situation was clear to Riis. "I lay down on my bed and cried," Riis wrote in his diary. In pencil, he added in the margin of Niels Edvard's letter, "Elisabeth is free." He added in his diary: "In God's name, I only now see that there is a higher and mightier power. And I now leave my fate to Him because I know He will take care of me and her. Now I know that, in time, she will be mine and all my earthly goals be reached."

Then and there Riis came up with a bold plan: He would work toward becoming financially independent; and since owning his own business would, he felt, make him less vulnerable, it occurred to him that buying the *South Brooklyn News* would enable him to reach this objective.

While Riis was making good money and spent little, if any, of it, he still had savings of only $75, not nearly enough to purchase the paper. He figured that the asking price would be approximately $2,500, an amount he could never raise. On January 24, after a few weeks of careful consideration, he approached the owners with an offer. He would give them a down payment of $75 and then $600 to be paid in monthly installments of $200. The price was fair, Riis argued, because the only real value in the paper was the old typesetting machine. The owners accepted his offer. Talmage, Delmar, and their partners must not have had much faith in the paper and were probably relieved to get rid of it. Thrilled by his good fortune, Riis, who was now not only an editor and a reporter but a publisher, felt confident that he could earn enough money to support himself and Elisabeth.

He was clearly fueled by more than his marital plans, however. Riis had found his calling in journalism. Though his overwhelming workload had driven him several times to consider quitting, change was unlikely at this point. At a prayer meeting he had heard Brooklyn's formidable preacher Henry Ward Beecher and was so moved he had revived the idea, contemplated in 1871 in Buffalo, of becoming a missionary. During a revival meeting in the local Eighteenth Street Methodist Church, the idea of entering the clergy once took hold. But the revivalist preacher, Ichabod Simmons, whose fiery sermon had inspired Riis, discouraged him. According to Riis's memoirs, Simmons said to him: "No, no, Jacob, not that. We have preachers enough. What the world needs is conse-crated pens.'"

※

HE IMMERSED HIMSELF in his new job as publisher with almost manic effort, which indeed was needed to make the *South Brooklyn News* prof-itable. He wrote nonstop and was responsible for practically all of the stories in the paper as well as the reporting. "I kept two printers busy all day, every day," he wrote in his memoirs. In his spare time he went from one business to the next selling advertising space. The local mor-tician was one of his most faithful advertisers. Once a week Riis carried the heavy printing plates to the printers on Spruce Street in Manhattan at Printing Square, where all of New York's bigger papers and printers were located. He would then go home, only to return after midnight to pick up the finished papers, which he singlehandedly carried back to his office. Grabbing a few hours for a nap, he curled up in his office and slept until dawn, often using a stack of newly printed papers as his pil-low. In the early hours of the morning the paper boy woke him up and collected the papers for distribution.

Riis worked tirelessly, and it paid off: Circulation increased, and the paper gained the respect of its readers and became influential in the community. Not only was Riis able to make all his payments, he earned enough money to set some aside. On August 16, 1875, he had paid off his last installment. The time had come to write to Elisabeth. As on Christmas Eve less than eight months earlier, Riis was overwhelmed by

Niels Edvard Riis (top left); Riis's mother, Caroline (top right); and Riis's two older brothers, Peter Ditlev (bottom left) and Sophus Charles (bottom right). Both died young, as did most of Niels Edward and Caroline's fourteen children.

Elisabeth Giørtz's stepparents, the industrialist Balthasar Giørtz and his wife, Clara.

The Castle, the luxurious childhood home of Elisabeth.

Ribe under water. Flooding was common in the winter.

Riis's first photograph, taken in January 1888. An open trench, potter's field,
Hart Island, burial ground for the city's poor

Gravediggers at potter's field burying children's coffins. Photograph by Riis

The notorious Mulberry Bend, the most densely populated place in the world, and the place Riis detested the most. Photograph by Riis

One of the backyards of Mulberry Bend. Photograph by Riis

Little girl in a typical tenement hallway. Photograph by Riis

A tenement apartment without windows or any kind of ventilation.
An entire family often shared a room like this. Photograph by Riis

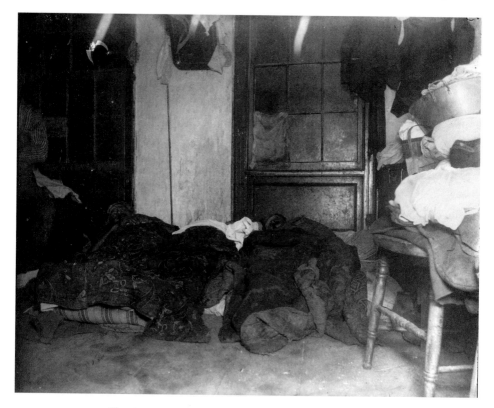

Sleeping men in a tenement apartment. Photograph by Riis

Men in a so-called two-cent restaurant. In *How the Other Half Lives*, Riis
wrote: "The privilege to sit all night on a chair, or sleep on a table, or in a bar-
rel, goes with each round of drinks." Photograph by Riis

Baxter Street Court, 22 Baxter Street. Courts like these were the only places children could play apart from the streets. Photograph by Riis

The police reporters at 301 Mulberry Street. Photograph by Riis

Police hunting pirates on the Hudson River. Riis often followed the police
on nightly patrols like these. Photograph by Riis

Police Chief Thomas Byrnes's infamous rogues' gallery at police headquarters, 300 Mulberry Street. Photograph by Riis

HIGHWAYMAN AT 17

BURGLAR AT 17

MURDERER AT 19
HANGED AT THE TOMBS

PICKPOCKET AT 15

BURGLAR AT 18

Photographs in the rogues' gallery. A closer look shows that many of these
allegedly hardened criminals were just boys, as Riis points out here.
Photographs by Riis

a range of conflicting emotions. Another letter had just arrived from his parents, informing him that his brothers Sophus and Peter Ditlev had died of tuberculosis, as had Aunt Bine. The news of his brothers' and his aunt's deaths was a sharp reminder of his own mortality. If Elisabeth turned him down, he wrote, "I will definitely try my luck in South America next year." He added inexplicably, "I hate all women except Elisabeth, I remember her with the greatest passion," a remark that perhaps suggests he had been jilted by another woman since arriving in the United States. No record of any such relationship exists, however.

After finishing his letter to Elisabeth, he felt restless and unable to fall asleep. Finally at daybreak he got up and walked directly to the post office to mail his letter. Now it was out of his hands. He had turned the last page in his diary and was determined not to write another word until he heard from Elisabeth.

※

AFTER HER PARENTS had turned her out of their house, Baumann had become Elisabeth's family. As his coffin was lowered into the ground next to his father's grave in the Garrison Cemetery in Copenhagen, a three-shot salute rang out. "The three shots went straight through [my] heart," Elisabeth later wrote to Christine.

One of Baumann's closest friends, Pastor Bulow, gave the eulogy. None of Elisabeth's relatives had come, and she undoubtedly felt alone and miserable. She remained with Baumann's mother after the funeral while trying to find some means of supporting herself. Her parents apparently had no intention of welcoming her back, but there must have been some form of communication between them; shortly after the funeral, Elisabeth moved in with relatives in Copenhagen. She resumed her musical training at Zahle's until the spring of 1875, then became a governess for the Dürings, a family with three daughters who lived in a small village near the town of Haderslev, in Jutland, not far from Ribe. Elisabeth found teaching frustrating; the girls, she told Christine, were "seriously unintelligent and at times, it requires much patience to teach them reading and especially music."

Though Captain Baron Otto Düring and his wife treated Elisabeth with kindness, she was unhappy in her position. She longed to reconcile with her parents and see her friends in Ribe. Eventually Balthasar and Clara Giørtz's hearts softened, and they invited Elisabeth to be with them for the summer. She spent six wonderful weeks in Ribe and dreaded her return to the Dürings'. Just as she was finishing packing, her mother entered her room and handed her a letter from Jacob Riis. Elisabeth had not given Riis much thought since he left for America, and she was surprised to receive a letter from him. His proposal, however, angered her; she perceived it as a transgression and expressed indignation in her reply to him, stressing that she would under no circumstances marry him. Elisabeth gave her letter to Riis's mother, who decided against forwarding it to her son.

❋

ELISABETH RETURNED to Haderslev. Fall set in with cold, rainy weather and short days. There was little to cheer her up, and she became, in her own words, "a pale, anemic, sorrowful girl to look at." In the evening she tried to busy herself with sewing, but her thoughts wandered. One night, when she was particularly restless, she remembered a conversation she had had with Baumann shortly before his death. He had gently admonished her to marry after his death, even if she did not love the man; it was better to be with a man who truly loved her than to be alone, he had said. Thinking back, Elisabeth wondered if Baumann had not obliquely been suggesting that she marry Riis. At the time Elisabeth had brushed the idea aside, not wanting to contemplate the possibility of Baumann's death. Baumann did not know Riis; Elisabeth had never talked about him. But Baumann had read the congratulatory letter Riis had sent Elisabeth upon their engagement and had surely understood that he loved Elisabeth.

Riis had loved her faithfully for twelve years, Elisabeth realized. By October he was constantly on her mind. She needed, as she wrote Christine, "to be loved. I hope you can understand that when you have been through what I have, it can seem a great gift to be loved by someone whom you may not have appreciated—can you understand this? And can you understand that I think I could be fulfilled by being there for someone who loves me with all his heart and will always be faithful to me?"

One evening in October, Elisabeth found it impossible to sleep before she had imparted her changed position in a letter to Riis.

Dear Jacob,

Please do not be angry with me for writing to you like this after all that has happened between us. But the thing is, my heart is so uneasy, and so many thoughts fill my mind that I simply must speak—please do not think me unwomanly, but hear me out and you will know why I could not have stopped myself from speaking even to save my life. I have not had a peaceful moment since I sent my last letter to you. When I sent it, there was no doubt in my mind as to my answer to your proposal. I knew I did not love you and therefore said no. But the very next day when the letter had been sent, a thought hit me like lightning: I could have said yes, perhaps my feelings for you were not those of a woman in love, but with time I might have learned to love you; you are noble, loving and a good Christian, and you would love me faithfully if I were to become yours. Then I would have someone to live for again, to live the rest of my life for, a wonderful sacrifice, I think. These were my thoughts, Riis, and I could not chase them away, and they kept me awake at night and now, after two weeks of thinking and contemplating, I am writing to you to tell you all, you my childhood friend. You have loved me faithfully for many long years though I have given you no hope, on the contrary I have caused you much pain. If you will have me as I am with the kind of love I can give you, I am yours from this moment on, and I will give you my hand in marriage. I cannot give you beauty, wealth or passion, I can only give you a heart which has loved, been hurt and longs for true love, oh, I will with great joy allow myself to be loved by you. I have been thinking perhaps I will disappoint you when you see me as I really am, but I pray, you will lead and guide me. You are good and strong, and together we will strive for all that is good and noble in life, will we not? I will do all that is in my power to be a good wife to you.

But let us keep this to ourselves for now, do not even tell your mother. I have not told my parents that I am writing these words to you and do not want them to hear of this news from strangers. And I do not wish to tell them before you are here, too. Can you possibly come home this summer? I think I will be in Ribe then, and we could meet and plan everything.

Until then my decision must remain a secret. Write me as soon as you can, and promise me in your letter that you will not breathe a word of this to anyone. And tell me you are happy about the turn of events. Although there is not much to be happy about, I think you might in fact be happy, but be careful that your joy will not be read between the lines of the letters you send home to Denmark, except of course in the letters you send to me. And will you not, please, send me your photo that I might familiarize myself with the way you look now. Me, I am a teacher here, but you probably already know that from your parents, though I will not speak of that just now. I can think of only one thing now, that I am your bride—how mysterious are the ways in which Our Lord works, only a fortnight ago I should have thought this impossible, but I am sure it was God who helped me think of this solution. May He bless our union. Please feel no anger toward me because of the things I wrote in my previous letter, which caused you a disappointment you could have been spared. Listen to me, please, don't be angry. And now farewell, I trust you to keep all this to yourself until we meet. I long to hear from you, and oh, I seem already to miss you. I enclose a little flower for you, and it is this flower that brings you these wonderful tidings from Denmark, and in my thoughts I am also sending you your first kiss from your future bride.

Elisabeth

"I came in late from work," Riis wrote in his diary, ". . . and found the letter from Elisabeth which brought joy and sunshine to my heart. God bless her. She is my bride now, and so ends this chapter of my unsettled life with a blessing. In the name of Our Lord, Elisabeth is my bride, my betrothed at last."

❋

THAT EVENING and all through the night Riis paced the floor of his small room, too excited to sleep. The landlord, who lived in the apartment below, heard him and, fearing something was wrong, went up to check on him. A jubilant Riis opened the door, and it required only a brief glance at his young tenant's face for the landlord to understand that Elisabeth had finally consented to marry him. Like all of Riis's acquaintances the landlord knew about her. Now he uttered a heartfelt, "Wish you joy, old man."

PART TWO

❖

Riis and the Other Half

10

• ◆ •

"Fat and Strong"

O N A RAINY AFTERNOON in Hamburg, Germany, Jacob Riis, confused and nervous, accidentally boarded a train bound for Holstein. When he finally discovered his mistake, three hours later, he realized he could not catch another train back and would have to spend the night in an unfamiliar town. He was furious, though the irony of the situation cannot have escaped him. He had spent close to six years in America, thousands of miles away from home and the woman he loved, yet now his impatience and agitation had cost him one more day. Taking a room at an inn, he tried unsuccessfully to calm down and fall asleep. At last, several hours before daybreak, he caught the first train back to Hamburg, where the steamer that had brought him from New York to Europe had docked the day before. In the afternoon he continued on to Denmark.

Riis made the journey back to his homeland as New Year's Eve yielded to 1876, a historically significant year for the United States. The country would celebrate its centennial. Lieutenant Colonel George Armstrong Custer and the Seventh Cavalry would be killed at Little Bighorn, an incomparably disastrous military defeat, and the Democratic candidate for president, Samuel Tilden, winner of the popular vote, would lose to Rutherford Hayes after a controversial electoral dispute, an outcome that in effect ended Reconstruction.

Thoughts of America were far from Riis's mind, however, as he sat restlessly in his compartment, awaiting arrival in Ribe. He had had the compartment to himself since crossing the border into Denmark, with ample opportunity to take in the familiar landscapes of his childhood: the flat marshes under the sky, so immense it seemed to swallow time, and the great heath, which Ripensers called the desert. It was a quiet, open, unindustrialized world, in stark contrast to New York City's harbors, smokestacks, and masses of people. By nightfall the train stopped at a desolate whistle-stop a few kilometers from Ribe, and Riis heard a familiar voice call out, "This way, Herr Doctor." The voice belonged to Ribe's district medical officer. "There is room in here," he continued, now addressing the conductor.

The medical officer accompanied a white-haired man. Riis was at pains, in his memoirs, to note that he immediately recognized the man as his father, though he had aged considerably. He jumped out of his seat and extended his hand in greeting. A look of shock registered on Niels Edvard's face; he had known nothing of Riis's homecoming. Riis later wrote that Niels Edvard must have thought he was seeing a ghost of yet another departed son.

Riis had kept both his travel plans and his upcoming marriage to Elisabeth secret, though every letter home had betrayed his newfound exuberance. His mother, who had finally dispatched Elisabeth's letter of rejection, had expected him to be devastated, and both parents were frankly baffled by the inexplicable joy his letters displayed. Certainly the Riises had never believed that their son would return to Denmark. Just shy of sixty, Niels Edvard had been irrevocably changed by the losses of the past several years.

"Bless my soul if here is not Jacob," he said, incredulous.

✻

THE REUNION that afternoon in the small red-brick building on Sortebrødregade was a happy one, according to Riis's memoirs, though as he also noted, the family was marked by a profound sadness. The deaths of Peter Ditlev and Sophus Charles had ravaged Riis's parents. As the young men had lain dying, Caroline had tried to keep up their spirits, but she had known that neither would recover.

Riis had not yet revealed what had occasioned his return to Ribe. His parents guessed it when, after tea, he told them that there was something he had to do. Watching their son cross the arched bridge and head with great determination toward The Castle, the couple, still ignorant of Elisabeth's consent, braced themselves for the return of a broken-hearted son.

✳

Riis later recalled feeling only slightly nervous about his reunion with Elisabeth. Confident that he had become a man of means, he knew that Elisabeth's parents could no longer reject him on the basis of insufficient income. When Elisabeth's letter had arrived in the fall of 1875, the *South Brooklyn News* was a prosperous paper. In fact, it was doing so well that the former owners regretted selling it to Riis; although he had turned out to be an accomplished newspaperman, he was clearly not *their* man. The Democratic Party bosses had mistakenly assumed that Riis would back their candidates. During a local election, however, Riis had chosen to support a Republican candidate, Police Captain John Mackellar, one of his few friends in Brooklyn. No doubt influenced by the corruption scandal surrounding William Magear "Boss" Tweed, whose defrauding of the city resulted in his arrest in 1871, Riis staunchly refused to comply.

Thus when Riis was preparing to leave for Denmark, the former owners jumped at the chance of recapturing the paper. They offered him $3,000, five times the purchase price. The sale of the paper hastened Riis's departure for Denmark; he had not intended to leave until the summer of 1876. Throughout the fall of 1875, Riis had written daily to Elisabeth, and with each letter he had moved his travel date up until one day he suddenly announced he was on his way.

✳

IT WAS DARK when Riis knocked on The Castle's door. Still, he could clearly make out the features of the person who opened the door for him. The light from the hall fell on his face, and Riis recognized the servant who had taken note of him standing under Elisabeth's window on the day of his departure for America. The servant also recognized Riis and in a loud, strong voice called for Elisabeth. From inside Riis could hear a voice inquire, "Is it him?"

According to Riis's memoirs he was taken into the living room, where the entire Giørtz family was gathered. An awkward silence fell, not broken until Riis asked Elisabeth if she remembered a skating incident from their childhood. They had been on a pond when the ice suddenly broke. He had saved her and carried her ashore, he recounted. According to Riis's memoirs, Elisabeth asked, "Was I heavy?"—a nonsensical rejoinder that made them both laugh.

However, according to a letter from Emma Reinsholm sent to Riis's daughter Katie several years after his death, the mood at The Castle that evening was far from lighthearted. Reinsholm recounted that the meeting with Elisabeth and her parents was so humiliating that, as a form of self-punishment, Riis deliberately went to The Castle on subsequent visits to Denmark in order to remind himself of it.

Balthasar Giørtz in particular remained unimpressed with Riis. Perhaps he still saw in him nothing but a poor carpenter, or perhaps his cause for hesitation lay elsewhere. The war of 1864 had left Denmark impoverished, and like so many other businesses Giørtz's cotton mill had faltered. A few years later, following several setbacks, Giørtz went bankrupt. Whatever his reasons were, he refused to give the couple his blessing. Instead, as he had done once before, Giørtz turned to his daughter and gave her a terrible ultimatum: She had to choose between her family and Riis.

Elisabeth did not give him a verbal answer, but her gesture spoke louder than any words. Defying her parents, Elisabeth, who seemed as headstrong as her future husband once she set her mind on something, crossed the room with elegant composure and calmly put her hand in Riis's.

❊

THE WEDDING TOOK PLACE at Ribe Cathedral on March 5, 1876. Very little is known about the ceremony, which went unmentioned in the *Ribe Stiftstidende*. Neither the Riis nor Giørtz family kept any record of the event. According to the church register, two altar candles were lit during the service, a considerable expense. There was a small reception at The Castle. Not surprisingly, Riis himself recalled the wedding as a grand event. According to his memoirs, townspeople filled the streets and gathered around the couple as they emerged from the cathedral, showering them with fresh flowers from the local greenhouses while the bells of the cathedral chimed.

For the guests and the citizens of Ribe the reality of the wedding was somewhat more sober. Giørtz was displeased, which everyone in Ribe knew. Riis was not the son-in-law he had envisioned for Elisabeth, and the wedding itself paled next to Elisabeth's romantic engagement to the dashing Lieutenant Baumann. Giørtz was no longer the rich and power-ful man he had once been, rendering the wedding less splendid than it might have been.

Even Elisabeth had changed. No longer the cheerful, heedless "prin-cess" of earlier years, running blithely through suitors, the death of her first fiancé and subsequent estrangement from her parents had brought about an irrevocable shift in outlook. And then there was Riis, the young rebel who had not accepted his place in society but had argued openly with the then mighty Giørtz at a ball and had later chosen to leave Ribe for the New World, to many a grave insult to the Old Town.

Despite this inauspicious sendoff, married life agreed with Riis. In the following months he "grew," as he later wrote, "fat and strong, whereas [before I] had been lean and poor." Elisabeth also seemed to embrace married life. When the couple arrived in New York in the early spring of 1876, she was already pregnant with their first child. That they would settle in the New World had been a given. Elisabeth was eager to start fresh and put her tragic past and family troubles behind her, and for Riis Denmark had little to offer compared to the States, where he was a highly respected professional. In Denmark he would never be able to rise above the status of a carpenter.

Their first home was a few modest rooms in a boardinghouse near Prospect Park. Elisabeth was naturally overwhelmed by the city, at the time the country's third largest. Of 250,000 available housing plots in Brooklyn, 45,000 were developed, and each year 3,000 new houses were built, 13 miles of paved road laid, and 1,500 gas streetlamps erected. There were 161 churches and 1,032 factories. On the harbor endless rows of warehouses looked out on the East River. No fewer than 14 large steamboats crossed the river at any given time, night and day, carrying between 40 and 50 million passengers annually. A roundtrip ticket cost two cents. At the time of the Riises' arrival, construction of the Brooklyn Bridge was not yet completed, but its majestic towers rose high above the skyline, like gigantic monuments to the young nation's burgeoning industrialization.

Like Manhattan, Brooklyn was a city of immigrants, with half of its citizens born outside the United States. Germans, Irishmen, and, increasingly, Scandinavians settled here in small enclaves—there was even a "Little Denmark," populated by 2,000 Danish immigrants. The *South Brooklyn News* had its offices in Little Denmark, and it was here that the Riises settled.

Elisabeth was almost immediately overcome by homesickness. The fact that she was going through her first pregnancy, was suddenly forced to economize, and had to do all the household chores herself did not make her situation any easier. At home in Denmark, despite the period of estrangement from her parents during Baumann's illness, when she had experienced relative poverty, she had been used to a life of leisure, with a staff to take care of all household tasks. In a small, cramped apartment in a huge, noisy city, where it seemed a thousand different languages were spoken, Elisabeth felt lost. Fortunately, she spoke English well enough to be able to shop and run errands on her own. According to Riis's memoirs, she never complained or mentioned her homesickness, which suggests that she was determined to make a success of life with her new husband.

✳

LITTLE IS KNOWN about the Riises' first years together; Elisabeth apparently did not keep a diary, and none of her letters have survived. Riis also no longer kept a diary, and in his memoirs their first years are mentioned only in passing, usually in the form of a humorous anec-dote. Curiously, Elisabeth almost disappears from Riis's life story once she becomes part of it. There is no mention of their children's early years; Riis does not note the birth of their first child, George Edward Valdemar, on February 22, 1877.

Elisabeth, accustomed to having a cook, had only a perfunctory knowledge of the culinary arts. Riis was no gourmet cook either, and their first cooking ventures were more comical than gastronomical. It took Elisabeth some time to figure out how to make bread dough rise, resulting in many a hard, flat loaf. She was equally ignorant of how to roast a chicken, so instead they seem to have fried it. "I mind [sic] our first chicken. I cannot to this day imagine what was the matter with that strange bird," Riis wrote. Though they kept turning up the heat, the chicken refused to turn brown and crisp. "The skin was all drawn tight over the bones like the covering on an umbrella frame, and there was no end of fat in the pan that we didn't know what to do with."

According to a letter Riis wrote years later to a friend, the editor and publisher Richard W. Gilder, Elisabeth was melancholic on their first Christmas. She did not complain or talk about it, Riis wrote; he could see it in her eyes. To lift her spirits he gave her a painting of the Good Shepherd tending his sheep. There was a certain gentleness in the eyes of the lambs that reminded him of his wife. Elisabeth hung it in their bedroom. It was this painting that gave rise to Elisabeth's nickname; Riis from then on called her his "lamb."

Elisabeth clearly had similar feelings of tenderness for Riis. Letters she wrote to him in 1879, three years after the couple had first arrived in the United States, exude loving affection, though they also disclose how lonely Elisabeth was and how much the two lived apart. They already had two children, their firstborn—whom they now called Ed—

and Clara. When Elisabeth had finished the housework and tucked the children in at night, she would write letters to Riis and leave them out for him on the mantel. Riis was working long hours in the city and frequently arrived home hours after his wife and children had gone to bed; he left in the morning before they had risen. To make up for the time spent apart, he habitually wrote her little notes, which he then dispatched by courier to Brooklyn. When she responded, she addressed him as *Musling*—clam or mussel in Danish—and she wrote about herself in the third person as his lamb.

Tuesday night

My darling Musling,

Both nurslings are in bed. The older one is asleep and the little one is in her cradle, which I am rocking fervently while I'm writing this letter to you. Thank you ever so much for the lovely note you sent me this morning: yes, please do write me every morning, otherwise I shall feel so deprived. And Musling knows without his love I cannot live, does he not? Thank God you are well and happy—it will be lovely to see you a little tomorrow night. We see each other so seldom.

Riis soon discovered that running a household was a costly affair, and he noticed that his small savings were dwindling fast. In the summer of 1876, though, there was still money in the bank, and Riis was newly employed by the *South Brooklyn News*. He had signed an agreement with the owners, promising not to put out any publication of his own for a period of five years. He was not particularly happy with his work; he missed being in charge and having the freedom to vent his indignation in the columns of the paper. Nevertheless, he initiated several reformist campaigns. Directly after returning from Denmark he wrote a series of articles on boardinghouses, maintaining that they overcharged for often small and dingy rooms. He also took a stand against a priest who preached that reading a newspaper on Sundays was a sin and argued for legislation outlawing Sunday sales. Such reform-spirited campaigns would later become Riis's trademark.

The owners tolerated Riis's activism but continued to object to the fact that he did not support the straight Democratic ticket, and in the early spring both parties realized it was time to part company. Riis was out of work again.

⁂

THOUGH THIS PERIOD of unemployment occurred when Elisabeth was pregnant with Ed, it did not seem to cause Riis much distress. He had faith in the future. He felt confident some kind of job opportunity would come along, an attitude characteristic of many of his new countrymen. "A chief reason why I liked this country from the very beginning was that it made no difference what a man was doing, as long as it was some honest, decent work," Riis wrote in his memoirs. He was free of the restraints of the European employment and class system and could choose a new line of work if he wanted or needed to. He still believed journalism to be his true calling, but he also realized that for a family man the work was demanding and paid poorly. Riis reasoned that there must be an easier way to make a living. He had a magic lantern stored in his basement, a slide projector bought on impulse. When he lost his job, he remembered the projector and thought he could put it to good use, perhaps even turn a profit. The magic lantern, originally lit by a candle, was not a new invention; it had existed since the 1650s. In Europe and later in the United States, traveling showmen used magic lanterns, projecting pictures onto screens set up in barns, theaters, churches, and on the streets. The shows varied greatly in style, with some showmen displaying pictures of monstrous animals and making wild roars as accompaniment. Others told fables, and some showed works of art.

By the time Riis bought his magic lantern, a new and better light source had been invented. A mix of oxygen and hydrogen was poured onto a piece of limestone, which, when ignited, produced a strong, bright light. With John Mackellar and another friend, Ed Wells, Riis set to work learning the new technique. Riis and Ed Wells founded their own small company once they understood the procedure. The two traveled the countryside of Long Island showing advertisements for farm-supply stores in Brooklyn. Their business venture was so profitable it supported both men. In the fall, when the farmers no longer came to the city for supplies, Riis and Wells moved their operation to Brooklyn and set up their show between Fulton Street and Atlantic Avenue, displaying ads for local stores.

In the summer of 1877, they decided to expand their territory. They traveled to Elmira, a small New York railroad town on the Pennsylvania border. Had the two eager businessmen been less intent on making money and more on keeping abreast with the news, they would have realized that visiting railroad towns where union agitation and labor trouble smoldered was indeed a bad idea. Their visit to Elmira almost cost them their lives.

❋

THE RAILROAD INDUSTRY, after its unprecedented expansion following the Civil War, was facing tough times. During a blizzard on December 29, 1876, a huge wrought iron truss bridge crossing the Ashtabula River in Ohio had collapsed. All but the first of two locomotives, which made it safely to the far abutment, fell into the ravine sixty-nine feet below, and most of the 159 passengers died, the majority in fires set by kerosene stoves and lamps. Almost a third of the passengers were so badly burned that identification was impossible. Not since Camp Hill in 1856, where two trains collided head-on, had there been an accident of such scale, and it sent shockwaves through the industry.

Only hours later the industry was hit by another jolt: Workers at the Grand Trunk Railway, in Canada, went on strike. It was one of the first strikes in North America to succeed; standing united, the workers discovered they had real power, and management was forced on January 3, 1877, to agree to their demands. When, on the following day, the greatest rail tycoon of the century, Commodore Vanderbilt, died, it was believed that the era of big business in its purely capitalist form had come to an end. In fact, however, once the railroad had recovered from the strike, management pulled on the iron glove and reneged.

The United States had still not recovered from the financial crisis caused by the bank panic of 1873, which had sent the country spiraling into depression. The railroads therefore felt justified in slashing wages by 25 percent rather than raising them. Their ploy backfired, however.

That summer, thereafter known as "the bloody summer," strikes in major cities from coast to coast found workers, unable to feed their families on their previous wages, defending themselves against armed troops.

The wave of violence was provoked by the Pennsylvania Railroad's decision to further reduce wages by 10 percent. Strikes spread to Maryland and West Virginia. Entire neighborhoods in Pittsburgh were set ablaze, and a huge rail depot was set on fire, destroying 104 locomotives and 500 railroad cars. "Pittsburg[h] at the Mercy of a Lawless Mob," read a headline in the New York Times, the accompanying article displaying no sympathy for the strikers.

As the situation escalated, a militia of 650 was ordered to Pittsburgh. In the resultant panic and confusion the militia shot randomly into a crowd, killing 25 men. The Pittsburgh strike was eventually crushed, but others soon erupted in Pennsylvania—in Altoona, Easton, Harrisburg, Reading, Johnstown, Bethlehem, Philadelphia, and Scranton—and in Elmira, New York.

Riis and Wells arrived in Elmira just as the situation was becoming critical. They were struggling to set up a canvas screen near the bridge crossing the Chemung River when strikers began gathering on one side of the bridge as management, militia, and scabs gathered on the other. Riis and Wells were so busy battling the obstinate canvas in the wind that they did not notice the crowds. The militia was convinced Riis and Wells were union people sending signals to the strikers, and before the two bewildered men knew what was going on, they had been overpowered and put on a train back to New York City.

Describing the event twenty-five years later in his memoirs, Riis referred to the strikers as lawless troublemakers and underscored that he had nothing to do with the strike itself; nor did he believe strikes to be a valid political tool. He also noted that he had no empathy for the workers, and that those who had initiated and organized the strike should be blamed for the resulting conflicts. Although Riis generally sympathized with the poor, he did not support the right to strike and did not sympathize with socialist ideas and practices. Even as a very young man, it will be recalled, he derided the communist who came to recruit sympathizers at the shipyard in Buffalo where he briefly worked.

As a reformer and activist in the fight against poverty and poor housing conditions in the big cities, Riis was remarkably forward-thinking,
but his brand of activism was of a centrist nature. He believed in modify-
ing and making changes to the existing social order rather than submit-
ting it to sweeping change. His intention was to convince the middle
and upper classes that taking an active, Christian interest in helping the
poor was crucial if they did not want to prepare American ground for
communist revolution.

Much later Riis embraced socialism, comparing it to the purest form
of Christianity. By the time this change occurred, however, he was no
longer a political player.

※

THE ROUGH TREATMENT Riis and Wells received in Elmira led to
the dissolution of their business. Due to the strikes there were no trains
to New York City, and the two advertisers were stranded in Scranton,
Pennsylvania, where they were set upon by a throng of striking miners. The mayor of Scranton arrived and tried unsuccessfully to appease
the miners; a brick hit him so hard in the back of his head that he spit
blood. The militia opened fire, and a man was shot dead at Riis's feet.
"In all my life I never ran so fast," Riis recalled in his memoirs.

Riis and Wells made it out of town on foot, and while walking north
on the dusty country roads, they unanimously agreed to quit advertising.
After two days of walking they reached Elisabeth and six-month-old Ed,
who were spending part of the summer in a cabin in upstate New York.

11

• ◆ •

Police Reporter

THE FIRST TIME forty-year-old William Franklin Gore Shanks, metropolitan editor of the *New York Tribune*, was approached about a job by his Danish neighbor, he told Riis that he didn't have enough experience to work at the *Tribune*. That was in the late summer of 1877. Shanks lived at 396 Ninth Street, near Prospect Park, and knew Riis as a newspaperman. Shanks was familiar with the *South Brooklyn News* and was aware that Riis had published the paper himself, without staff.

Still, it was one thing to run a small local paper and an entirely different matter to be a reporter for one of the city's flagship papers. The most important paper in the city was the dynamic *New York Herald*, which, with a daily circulation of 170,000, was the largest in the world. No other newspaper employed as many reporters, and no other paper launched as many daring projects as the *Herald*. Its eccentric, temperamental, domineering, and often inebriated owner and editor in chief, James Gordon Bennett Jr., Newspaper Row's *enfant terrible*, would stop at nothing to get a good story. It was Bennett who in 1869 sent reporter Henry Morton Stanley on a large-scale expedition to Africa in search of the missing Scottish missionary-explorer David Livingstone. It took three years for Stanley to track down the elusive Livingstone—three

133

years of high adventure and intense danger. Stanley's travel pieces from the jungles of Africa were an instant hit, syndicated to papers all over the world. His immortal greeting at the successful completion of his search—"Dr. Livingstone, I presume?"—became one of the catchphrases of the century.

The *Tribune* was also eclipsed in circulation by the *New York Sun*, owned and edited by the highly esteemed Charles A. Dana, former editor of the *Tribune*. This was the same Dana whom Riis had contacted during his first months in the United States, hoping that Dana could arrange his enlistment in the French army. The *Sun* was widely regarded as a newspaperman's newspaper, known for its crisp style and thorough editing. With a circulation of 130,000, it also ranked as one of the biggest papers in the country.

Though the *Tribune*, with its circulation of 40,000, was surpassed by both the *Herald* and the *Sun*, it was an influential paper. Owing to its talented founder and editor, Horace Greeley, the paper had been one of the leading publications in the country almost from the point of its inception in 1841 until the Civil War. Greeley's visionary and politically forceful editorials frequently acted as inspiration and guidance for the political elite. Greeley was in control at the *Tribune* until his death in 1872.

Born in 1811, he was a legendary figure in the publishing world, having risen from humble origins to become both influential and affluent. Born to a poor farmer in Amherst, he grew up in rural New Hampshire, taught himself to read at the age of three, and by the time he was five read everything his parents kept in the house: newspapers, the Bible, Shakespeare. Neighbors and friends were so proud of his academic prowess that they took up a collection for him to attend the nearby Phillips Exeter Academy. Greeley's father, however, denied him the opportunity. He needed all of his children to work on the farm and refused to send his son off to school. But as time passed, the father was forced to acknowledge that his small, bookish son was unfit for hard labor. Reluctantly he let him apprentice as a printer.

At the age of twenty, Greeley moved to New York City, working at low-paying printing jobs. The ambitious young man moved up the ranks in the business, and in 1841 he established his own paper, the *New-York Daily Tribune*, which quickly became a success. As editor in chief, Greeley became known for his Progressive stand. He flirted with socialism and supported Prohibition, as did most reformers at the time. He believed in increasing immigration into the United States and supported the passage of the Homestead Act. He argued for far-reaching social reforms in New York City, such as shorter workdays (down from twelve hours to ten). In his editorials Greeley also spoke out vehemently against slavery and was, for a while, a strong supporter of Abraham Lincoln, whose election he greatly influenced.

Greeley's political power was undeniable. During the Civil War, however, he grew ambivalent about the way Lincoln handled the war, and his wavering eventually cost him both his political clout and a significant portion of his readership. Before the war ended, Greeley withdrew his ardent support for Lincoln and spoke against his reelection, calling for an immediate peace agreement between the North and the South—highly unpopular standpoints that seriously damaged his reputation.

His increasing ambivalence toward the president and, by extension, the Republican Party later moved him to accept, if reluctantly, the Democratic candidacy for president in 1872. He was to run against the popular war hero Ulysses S. Grant, who was mired in scandal and, according to traditional political thought, should have been an easy opponent to beat; but Greeley's campaign was a disaster. Many of his potential supporters felt he had deserted the Progressive cause (moderate Republicans like Greeley were prominent among Progressive forces in the country), and Greeley, who had always had a great command of the written word, turned out to be a poor public speaker, thus further damaging his campaign.

The fact that he harbored serious doubts about his candidacy for the Democratic Party also had an impact on his campaign. The worst blow, however, was the untimely death of his wife, Mary Young Cheney Greeley, in the middle of the campaign. Greeley suffered a thunderous defeat, the worst in the nation's history, and died a broken man within a month of the election.

Greeley had been an easily recognizable figure in the streets of New York. With his stooping posture, long, streaming hair, sizable hats, and long coats with deep pockets stuffed with the day's papers, he looked decidedly Dickensian. When he died, many people thought the paper would die with him—after all, Greeley *was* the *Tribune*. However, his successor, Whitelaw Reid, ambitious and competent if a bit colorless, kept the paper not only running but running well. By marrying one of the country's wealthiest women, Elisabeth Mills, the daughter of banker-philanthropist Darius Ogden Mills, he ensured the paper's financial survival for decades. After having taken over as editor in chief and owner of the *Tribune*, Reid immediately began making sweeping changes. His first major undertaking was to demolish the building that had housed the *Tribune* since its inception and hire the acclaimed architect Morris Hunt to design new offices for the paper.

Reid's actions sent a clear message to readers and the press: The *Tribune* was as strong as ever and would remain a heavyweight in the publishing world. The new building was spectacular, so tall it became one of the first in New York to require an elevator. A huge tower, 300 feet tall, further enhanced the structure and made it New York's second tallest building. Next, Reid began hiring a string of well-known writers. Henry James was on staff for a while, working as the paper's Paris correspondent.

A few weeks after turning Riis away, Shanks suddenly had a change of heart and employed him as a general reporter on a trial basis. The rationale behind his decision remains a mystery. He may have been motivated by compassion, hiring Riis simply because he was struggling and had a family to support. It is more likely that Shanks realized Riis was a reporter who would never shy away from hard work and long hours—an important asset in the competitive field of local news.

Shanks himself was a hardworking man. Born in Kentucky, he started his career as a journalist writing for local papers. When the Civil War erupted, he was hired by the *New York Herald* as a war correspondent. After the war he relocated to New York and became a writer and editor at *Harper's Weekly*. In addition, Shanks wrote numerous well-received books and plays. For a short time, before his employment at the

Tribune, he was the Washington correspondent for the *New York Times*. At the *Tribune* he initially worked as the foreign affairs editor before rising in the ranks to become editor of the city desk, in many respects the most demanding job in the business. Local news constituted a paper's soul, and readers were highly demanding. Breaking news arrived minutes before deadline and reporters scrambled to get their stories together before the presses started rolling.

Even while holding this position, Shanks continued to churn out books on the side. Perhaps it was because he recognized a similar industriousness in Riis that Shanks was eventually compelled to offer him the job. His intuition concerning Riis may also have been based on his uncanny ability to predict the direction in which the press was moving. American journalism was in many ways undergoing radical change. Because it had become economically feasible to mass-produce newspapers, most of the larger papers could increase their circulation, resulting in an increase in advertising revenue. Thus newspapers no longer had to rely on party subsidies, and gained the freedom to examine political institutions, political issues, and the politicians themselves objectively and critically. In-depth investigative reporting began taking precedence over regular news at the most ambitious and serious papers. Reporters no longer simply reported news, they had begun writing so as to engage and attract readers' attention. Vivid and colorful human interest stories were gaining ground as were journalistic campaigns written by hard-nosed reporters with something on their mind.

※

INVESTIGATIVE REPORTING achieved its breakthrough with a campaign led by the *New York Times* and *Harper's Weekly* in 1871 against Boss Tweed. From the throne of Tammany Hall, Tweed and his Ring swindled up to $200 million from the city over a decade-long period. The deceit eventually proved too much for Tweed's bookkeeper, James Watson. Disillusioned and distraught, Watson leaked information on the corruption to the press. It was the massive misappropriation of tax dollars during the construction of the municipal courthouse—now known as the Tweed building—that proved the turning point for Watson. The building ended up costing taxpayers more than $12 million, most of which found its way into the already well-lined pockets of the Tweed Ring. Watson, after deciding he could no longer be party to the fraud, gathered up his reports and financial records and brought them to the editorial offices of several papers, among them the *New York Herald* and the *Sun*. Neither paper had the courage to publish the story; instead, the *New York Times* and *Harper's* did. The scathing, satirical Tweed cartoons in *Harper's* drawn by Thomas Nast, combined with the *Times's* investigative reporting, initiated the downfall of the Ring.

Under Whitelaw Reid's leadership the *Tribune* had become a more conservative paper than it had been during Greeley's reign. Reid succeeded in breaking several strikes at the paper and also kept the paper's printing trade workers from joining a union. Nevertheless, he understood the value of investigative reporting and won recognition for a series of articles on attempted election fraud in 1876, the year Riis became a staff writer. The series revealed that the nephew of Samuel J. Tilden, the Democratic candidate for president, had tried to buy votes for his uncle.

Riis would rise to become one of the *Tribune's* great investigative reporters. Today, of course, he is mostly known for his groundbreaking exposés of how the other half lived, but it was as a reporter that he made his first mark in the newspaper world.

※

INITIALLY, RIIS'S WORK at the *Tribune* was not much different from his job at the New York News Association. From early morning until late at night he walked the streets in search of newsworthy stories about anything and everything. There had been no improvement in salary.

During one of the worst blizzards in New York's history, which hit the city on Friday, February 1, 1878, Riis landed what he thought was a great scoop. Huge waves lashed the coast, with Coney Island especially hard hit: Many of the little cabins on the beach, housing hotel staff and the coast guard, were washed into the sea, and the hotels themselves suffered extensive damage. As the storm churned and the air turned into a thick, icy mass, Riis was attempting to make his way from downtown to Coney Island. By the time he reached Sheepshead Bay, he was soaked, exhausted, and miserable. To his horror he discovered that all ferries to Coney Island had been canceled because of the storm. Riis landed his story about the devastation based on interviews with people who had left Coney Island during the day and had witnessed the storm's destruction, and from Sheepshead Bay hoteliers with a "laudable desire not to see an enterprising reporter cheated out of his rightful 'space,'" as Riis later wrote. None of the other papers got a reporter as far as Sheepshead Bay, and the *Tribune* had an exclusive. Still, Shanks was not at all pleased.

The article read like fiction. Either Riis's subjects had exaggerated and he had not challenged their hyperbole, or he had given rein to his own imagination. The headline was dramatic:

SEVEN LIVES LOST AT CONEY ISLAND. THE BEACH DEVASTATED BY TWO IMMENSE TIDAL WAVES—THREE WOMEN DROWNED— HOTELS AND OTHER PROPERTY DESTROYED.

Riis described how a coast guard cabin had been sucked into the sea, leaving only a stove where it had stood. There was a story about a cat and a dog who survived by climbing onto a wooden board and sailed until morning, when they landed unharmed. A barn with a horse tied up inside had also been swept away by the waves, according to witnesses, only to land on the beach the next morning, intact and with the horse still securely tied.

On the morning of February 2, the day the article ran, Shanks called Riis into his office and took him to task for relying on unsubstantiated, secondhand accounts. Shanks admitted to Riis that maybe, just maybe, the part about the cabin and the stove was true, but the stories about the cat and the dog sailing on a board and the floating barn with the horse were just too far-fetched.

Riis was working hard for a low salary at the *Tribune*, earning not nearly enough to cover the family's expenses. He was a reporter for one of the city's major newspapers, yet he could barely support his family. After six months on the job he decided to quit, placing a letter of resignation on Shanks's desk. A few hours later, he noticed that his letter was lying there unopened. He snatched it and went back to work.

The following evening, Riis had just covered a meeting uptown and was hurrying downtown to write and file his story. As he approached the *Tribune* building, running down Spruce Street, a gust of wind hurled him around the corner and he collided with Shanks, who had just emerged with a colleague. Shanks was knocked to the ground.

"Is that the way you treat your city editor, Riis?" asked Shanks, as Riis handed him his hat. According to Riis, the following exchange occurred:

"It was the wind, sir, and I was running."

"Running! What is up that set you going at that rate?"

Riis told him about the meeting uptown and his impending deadline.

"And do you always run like that when you are out on assignments?" Shanks asked.

"When it is late like this, yes. How else would I get my copy in?"

The next morning Riis was again summoned to Shanks's office. Convinced he was going to be fired, he was full of foreboding, but Shanks had something entirely different in mind.

> "Mr. Riis," he began stiffly, "you knocked me over last night without cause. . . . Nice thing for a reporter to do to his commanding officer. Now, sir! this will not do. We must find some way of preventing it in the future. Our man at Police Headquarters has left. I am going to send you up there in his place. You can run there all you want to, and you will want to all you can. It is a place that needs a man who will run to get his copy in and tell the truth and stick to it."

"And with this kind of an introduction I was sent off to Mulberry Street," Riis wrote, "where I was to find my lifework."

❋

DURING THE 1800s grave robbing was a lucrative business. Doctors, often short of bodies to dissect, were willing to pay for cadavers and to accept the typically no-questions-asked premise of many transactions. The most profitable form of grave robbing was kidnapping the corpses of the wealthy for ransom. Cadaver thieves extorted huge sums of money from relatives, who would pay anything to retrieve the body of a loved one.

The 1878 robbery of the corpse of department-store magnate Alexander T. Stewart, the so-called Merchant Prince of Manhattan, unfolded like a classic whodunit. On the night of November 7, while the wind was howling through the trees and the rain poured down relentlessly, a team of sophisticated robbers emptied vault 112 in St. Mark's Cemetery, on Second Avenue between Eleventh and Twelfth streets. Stewart, who died in the spring of 1876, had owned several stores in the city, among them the gigantic Iron Palace on Broadway, between Ninth and Tenth streets. At five stories, it took up an entire block and was considered to be the greatest department store in the world. Stewart, a thin redhead with cold gray eyes, had been respected for his wealth but generally disliked, his reputation that of a miser and a ruthless employer. Only a handful of people knew where his body was buried, and the mystery of how it was found and removed from its underground tomb remains unsolved. Vault 112 housed three caskets. As the rain turned to sleet, the robbers scaled the tall spiked iron fence surrounding the cemetery and went straight to work on the correct casket, tearing the lid off. When the body came in contact with fresh air, it dissolved into a slimy, foul-smelling mass. The robbers stuffed it into a bag and escaped unnoticed.

The story of the theft made front-page news. City police and detectives were under tremendous pressure to capture the thieves, and Stewart's widow offered a reward of $25,000 for any information leading to their arrest. Presumably a discreet return of the body had been planned, and the pickup of the ransom, but in the frenzy of the entirely unexpected press coverage the robbers undoubtedly felt their only course of action was to lay low or, if not, face arrest; so they made no contact with Stewart's widow, and the police had no clues and no idea where to begin looking for the robbers or the body.

The detectives assigned to the case worked with the press to create the false appearance of good progress. On November 17, the *New*

York Times reported that the police were about to make a major break-through. Two days later the paper informed its readers that the police would apprehend the robbers soon. There was one paper, however, that held out against the upbeat stories about a forthcoming arrest, disclosing that the police had in fact nothing to go on. "GRAVE-ROBBERS UNCAUGHT," read one of its headlines, and the article continued: "All sorts of rumors claiming that the body of Mr. Stewart had been discovered, now here and now there, and innumerable theories as to the manner and direction in which the body had been removed were circulating and the police were busy with a dozen clues, none of which led to the capture of the perpetrators."

The *New York Tribune* was the lone voice of reason; the dissenting articles were written by Jacob Riis, the paper's new police reporter. Management had been ill at ease about the course of action Riis had wanted to take, afraid to jeopardize the prestige the paper enjoyed due to the recent exposé of attempted election fraud. They made it clear to Riis, his colleague Amos Ensign, and Shanks, who both worked with him on the story, that if they were wrong they would all be fired.

"I slept little or none during that month of intense work and excitement, but spent my days as my nights sifting every scrap of evidence," Riis recalled in his autobiography. He went to extreme lengths to find out what the detectives knew about the case. One night, he jumped into the police chief's carriage, hoping to glean some news from a conversation with officers. It was quickly discovered that he was a reporter, and he was thrown out.

There was a lot at stake for Riis, who could ill afford to lose his job, yet he never wavered. In the end he emerged victorious, and the other papers were put to shame, when the police admitted that the trail had gone cold and that they most likely would never solve the case of the theft of Alexander T. Stewart's body. Riis was duly recognized for his courage at the paper. In an internal memorandum, Shanks praised his work, saying Riis had made "the *Tribune* police reports the best in the city." Riis was given a raise in pay for his efforts.

❄

THE RAISE CAME only six months after Riis had taken the job, and in hindsight it may be viewed as the first clear sign that he would one day become a renowned police reporter. Still, recognition came none too soon. Riis's work was exceedingly demanding, and he had often been tempted to quit. When he got the job, he had immediately wired Elisabeth the good news: "Got staff appointment, Police Headquarters. $25 a week. Hurrah!" But it was unusually taxing work that awaited him. The cramped office, at 301 Mulberry Street, some twenty blocks uptown from Newspaper Row, accommodated police reporters from all the papers except the *Evening Post*, which saw itself as too refined to cover crime. Otherwise they were all there: the *Sun*, the *Tribune*, the *Herald*, the *Times*, the *Daily News*, the *Mail & Express*, and the *New York World*. Directly across the street was the Central Department of the Metropolitan Police, a four-story marble building housing the New York City police force and nicknamed the Marble Palace.

Riis's beat was much broader than he had expected. Apart from crime and the police he also had to cover fires, the Health Department, the Coroner's Office, and the License Office. He wrote about everything from deaths, accidents, crimes, fires, murders, brawls, fraud, and embezzlement to epidemics of cholera, smallpox, typhus, yellow fever, and tuberculosis, as well as the many foodborne diseases that ravaged the city. Riis followed the police on patrol in all kinds of weather and at all hours. He went out with inspectors on hot, humid summer days, inspecting the excruciatingly claustrophobic tenements.

As Riis put it, "it was my task to cover . . . all the news that means trouble to someone." He was assured that his stories would be prominently featured because they dealt with subjects people loved to read about; death and mayhem sold papers. Riis saw more human pain and misery on a weekly basis than most people did in a lifetime. Although once he had gotten his raise the job allowed him to support his family, he worked mainly nights and early mornings. His new colleagues, with the express purpose of belittling him, referred to him as the Dutchman, by now an all-too-familiar sobriquet.

There were usually about thirty reporters at work in the office. It was a cliquey group, and they had made a virtue out of working as little as possible, often basing their stories exclusively on police bulletins, which were posted on boards at police headquarters. There was tacit agreement among the reporters as to which stories they would cover; nobody had to bother with the tedious work of digging up stories or worry about the competition. The goal was to free up as much time as possible for playing cards.

Riis did not care for card games, and the other reporters soon realized that he did not fit the Mulberry mold. Riis was driven and wanted to work hard. He still remembered the Sheepshead Bay story, and knew what could happen if you did not do your own research and did not base your stories on firsthand accounts.

Riis did rely to some extent on police bulletins, using them as a stepping-stone for further investigation—an approach that annoyed his colleagues and upset the established order. If he filed superior stories, editors were likely to demand more from their reporters or perhaps even fire them. The other reporters decided to make Riis's life at 301 Mulberry Street miserable; to crush him before he became too successful. When news came in from police officers, they would deliberately forget to tell Riis. Several times he missed big stories that were prominently featured in other papers. On one such occasion, a *Tribune* editor recommended that Riis be fired, but Shanks intervened and saved his young protégé from losing his job.

Shanks's support gave Riis a much-needed psychological boost, and he threw himself into his work with renewed energy, intent on proving to himself and to Shanks that he was up to the task. He became almost obsessed with beating colleagues at their own game—going further to get a story, showing up earlier for work, getting the scoop while making sure the other reporters were not informed at all. A war had broken out on Mulberry Street.

In retaliation, Riis's opponents began stealing his wires—the *Tribune*, which was affiliated with the Associated Press, was the only paper in the building with a telegraph line—and replacing them with bogus wires, prompting Riis to head out, sometimes in the middle of the night, chasing phantom stories. When Riis returned from fruitless expeditions, his colleagues welcomed him with gleeful chuckles. One night, pursuing yet another nonexistent lead, Riis happened to stumble upon an important piece of news. He returned at 2:00 PM to find the other reporters assembled at the top of the stairs, ready to enjoy a good laugh at his expense. Riis walked past them without a word, went to his desk, wrote his story, and wired it. Since he was the only one with access to a telegraph, he was able to file the story before deadline and the *Tribune* was able to go solo with the story the next day. Riis had beat his competition.

It was not much later that he correctly claimed the police had no clues in the case of the Alexander T. Stewart's missing body. With this he finally won the respect and admiration of his peers. Eventually, he came to be seen as the best police reporter in New York. Normally humble about his accomplishments, Riis did make note of the nickname given to him by his formerly ill-disposed colleagues: "the 'boss reporter' in Mulberry Street"—"the only renown I have ever coveted or cared to have."

✳

POLICE HEADQUARTERS had originally been built as a bulwark against the draft riots of 1863, when starving and disillusioned Irish immigrants resisted being conscripted into the Union army. More than just a reaction to the draft, the riots became a referendum on living conditions in the tenements. The level of pent-up frustration and anger let loose was unprecedented in the city's history. The military was eventually called in to quell the rioters, resulting in several hundred fatalities.

Mulberry Street had changed considerably by the time Riis arrived in 1878, but there was still much hectic activity in the dark, narrow, cobblestone alleyways, enclosed by cramped tenements. Shiny horse-drawn patrol wagons and black police vans, known as Black Marias and used for transporting prisoners, drove by constantly en route to police headquarters. Milling in and out of the building were officers in heavy blue uniforms and dome-shaped helmets, police in civilian clothes, and errand boys. The police normally used the main entrance, but when they were trying to keep something quiet or avoid reporters, they entered through the back door, near the Health Department. Prominent politicians went in the back door for secret meetings with the four politically appointed police commissioners who headed up the police force.

It was also used when the most notorious of the city's criminals were brought in for interrogation. Detective and, later, Police Chief Thomas F. Byrnes's infamous third degree was conducted in the so-called chamber of horrors. According to those who had witnessed an interrogation, this room had only one redeeming quality: its lovely carpet. Everything else in the room was chosen by Byrnes to break down prisoners' defenses. There were confiscated weapons; four black hoods, worn by four killers at their executions; a bloodstained shirt that had belonged to a young man named Benjamin Nathan, killed by multiple stab wounds in the summer of 1870. And there was a wide assortment of tools used in various thefts: tools for opening a safe, such as a diamond drill and a muffled hammer; famous river pirates' equipment, including devices for opening barrels, lockers, and sea chests. These items were all displayed in a glass case, serving as a reminder that even the smartest and most hardened of criminals could not escape the wrath of Detective Byrnes.

From their side of the street the reporters had a full view of police headquarters and could observe officers haul in prostitutes (every fourth woman arrested was a prostitute), pocket thieves, burglars, crooks, con men, drunks, assailants, troublemakers, striking workers, the mentally ill. Many prisoners had been beaten severely by arresting officers before they were taken into custody. Basement jail cells were almost always filled to capacity. Police officers, or "bluecoats," were unsparing in their use of the nightstick, which could paralyze with one blow. These long clubs were made of locust, a fine, straight-grain, stress-resistant wood that made a distinct singing noise when brought through the air. The song of the nightstick was familiar to, and dreaded by, all tenement dwellers in the city.

A tangled web of what seemed like millions of thick telegraph wires connected headquarters with the city's thirty-six precincts. In-house communication, however, was still carried out the old-fashioned way: Messages were shouted down the hallways. A gong was also employed, with specific rhythms for events such as fire. The reporters could of course distinguish the different rhythms, and kept abreast of police news by shouting from their office windows to the officers in the street.

The impressive collection of mug shots that hung at headquarters was used as a point of reference for both officers and reporters.

For curious New Yorkers and out-of-town tourists, Captain Byrnes's rogues' gallery—a term he popularized—was viewed as a great attraction. Sixteen hundred faces peered out at onlookers and, Byrnes hoped, served as a deterrent to criminals.

※

THREE THOUSAND MEN served on the police force during the 1880s and 1890s. Considering the size of the city, it was a relatively small force, yet they arrested more than 100,000 people a year. According to confirmed reports from the time, police officers severely beat at least two thousand of those arrested, but in all probability the number must have been much higher. Each year, approximately 500 infants set out to die by their parents were rescued by the police and brought to orphanages. The police saved at least 50 or more people from drowning in the Hudson River annually.

The force, made up mostly of Irish immigrants and their descendants, featured characters whose toughness rivaled that of the criminals in Byrnes's rogues' gallery. During Riis's tenure on Mulberry Street, Alexander S. Williams, a former shipbuilder from Nova Scotia, was among the most feared police captains in the city. "Clubber" Williams loved to make his nightstick sing, and he had a reputation for taking bribes from brothel and bar owners. By the time he made captain of the precinct south of Fourteenth Street, an area he christened the Tenderloin because of the opportunities it offered for graft, he had amassed a fortune of $300,000—a huge sum at the time—and owned two mansions and a yacht.

Thomas F. Byrnes, born in Dublin, had a walrus mustache and deep-set, piercing eyes. His career took off in 1878 when he solved the Manhattan Savings Institution robbery, the largest bank heist of the nineteenth century. Career thief George Leonidas Leslie and a gang of equally experienced robbers stole over $2.7 million but were all apprehended within a few months by Byrnes. The press—Riis covered the case for the *Tribune*—hailed Byrnes as a hero, and he was appointed chief detective at headquarters in 1883. The department had had a dismal track record, but under the talented leadership of the bulky, volatile Byrnes, it excelled and solved so many cases it was nicknamed America's

Scotland Yard. Byrnes became friends with some of the city's richest men, who appreciated his ability to keep the downtown area south of Fulton Street—where Wall Street is located—crime free. Byrnes himself called Fulton Street the city's "crime dead line": Robbers and thieves caught south of Fulton were so severely punished by Byrnes's army of officers that most of them never ventured beyond the dead line again.

Financier Jay Gould paid Byrnes a small fortune for keeping Wall Street free of crime, and most respectable citizens turned a blind eye to the detective's questionable tactics. Byrnes's powerful friends included individuals from the criminal underworld, and his network of law-breaking buddies eventually became so extensive that at times it was difficult to tell on which side of the law he belonged. Despite his dubious methods and corrupt character, he was a resourceful and efficient policeman who contained crime while modernizing the police force.

※

RIIS HAD A PRONOUNCED love-hate relationship with the New York police force, forever defined by the night in 1870 when his dog was brutalized outside the lodging house on Church Street. As a police reporter, Riis learned that the officers on the force were not only brutal but corrupt. In a remarkably critical article written in 1884, Riis made his readers aware of widespread corruption. He asserted that the force was in league with the criminal underworld, claimed that the majority of officers were useless, and called for radical reform.

The article undoubtedly made him unpopular on Mulberry Street, yet Riis wisely refrained from indicting Byrnes himself. Instead, he referred to Byrnes as one of the few outstanding officers on the force. He was of course aware that Byrnes was as guilty of corruption as others, but as a reporter he could not afford to jeopardize his relationship with the top brass. If these relations were broken, he would lose access to important news.

Riis's dilemma was one shared by all reporters, then and now. On the one hand, the reporter is a watchdog, hired to keep a critical eye on institutions and private persons. On the other hand, these institutions and individuals are the reporter's most important sources. Thus a relationship of mutual respect and trust between the two parties is often in the interests of all. Riis discovered quickly that one way of maintaining this fine balance was through off-the-record interviews, where the source can reveal everything, having been assured that the reporter will not quote him directly or print information the source prefers to keep out of the public eye.

"The department reporter has his field as carefully laid out for him every day as any physician who starts out on his route . . . he is friend, companion, and often counsellor to the officials with whom he comes in contact—always supposing that he is not fighting them in open war," Riis said of his approach.

> He may serve a Republican paper and the President of the Police Board may be a Democrat of Democrats; yet in the privacy of his office he will talk as freely to the reporter as if he were his most intimate party friend, knowing that he will not publish what is said in confidence. This is the reporter's capital, without which he cannot in the long run do business.

Riis made use of other methods to keep in good standing with his sources, which were in fact much more effective, albeit not suitable to be printed in his memoirs. From time to time he wrote articles praising the people and institutions he depended upon for information and tips—stories with a message that he knew the subject wanted to impart to the public. Sometimes he was commissioned to write such stories. One example of Riis's venture into this kind of ethically questionable journalism—puff pieces—was a story, praising the bluecoats, written shortly after his highly critical article that called for a radical reform of the force. The story carried the following headlines:

TALENT ON THE FORCE

Striking Individuals Lurking
Within the City's Bluecoats

Bravery and Genius in New York's Police
Which Seldom Meet the Public Eye—Sportsmen,
Musicians and an Old Indian Scout

Praising the very men he had called useless, and commending them on their many heroic acts, Riis focused specifically on an officer who maintained strong faith in God. His goal was clearly to assure his readers that even though it sometimes did not seem so, there were many devout officers on the force. Riis even dropped a few words of praise for Clubber Williams.

In an article on Inspector Henry Steers, which ran on the anniversary of the officer's thirty-second year on the force, Riis wrote of "an old man with a young heart beneath a blue coat."

> He is old in faithful service, if not in years. The storms of fifty-seven winters have not whitened his looks. His heart is young because he is good and brave. To-day he has worn the policeman's coat thirty-two years. In all that time no voice save that of the malefactor's has been lifted in reproach of inspector Henry V. Steers. . . . His ready courage and strong arm availed there to save more than a few unfortunates from drowning. As Roundsman he fought a Sixth Ward mob in the dark days of the draft riots. Some time later, on duty in the Eighth Ward, he fought a band of burglars in a bonded warehouse single-handed, put them to flight and chased them over the roofs of the neighboring tenements. Leaping across an alleyway he fell and broke his ankle. It is characteristic of the man, that though thus disabled, he brought his men to bay and arrested them.

Riis's transgressions were a minor concession for being able to follow health commissioners and policemen on their patrols into the darkest corners of New York's tenements. Riis not only developed his writing by reporting on these journeys, but he also sharpened his devotion to reform. Seeing the circumstances under which so many of New York's tenement dwellers lived moved him deeply, and he was in turn able to move his readers, letting them travel vicariously through his articles. One night, he followed the police on a raid of a stale-beer dive:

> I went along as a kind of war correspondent—[we] groped [our] way in single file through the narrow rift between slimy walls to the tenements in the rear. Twice during our trip we stumbled over tramps, both women, asleep

in the passage. They were quietly passed to the rear, receiving sundry prods and punches on the trip, and headed for the station in the grip of a policeman as a sort of advance guard of the coming army. After what seemed half a mile of groping in the dark we emerged finally into the alley proper, where light escaping through the cracks of closed shutters on both sides enabled us to make out the contour of three rickety frame tenements. Snatches of ribald songs and peals of coarse laughter reached us from now this, now that of the unseen burrows.

"School is in," said the Sergeant drily as we stumbled down the worn steps of the next cellar-way. A kick of his boot-heel sent the door flying into the room.

A room perhaps a dozen feet square, with walls and ceiling that might once have been clean—assuredly the floor had not in the memory of man, if indeed there was other floor than hard-trodden mud—but were now covered with a brown crust that, touched with the end of a club, came off in shuddering showers of crawling bugs, revealing the blacker filth beneath. Grouped about a beer-keg that was propped on the wreck of a broken chair, a foul and ragged host of men and women, on boxes, benches, and stools. Tomato-cans filled at the keg were passed from hand to hand. In the centre of the group a sallow, wrinkled hag, evidently the ruler of the feast, dealt out the hideous stuff. A pile of copper coins rattled in her apron, the very pennies received with such showers of blessings upon the giver that afternoon; the faces of some of the women were familiar enough from the streets as those of beggars forever whining for a penny, "to keep a family from starving." Their whine and boisterous hilarity were alike hushed now. In sullen, cowed submission they sat, evidently knowing what to expect. At the first glimpse of the uniform in the open door some in the group, customers with a record probably, had turned their heads away to avoid the searching glance of the officer; while a few, less used to such scenes, stared defiantly.

A single stride took the sergeant into the middle of the room, and with a swinging blow of his club he knocked the faucet out of the keg and the halffilled can from the boss hag's hand. As the contents of both splashed upon the floor, half a dozen of the group made a sudden dash, and with shoulders humped above their heads to shield their skulls against the dreaded locust broke for the door. They had not counted upon the policemen outside. There was a brief struggle, two or three heavy thumps, and the runaways were brought back to where their comrades crouched in dogged silence.

What Riis observed was quite familiar to him. He knew what it meant to eke out an existence in the slums. He had escaped this lot and moved up in society, but his vastly improved circumstances did not alter his perspective, and in fact only intensified it: The conditions under which people lived here were intolerable to him.

12

Anatomy of the Slums

O N June 13, 1871, the steamer *Thyringia*, carrying 800 passengers, docked at Castle Garden. A young Danish missionary
student on board, Rasmus Andersen, described the spring day in his
diary as "sunny and mild." With intense delight, he also noted the sweet
scent of hay coming in from Staten Island. "It was such a lovely fra-
grance that greeted us," he wrote. Andersen had traveled third class
and was the youngest member of a delegation of three Danish clergy-
men, including a pastor, A.L.C. Grove-Rasmussen, and a lay preacher,
A. S. Nielsen, commissioned by an intricately named Danish National
Church committee—The Commission for the Advancement of the
Gospel Among Danes in North America—to set up a church for Danish
immigrants in America. Christians at home were concerned that their
fellow Danes in America would otherwise forget their faith. According
to one of Pastor Grove-Rasmussen's first letters home, the Commission
had been right to worry. "The Danes I have met thus far have indeed
abandoned their Christian faith in their pursuit of material wealth—it
seems this is all they think about."

The small delegation stayed only a few days in New York before
heading for the Midwest, where most Danish immigrants had settled.
Apart from establishing churches, they were also authorized to preach

and function as clergy advisors. The journey west, however, came to a sudden halt for Andersen when he contracted smallpox and was hospitalized in Chicago. His travel companions did not wait for him to recover, nor did they help him pay his considerable hospital bills, which ended up ruining him. He was in low spirits when he was finally able to continue his journey.

To his great dismay, he discovered that none of the Danes he met in Wisconsin were interested in his services. He realized that unless he became ordained in the United States it would be difficult for him to get a parish of his own. To that end, he entered the Augsburg Theological Seminary, in Marshall, Wisconsin. It was run by the Norwegian-Danish Conference, which did not adhere to Danish Lutheran Church teaching. Andersen could not therefore be ordained, but the schooling enabled him to acquire a small Danish parish in Waupaca, Wisconsin, where he settled and later married. Eventually, however, with the influx of Baptists, Methodists, Seventh-day Adventists, and other modern denominations to the area, his congregation dwindled. The rival denominations were more forgiving than the Danish Lutheran Church and their services vastly more entertaining and lively than the solemn Danish services.

Andersen next took a job representing the Danish National Church in New York, where he was to contact Danes who had just arrived in the United States through Castle Garden. It was thought that recruiting Danes off the boat would be more effective than waiting till they had settled and become accustomed to life in America. Still, the work was far more difficult than Andersen could have imagined. The new arrivals were disinclined to join his congregation in Brooklyn, where a fair number settled. Despite limited funds, Andersen acquired a small attic in Fallesen's Coach Works, on the corner of Twenty-second Street and Third Avenue, which he converted into a chapel. His congregation, admittedly small, was mostly made up of Norwegians, who complained incessantly about his uniquely Danish interpretation of Lutheranism, though there was one regular churchgoer who was always satisfied: Jacob Riis.

As the young editor of the *South Brooklyn News* Riis had cherished the services of Brother Ichabod Simmons and Henry Ward Beecher, and he now became one of Andersen's most devout parishioners. "Everything was dusty and dirty," Andersen wrote of his small attic chapel, "we had to give it all a good wash, arrange the few benches as best we could, and for an altar we hung Dannebrog on the wall and placed a small table with a white tablecloth in front of it. We had no lamps, and I thought I would have to buy them myself, but then Jacob A. Riis came in, left again and soon returned with a couple of lamps and a can of lamp-oil."

In 1879 Riis offered to write letters to every Dane in the neighborhood, encouraging them to join Andersen's congregation, but his efforts were met with a decidedly mixed reaction, if not outright suspicion. Having worked for two years at the *Tribune*, Riis had attained a social status unobtainable for most immigrants, and many in the congregation perceived him as a social climber. In a culture where self-effacement was seen as a virtue, Riis, who had assimilated with relative ease, spoke the language fluently, and supported a thriving family, came across as overly confident and self-assured. Many frankly envied his success, finding it insufferable because it set their own precarious situations in sharp contrast. Riis's personal mannerisms could be offputting as well. He spoke loudly and animatedly when he was excited, and he could be curt and arrogant when displeased, conduct considered socially unacceptable by many Danes.

After his death Riis was hailed as a great friend of Danish immigrants, someone who was always willing to lend a helping hand. In reality, however, Riis was quite impatient with most of his fellow immigrants; he was quick to judge and condemn those who failed to assimilate, and he did not refrain from expressing his contempt. The musician Victor Bancke recalled coming to New York with a friend in 1893. The two men went to see Riis in the hope that he might help them find employment. They were kept waiting for an hour, whereupon Riis, "a small man, who moved about quickly and seemed extremely busy," encountered them in his office.

"What do you want?" he brusquely asked.

I introduced myself and my friend and gave him our letter [of recommendation]. When he had finished reading it, he asked: "Who is Bancke?"

"That's me," I replied, to which he responded with the following:

"Do you realize that it's a moral outrage to send starving musicians over here? Within a year you will be in the poorhouse, did you know that? But I can assure you that I will put an end to the immigration of such personages. This very day, I will write a story to the Danish press and not mince words."

And there we were, both of us dumbfounded.

"Is that all you can tell us?" I asked.

"Yes," he shouted, "and get yourselves home, the sooner the better."

Bancke and his friend were not the only ones given the brush-off by Riis. A parishioner in Andersen's congregation was so incensed by Riis that he wrote to him, "You have no soul and should not attend the Danish Church." Andersen, who had become a good friend of Riis's, was forced to tell him that his help was not needed in building what would later become the Danish Seamen's Church in Brooklyn.

Riis's efforts to aid the church, however unappreciated, speak to his enormous energy and well-intentioned inclination to be active in the community; they reveal, too, a restlessness that could not be satisfied. Not given to introspection, Riis rarely read fiction except for the Dickens and Hans Christian Andersen he had devoured as a young man; nor did he enjoy the theater or attend concerts. The few times he mentioned a play in his diaries or letters, he did so with the utmost disdain, calling it a waste of time. Instead he put his heart and soul into his work. His passion for work made him less than an ideal husband and father. Though the family grew quickly—Elisabeth gave birth in 1882 to a second son, John, when, Clara, born in July 1879, was three—Riis fell into a chair, grumpy and unapproachable, upon returning from work, and left for other engagements after a hasty dinner. Like his father, he could be quite harsh with his children and did not hesitate to spank them when they misbehaved. "He was a loving and good father, but he never spoiled us! When we needed a spanking, we got them," his youngest daughter, Kate, related many years later.

Riis delegated to Elisabeth the job of insuring that their children were properly educated. Despite his public outrage over the fact that children in the slums were often denied schooling, neglect he called "one of our time's greatest social calamities," he did not participate actively in his own children's education, apart from expressing a hope that they would pursue careers in social work. Considering Riis's long workdays and multiple projects, he may simply have been exhausted and absentminded when he was home, unable to summon the energy to be involved. Riis's intensity drove him to overwork, and the calling for which he yearned was beginning to manifest itself. It was at this point that Riis began to see himself as a man on a mission, as someone whose journalistic work could make a difference for the people in the slums.

With a weekly paycheck of $25 he earned ten times more than the poorest families in the slums. Still, he made only $10 more than the most successful, yet still poor, slum families. In an age before retirement plans and health insurance, Riis knew that he was only an accident or serious illness away from the gutter unless he could maintain a healthy savings account. Like most middle-class families, however, he did not make enough money to save much. Even later, when he earned considerably more, the family still did not seem to be able to save; and in this they were no different from other comparatively well-off families.

Rent was steadily increasing in Brooklyn, and it seemed to Riis that he had to run faster and faster and work harder and harder to make ends meet. In the early 1880s he took an extra job as a correspondent for the Danish daily *Nationaltidende*. It is astounding that he found time to deliver a great number of feature stories to this paper while simultaneously working for the *Tribune*, a job that included feeding the Associated Press. His features in the *Nationaltidende* were often several-thousand-word articles with detailed and spirited accounts of everything from presidential elections and the Wild West to everyday life. Many of the stories had a high quotient of the absurd. In the fall of 1884 he wrote about a murderer who survived his own hanging:

> An argument against hanging as a viable death penalty walks about in Texas in the form of a Negro who recently survived a hanging. He had been sentenced to death after being found guilty in the molestation of a white girl. He hung from the rope for 40 minutes until he ceased breathing and was

declared dead. He was then cut down and given to his aging father, who loaded him onto a wood-cart without suspension and drove him back to his shack a few miles outside town. During the rough ride, the hanged man was jolted back to life, scaring his father half to death. The question now plaguing the authorities is what to do with the revived. Officially he is a hanged man and declared dead by the Sheriff and twelve impartial men and can therefore not be considered a human being under the law. But he is in fact alive and is threatening to pummel the hangman. . . . Arresting a dead man, however, is out of the question. It is a peculiar dilemma, which Texas authorities might best get around by sending for Sitting Bull and his Indians, who are currently on display here in New York.

Riis's pace of production was staggering, and stories such as the following surely resonated with him:

Secretary of the Treasury Folger died in a most American fashion the other day. He literally worked himself to death. Folger was known as the politician who suffered the worst defeat in years in the New York gubernatorial election two years ago, when the Democrats' candidate, Cleveland, beat him with a majority vote of more than 192,000. Still, Folger was an honorable man, who worked himself to death in his post, never delegating any of his assignments to thievish subordinates.

By 1886 Riis was working so hard that he collapsed. He wrote to his editors:

I telephoned the office just now that I could not come to work. I ask that I may be excused till I am able. I trust and hope to a merciful God that that may be tomorrow, or soon. You know I would not desert you at this time, if I was physically and mentally able to work. I am not. I can not tell what is the matter with me, but the doctor says that I must rest, rest until it goes over. God grant that may be soon. The worst is I am discouraged, disheartened, and that prevents me from pulling myself together. There is so much work waiting to be done.

Diagnosed with nervous exhaustion, Riis credited his eventual recovery to his obsession with his work: describing life in the slums.

✳

THE SLUMS WERE at their worst on hot summer days, when the temperature hovered around 100 degrees, with 90 percent humidity. In the alleys separating tenement houses, the thick air quivered. To preserve energy people took only small gulps of air—through the mouth, so the stench would not be overwhelming.

The reporter with the oval spectacles, bowler hat, wrinkled suit, and wispy mustache felt assured that he had seen everything, the worst of the worst—deaths, drunks, the depths of poverty-induced despair. He had spent hours in the alleys of Mulberry Bend, Gotham Court, and Hell's Kitchen within the dense blocks, sometimes five buildings deep. He had walked in all seasons and at all times of day.

But on a summer day in 1886, while tens of thousands took to the roofs and fire escapes for relief from the sweltering heat, Riis realized that he could still be horrified by new experiences. As so often before, he was following a group of health inspectors on their rounds. They were doctors on an impossible quest, trying to help infants and the elderly, who were most susceptible to heat-related diseases. In reality, the incident Riis witnessed, on Mott Street, was no worse than others he had seen, yet for some reason it made an indelible impression. There was a peculiar melancholic poetry to the scene, reminding Riis of an old saying he was soon to make his own: "We are all just God's children."

"The father's hands were crippled from lead poisoning," he later wrote.

He had not been able to work for a year. A contagious disease of the eyes, too long neglected, had made the mother and one of the boys nearly blind. The children cried with hunger. They had not broken their fast that day, and it was then near noon. For months the family had subsisted on two dollars a week from the priest, and a few loaves and a piece of corned beef which the sisters sent them on Saturday. The doctor gave direction for the treatment of the child, knowing that it was possible only to alleviate its sufferings until death should end them, and left some money for food for the rest. An hour later, when I returned, I found them feeding the dying child with ginger ale, bought for two cents a bottle at the peddler's cart down the street. A pitying neighbor had proposed it as the one thing she could think of as likely to make the child forget its misery.

✳

MULBERRY STREET was not far from where Riis had found himself on the verge of suicide in the fall of 1870; and Five Points and Chatham Square, where on cold nights he had sought shelter in stairways and had often been brutally awakened by the song of the nightstick and sent on his way, were less than a mile from his office. By the time he revisited Five Points as a reporter, its old wooden tenements had been torn down. The worst slum was now in the area just south of Bayard Street and north of Park Street, where Mulberry Street bent like an arm. It was Riis who coined the term Mulberry Bend. The name soon became synonymous with the city's most pestilential neighborhoods.

Mulberry Bend was lined by blocks of tenements. Dividing the rows of buildings was a labyrinth of alleys—Bottle Alley, Cat's Alley, Blind Man's Alley, Bandits' Roost. These narrow passageways led into back alleys, which were used as dumps and gave off a horrendous smell. Together the alleys formed a complex web; only people who traveled them on a regular basis knew their way around. Riis recalled getting lost repeatedly when he first explored the area as a reporter.

The influx of immigrants to the United States, which had been massive as early as the Civil War, reached new levels when Riis worked at the *Tribune*. Referred to as "the new immigration," this influx encompassed 60,000 arrivees per month, primarily desperately poor Italians, Eastern Europeans, and Russians, with the greater part of the Russian immigrants Jews fleeing the pogroms. The new wave of immigrants added to the already high population density, and housing rules slackened, rendering living conditions still worse than they had been. In 1888, Riis wrote, in *How the Other Half Lives*, 5,650 immigrants crowded into tenements on Baxter and Mulberry streets between Park and Bayard streets alone. "The degree to which the tenement-houses are packed can be understood only when seen," wrote Riis, in a feature headlined "VISIT-ING TENEMENT-HOUSES." A typical apartment was home to two families with children and a couple of workmen.

William T. Elsing, a pastor who worked in the tenements, described visiting a typical slum apartment in the late nineteenth century:

> The halls in nearly all the houses are more or less dark, even during the brightest part of the day. In the winter, just before the gas is lighted, dungeon darkness reigns. When groping my way in the passages I usually imitate the steam craft in a thick fog and give a danger-signal when I hear someone else approaching; but even when all is silent I proceed with caution, for more than once I have stumbled against a baby who was quietly sitting in the dark hall or on the stairs. In the old-style halls there is no way of getting light and air, except from the skylight in the roof, or from the glass transoms in the doors of the apartments. In the newer houses a scanty supply of air comes directly from the air-shafts at the side of the hall. The new houses are not much better lighted than the old ones. The air-shafts are too narrow to convey much light to the lower floors.

In 1879 the city stipulated that all rooms have access to fresh air and be of a certain size. Five- to seven-story so-called dumbbell tenements were constructed, allowing for windows to be added to back rooms so fresh air could enter from the narrow airshaft in the middle and air circulate through the apartments. Many of these new tenements were built along the streets of the Sixth Ward, where Riis had his office, and on the streets of the Tenth Ward east of the Bowery, now known as the Lower East Side but at the time referred to as Jew Town because of its large population of Eastern European Jews.

Ironically, the construction of the dumbbell tenements, intended to ensure a healthier living environment for the urban poor, caused indoor pollution. As sanitation was ineffective or in many places nonexistent, the airshafts were used for dumping waste, and the pollutant-filled air from these gigantic outdoor toilets filled the apartments. The construction of the dumbbell tenements had other flaws. Sound traveled well in the halls and corridors of these buildings, so when people walked up and down the stairs they could hear a loud chorus of echoes from residents' conversations and other activities.

Having arrived in the city when the number of tenements stood at 15,000, Riis saw that number double within ten years. The population of the slums had grown to a staggering one million by 1880, equal to the city's entire population only a decade earlier. The population explosion in itself would have caused a tremendous housing problem regardless of any measure of goodwill or legislation. Compared to London's slums, which were considered dangerously overcrowded, the New York tenements held twice the number of people per square mile and the area was by all accounts the most densely populated place in the world.

Mulberry Bend, the size of a small farm field (2.76 acres), had a population density of 2,047 per acre, as compared with New York's population density today, 104 per acre. In the hardest-hit neighborhoods, 50 percent of all children died before their fifth birthday. Typhus, cholera, smallpox, and yellow fever raged in the tenements and killed thousands every year. Between 1832 and 1892 New York suffered fifteen epidemics: in 1832, cholera; 1834, smallpox and cholera; from 1836 to 1837, measles and scarlet fever; in 1849, cholera (more than 5,000 died); in 1851, smallpox; 1854, cholera; 1865, smallpox; 1866, cholera; 1872, 1875, and 1881, smallpox; 1887, diphtheria; 1892, typhus and smallpox.

Each year about one hundred infants were found dead in the gutters of the slums; this was in addition to the approximately 500 babies abandoned by their parents on the streets, swaddled in rags or newspapers. When found by the police, the babies were first brought to Randall's Island, where, according to official statistics, half died within a few days. Those who survived were taken to the Foundling Asylum.

The suicide rate in the slums was high enough to warrant special study. In 1881, a randomly chosen year, 224 New Yorkers committed suicide; 8 out of 10 were immigrants, 173 were men, 63 shot themselves, 38 chose hanging, 28 used a knife or razor blade, 15 jumped to their deaths from buildings, 16 drowned, 6 committed suicide with gas, and 20 took poison.

According to Riis, Mulberry Bend had "never been other than a vast

human pig-sty. There is but one 'Bend' in the world, and it is enough."
It was in this pigsty that Riis matured as a reporter.

❋

IN HIS FIRST YEARS as a police reporter, Riis was deeply fascinated
by the world he covered: its sheer size and complexity, the mosaic of
human drama that unfolded in the dark alleys and cramped apartments.
His articles from this early period convey his awe and exuberance. He
was infatuated with the privilege he had been given of bearing witness
to life in the slums, and consumed with writing about it.

Though he had seen and experienced poverty as a young immigrant,
he had only seen a fraction of the slums. As a reporter he became a regular at the city's mortuaries, where the dead lay side by side in long rows.
He saw countless murder victims in the streets and visited the night-
marish prison and even more forbidding asylum located on Blackwell's
Island (now Roosevelt Island), in the East River. He called at the children's hospital on Randall's Island and spent hours in the poorhouses,
dumping grounds for the crippled and elderly, whose only hope of release
was an untimely death. More than 20,000 people lived in the poorhouses, in unimaginably tight spaces. Riis witnessed countless arrests
and police interrogations. He often went to potter's field on Hart Island,
at the western extremity of Long Island Sound, sailing with the gravediggers whose thankless job was burying the unknown and those too
poor to afford even the most modest of funerals.

The poor were laid to rest in simple pine coffins. To Riis, the sight of
miniature coffins, chilling testimony to how brief many children's lives
were, was especially hard to bear. As a reporter Riis had a special gift for
laying bare the extent of the misery by narrowing in on such gruesome
details. He proved to be a master at finding the dramatic angle for a story.
Like most reporters, he was also drawn to the morbid, the absurd, the
grotesque, and the repulsive—subjects that seized readers' attention.

Riis's style was influenced by the emergence in America of yellow
journalism, a highly sensationalized form of news reporting introduced—
some say invented—by Joseph Pulitzer, who in 1883 bought the floun-
dering New York World. Under his aggressive management, and with

sharp editorial focus on dramatic, attention-grabbing news, the paper became a success. Pulitzer's most notable innovation was the catchy, large, bold-faced headline, so compelling in appearance and content that few could resist buying the paper. Before Pulitzer, headlines had been set in almost the same font as the body of the paper, and front pages had carried so many stories that none stood out. Competition in the news business was fierce, and Pulitzer's new shade of journalism soon colored the entire sector. In a few years, the *New York World* became the country's biggest paper, and for its competitors the choice was simple: Follow suit or close.

Many of the stories Riis wrote for the news bureau were picked up by the *New York World*. Though he later became one of its detractors, he clearly mastered the genre to perfection:

THE RIVER'S UNKNOWN DEAD

The Ghastly Harvest That the Tide Brings In.

Scenes in the New York Morgue—The Unidentified Dead—
The River as a Favorite Mode of Suicide—
The Police, the Coroner and the "Found Drowned"

Frequent thunderstorms of late have literally raised the dead from our rivers. A big storm, like a naval parade or the saluting from Castle William of some foreign man-of-war, never fails to bring to light some of the hidden things of the river and people the Morgue with a ghastly throng. The first warm spell in the spring, when the sun's rays take the wintry chill off the water and tempt the small boy to play hooky from school and linger about the piers, have the same effect and bring the first of the year's heavy crop to the dead-house. Then the "floaters" that have lain frozen all winter on the bottom rise and are washed ashore by the tide. All the year through dead bodies are found in the rivers, but in the spring the

Season Opens at the Morgue

And at the Potter's Field. Jack Frost puts an end to it in November. In the brief six months how many an anxious query is answered by the waters,

how many a dreaded secret revealed! And, alas! How many a one is bur-
ied unfathomed, unsolved, to which henceforth forever the cemetery of the
unknown dead only holds the key.

Somewhere between a hundred and fifty and two hundred human bodies
are cast up by the rivers every year. . . . Sometimes it happens that the tide
casts up

A Body Entirely Nude,

As that of a woman that came in from the bay the other day, at Fort Ham-
ilton. In such cases the difficulty of identification is enormously increased.
Though this particular body was in a state of excellent preservation, it was
buried unrecognized, and with it all hope that it ever would be. The difficulty
of recognizing the features of the closest friend or relative after he or she has
been in the water a few days is great to most people . . .

To the Horrors of Death

And decay are sometimes added a broken head or mutilated limbs. A body
is washed up, with skull crushed in, or fearful cuts and bruises, suggesting
murder.

The article, written in 1885, continued for another two columns,
Riis relating what happened to bodies in the care of the authorities and
how the unidentified ended up in potter's field.

As early as the late 1870s, yellow journalism had become Riis's preferred style:

SENSATIONAL HAPPENINGS THAT RUN IN STREAKS

Fires, Crimes and Elopements that Run Together
and Startle Our People.

HOW THE UNWARY ARE ROBBED IN METROPOLITAN NEW YORK

THIS YEAR'S BABY CROP

Extraordinary Facts Concerning Abandoned Infants

MURDER'S STRANGE TOOLS

Ranging from Sisera's Nail to a Jersey Coffin-Lid

HUNTING RIVER PIRATES

Dangers Nightly Encountered by Police

OMINOUS SIGNALS

Fire Boxes Indicating Disaster and Death

CHAMBER OF HORRORS

Chief Byrnes's Unique but Ghastly Collection of Mementos

However, as he became more involved in the plight of the urban poor, Riis's style of writing became less sensational, evolving as he himself developed into a more serious journalist. Something changed in him forever when, as a bystander on Mott Street, he saw the grief on the faces of parents whose baby was dying. These were real people, not subjects to be exploited for a good story. From this point on Riis focused on showing the humanity of the poor: their hopes, fears, and dreams, and their willingness to help a neighbor in need in spite of their own hardships.

"The readiness of the poor to share what little they have with those who have even less is one of the few moral virtues of the tenements," he was to write in *How the Other Half Lives*. Riis endeavored to put a human face on poverty, stressing that slum dwellers were not a breed apart: "The mothers in their own way seem to love their children quite as much as mothers in the higher walks of life." He wrote, of a railroad car cleaner who died on the job and whose family awaited him at home:

In a rear room on the top floor of the tenement, No. 590 Second Avenue, a little woman went cheerfully about her work last evening getting supper ready for her husband, for whom the table was laid, at the open window a bright lad, half-grown, was watching the busy throng of shoppers. "Papa is late," he said; "I can't see him yet. It is nine o'clock."

"SOMETHING HAS KEPT HIM,"

said the little woman with a proudly contented smile. "He is at work now, you know. But he won't be longer than he can help. Won't he be glad to see this ham I bought for his lunch on Monday? Thank God, we can afford it now. You will hear his step on the stairs presently, Mike." But the steps of Michael Mahon would never more be heard on the stairs. While his wife and boy were keeping a loving watch for him at the window he was

LYING STARK AND DEAD

in the lumber room of a station on the Second Avenue Elevated Railroad far uptown. He had lain there since four o'clock, thrown to one side, like a dead dog, as little thought of. No one had heart or thought for the little home in the downtown tenement where the light would presently go out forever. No one left word to the wife. The man had been killed; so much brain and muscle wasted; so much of a loss.

MAHON WAS A CRIPPLE.

Though only forty-two years old, he walked like an old man, with difficulty. Only a week ago he had, after months of weary search for work, found employment as a car cleaner on the Second Avenue Elevated Railroad. He was stationed at One Hundred and Twentieth Street. In the effort to get out of the way of an uptown train, just at the end of the station platform, a few minutes after four o'clock he was caught by the engine, hurled across the track and crushed to a shapeless mass. They had to raise the heavy locomotive with levers to

GET HIS QUIVERING BODY OUT,

And then he was dead. To stop the flow of blood they wrapped his mangled head and chest around and around with cotton waste, and then laid the corpse on its face in the lumber-room at the end of the station; throwing over it an old piece of cloth. The police were informed and the railroad employees told them where the dead car cleaner had lived. An officer was sent to sit on the platform until a dead wagon came but no thought was taken by anyone of the waiting wife and child. The corpse still lay in the station when the reporter went up to find out about the killing at seven o'clock.

NO ONE COULD TELL ANYTHING
about it. The station agent shrugged his shoulders and said a man had been killed. It was all he knew. . . . There were others at the station no better posted. The main dispatcher at One Hundred and Twenty-seventh Street, Mr. Teebs, might tell.

But Mr. Teebs could tell nothing. It was not his concern people getting killed on that track. That was the affair of the trainmaster at Third Street and One Hundred and Twenty-seventh Street, if anybody's. He, Mr. Teebs, had nothing to do with it.

Mr. Wetmore was found. He had made his report to the superintendent and had nothing to say, would have nothing to say. It was not a matter of consequence anyway.

"NOT A MATTER OF CONSEQUENCE!"
said the indignant and shocked reporter. "Is it possible that you don't care, or that no one here cares whether a man was killed on your track or not?"

"Indeed, I don't, nor does the press either," was Mr. Wetmore's reply. "You can put that down."

IT WAS THE REPORTER
to whom the duty fell of carrying the message of death into that stricken home.

Riis employed many of the narrative techniques of Dickens and Hans Christian Andersen, and he expressed similar social criticism. Like Dickens and Andersen, he could be sentimental, moving readers to tears. And like his literary predecessors he had a tendency to portray the world of the poor in black and white, with good and evil sharply contrasted. The story about the car cleaner bears a striking resemblance to

Andersen's "Little Match Girl." Andersen's character lights match after match and warms herself in the lovely images conjured by the flames. The car cleaner's family warm themselves in the glow of a fantasy: a job that was supposed to have saved them from starvation.

Like Dickens and Andersen, Riis came to be seen as a spokesman for the poor and unfortunate, though Riis went a step further by engaging himself and becoming involved in the world he described. As a journalist he also expressed sharper and more explicit criticism of society by addressing specific issues. He became so intent on delivering his message, however, that some of his stories took on the tone of sermons. His overriding message was that the people living in the slums were victims of a manmade environment. The neglected and deteriorating houses had, Riis argued, an ill effect on both health and social behavior. Although many of Riis's colleagues were disgusted by his preachiness, and several of his editors were inclined to delete his personal commentary, Riis remained undeterred, and little by little his opinions were published more or less as he filed them, just as his facts were. The visionary Shanks, in particular, had come to believe that this police reporter had an important message to impart to the readership.

Hair-raising features on the slums were not uncommon in the New York papers. It was not exclusively Riis who wrote feature articles on the poor in the city. Most papers on occasion published what were called slumming stories, pieces in which a reporter took readers on a tour of the slums, allowing them to witness the horror from the comfort and safety of their own homes. To ensure that readers would not feel threatened by the world confronting them in the columns of their morning paper, reporters referred to the poor as "sinful," "degenerate," "wicked," "dim-witted," and "dangerous." It was important to represent the poor using words that suppressed their humanity. The poor were to be seen as a faceless mass—people with whom the reader could not identify. Viewed in this light, Riis's articles were radical.

Riis's work from the 1880s indicates that he was never able to shake the horrors and humiliation of his first few months in New York. He wrote extensively about suicide:

LIFE'S STRUGGLE TOO HARD

George Weiss, age forty-six, a German tailor, hanged himself in the rear ten-
ement at No. 217 Avenue A yesterday morning. To make sure of his work,
he prepared an extra noose and made it tight to the door-frame that served
him as a gibbet. But it was not needed. When Weiss was found he was dead.
Several letters that were scattered about were written by him. In one he said:
"I am starving and without means to satisfy my hunger. I am friendless and
alone. I have a wife who is well off and who has a good home, but she has no
pity for me. I do not care to live." "I am sad and disappointed." He wrote on
an odd scrap of paper: "My wife and children have no love for me." In a sort
of summing up of his debts, he directed the landlord to take his bed for the
month's rent and the baker his two pillows for a debt of $2. This paper ended
abruptly with a declaration: "I am going to kill myself forthwith. Farewell."

From the man's story, as told by his sympathetic neighbors, it appeared
that he had been living in the utmost poverty and almost at the point of star-
vation. He had once, it was said, been prosperous, and had lived in com-
parative affluence with his wife and six children, but discord crept into the
family and after a violent quarrel it was broken up two years ago.

At least one of Riis's stories concerned a young man who could not
be identified and whose body no one came to claim.

A young man about twenty years old, and of Hebrew origin, registered at
the Occidental Hotel, No. 341 Bowery, Friday evening, as M. Bauer of
Hartford, Conn. His appearance was peculiar. His face was shaven, but his
hair was so long that it fell about his shoulders, and his dark eyes had a look
which indicated that he was not entirely sane. He was given a room in one of
the upper stories. A servant tried the door of the room several times Saturday
and found it locked. Yesterday morning an attendant discovered that the door
of the room was still fastened on the inside, and on climbing up and looking
through the transom, he saw the body of Bauer lying on the bed. When the
door was forced open by the police it was discovered that the young man had
committed suicide by shooting himself through the head. From the appear-
ance of the body it was believed that the suicide was committed Friday night.
The clothing which the man wore was new and the pockets contained $20

and a silver watch and gold chain. A locket attached to the watch-chain bore the initials "L.R.," and contained the photographs of two elderly persons, who might have been the father and mother of the suicide. Nothing else was found which could furnish a clew to the identity of the young man. Coroner Brady yesterday took charge of the effects and sent the body to the morgue.

Surely Riis saw, in this lonely immigrant, what he himself might have become: yet another anonymous victim of poverty.

Riis's fascination with the subject of people who took their own lives drove him to write a feature on what was fast becoming known as the era of suicide—then considered, in certain scientific quarters, a contagious disease. Riis wrote that in 1850, one in 16,680 people had committed suicide; by 1874, the number had risen to one in every 5,515. The most common cause of suicide, Riis found, was "poverty or the fear of poverty." He told the story of a woman who threw herself and her four children in front of a train because she had lost her bank book— according to eyewitnesses, she had been hugging her youngest fiercely to her chest as the train hit. One man had soaked himself in lamp oil, lit a match, and set himself on fire. Another had knocked his brains out on a furnace. A farmer had decapitated himself with a scythe. A young couple took poison because they were "too tired" to carry on. They died in their bed, in each other's arms.

❀

MOST REPORTERS and writers who wrote about the slums focused primarily on suffering and squalor. In fact, of course, there was more to the slums than abject poverty. Hundreds of thousands of families lived relatively normal lives. They worked, although usually under deplorable conditions, paid rent, fed their children, and had hopes and dreams for the future. For a large number of immigrants, not least those who had escaped religious persecution in Russia and Eastern Europe, life in the tenements was an improvement on their old lives, offering a more dignified existence. Moreover, poverty was not a life sentence, as many writers—including, at times, Riis—seemed to want readers to believe. Even for tenement dwellers social mobility was possible, and a considerable number of families escaped the slums within a generation or two. Many early Irish and German settlers had already lifted themselves into the middle class.

Most reporters ignored the rich street life of the slums. Mulberry Bend, inhabited primarily by Italians, supported butchers, clothing stores, shoemakers, tailors, and lawyers' and doctors' offices. Vendors sold a multitude of goods, and throngs of shoppers and children milled around, laughter and music floating under the festoons of flapping laundry suspended between the buildings. These were largely self-contained, self-sustaining neighborhoods.

Riis's reasons for focusing on poverty and squalor were not exclusively politically motivated. As a reporter he simply saw more of the tragedy of the slums, especially at night, when, as he said, he could apprehend the true nature of things: "I walked every morning between two and four o'clock the whole length of Mulberry Street, through the Bend and across Five Points down to the Fulton Ferry. There were no cars on the Bowery, and I liked to walk, because I was able to observe the slum when off its guard. The instinct to pose is as strong there as it is on Fifth Avenue. It is a human impulse, I suppose." He also walked to and from the ferry every day rather than take a hansom or one of the sputtering trains that crossed the Bowery on gigantic iron rails. He wanted to see and feel his beat.

The slums were veritable hatching grounds for pocket thieves, and the men who ran the brothels and bars led organized gangs—the Fourth Avenue Tunnel Gang, Forty Little Thieves, the Gas House Gang, the Molasses Gang, the Hell's Kitchen Gang—drawn from the ranks of hard-core criminals. The notorious Whyos Gang, one of New York's most vicious in the 1880s and 1890s, originated in Mulberry Bend. According to a legend put forward by Herbert Asbury in his classic, highly entertaining, if somewhat exaggerated *The Gangs of New York*— source of inspiration for Martin Scorsese's movie of the same name—a prerequisite for membership was to have committed at least one murder. The Whyos robbed ships docked at the wharf or anchored in the East River. Though it is doubtful that all of its members were murderers, they were greatly feared. Hoggy Walsh, Fig McGerald, Bull Hurley, Googy

Corcoran, and Red Rocks Farrell, all violent criminals, were prominent members of the Whyos Gang.

Both as a matter of course and in response to the violent nature of the gangs, the police adopted brutal methods of their own. History had taught many officers to fight back or risk dying. Officers patrolling Hell's Kitchen, Mulberry Bend, and the Tenderloin, areas ruled almost entirely by gangs, made it a rule to stay together in groups of three or more for their own safety.

Civilian pedestrians did not have much to fear, as long as they kept to themselves. As Riis observed:

> I have often been asked if such slumming is not full of peril. No, not if you are there on business. Mere sightseeing at such unseasonable hours might easily be. But the man who is sober and minds his own business—which presupposes that he has business to mind there—runs no risk anywhere in New York, by night or by day. Such a man will take the other side of the street when he sees a gang ahead spoiling for a fight, and where he does go he will carry the quiet assumption of authority that comes with the consciousness of a right to be where he is.

Riis of course became a familiar figure in these neighborhoods. He was there every day, and people recognized the chain-smoking man who always carried a notepad. Known not as the Dutchman or Jake, as he was called by some, but as Doc, he was mistaken for a doctor because of the frequency with which he accompanied health inspectors on their rounds. Fortunately for Riis, doctors were in high demand and therefore safe in the slums.

But though Riis rarely met with violence, he didn't escape it entirely. One night, he heard someone yell "murder" from a bar on the corner of Crosby and Jersey streets. He headed in the direction of the shouting, entered the bar, and saw a full-fledged gang fight unfolding before his eyes. On the floor was the bar owner, unconscious and with a knife protruding from his neck. Around him sat a group of women, crying. Riis moved toward the body, and as he was kneeling to get a closer look at the wound, he heard the door slam behind him. As bottles flew through the air Riis instinctively pulled the knife out of the bar owner's neck and shouted, "Whose knife is this?" A bottle was hurled in his direction and he understood his involvement was unwelcome. He tried in vain to stanch the bar owner's blood with a sponge and bandages, procured from the women who surrounded the man. The brawl continued, and at length the police arrived.

Another night, Riis was turning a corner at his customary fast-paced gait and crashed into the Whyos Gang. The gang leader perceived it as provocation and pulled a knife on him. Riis could feel the knife go through his clothes and poke his ribs. The gang leader asked him what he thought about the knife. According to Riis's memoirs, he coolly pushed the man's hand away from his body, looked at the knife, and replied that he thought it was about two inches longer than the law allowed. Riis noted, "I knew even as I said it that I had cast the die; he held my life in his hand." The police arrived exactly as this near-fatal exchange occurred, at least in Riis's memory.

✻

LONG WORKING HOURS eventually took their toll; it was when the initial excitement of Riis's new beat had subsided that exhaustion began to set in and his passion became a backbreaking obsession. By the mid-1880s he felt utterly overwhelmed. He had seen too many infant corpses, too much crime and squalor. He had been in too many foul-smelling boardinghouses with too many vagrants living in one room. He had seen too many young women wither away in opium dens in Chinatown. Riis went to Shanks and informed him that he wanted to quit the beat, asking to be transferred back downtown to Newspaper Row, where he could work as a general reporter again. Shanks turned him down out of hand; Riis had simply become too valuable to be released. "Go back and stay," his boss replied, according to Riis's memoirs. "Unless I am much mistaken, you are finding something up there that needs you. Wait and see."

As always, Shanks had an intuitive sense of what was right for Riis.

13

The Reformers

R IIS WAS NOT ALONE in feeling overworked and stretched to the
limit. The city operated at a relentless pitch in the 1880s, a period
that brought tremendous technological innovation. The Brooklyn Bridge,
the world's largest suspension bridge, had been completed in 1883 and
was widely viewed as the eighth wonder of the world. With the bridge,
Brooklyn seemed to move closer to Manhattan, the two cities forming
a metropolis whose business and cultural reach extended far beyond its
borders. Sections of the elevated railway, known as the el, were being
constructed above traffic-clogged streets, and New Yorkers could get from
place to place more quickly and more easily. Bicycles had also become a
popular means of transportation, with cyclists cruising between hansoms,
carts, and omnibuses, adding to the general sense of chaos.

The 1880s also saw the dawn of the electrical age. Founded on Pearl
Street in 1882, Edison Electric Illuminating Company of New York sup-
plied generators that lit only a few lamps on one block; but in 1887
Edison's competitor, George Westinghouse, a spokesman for alternating current, spawned a competition to provide universal service. Soon
a complex web of electrical wires hung above the city, so thick in some
places that it blocked the sun. The web of wires grew even denser with
the advent of the telephone.

As life in the city became increasingly stressful, people began long-
ing for peace and quiet far away from lurching bikes, noisy trains, and
dangerous wires. Those who could afford it fled the city for the country and became commuters. It was a relief to leave the city at night and
get away from its incessant beat, massive crowds of people, heavy odors,
animals, trash heaps, fish stands, slaughter benches, overflowing trash
cans, and gasworks. A house in the country meant no longer having
to endure the exhausting struggle of pushing one's way down eternally
crowded streets, the neverending lines, and the cacophony of sounds
from neighing horses, metal-rimmed carriage wheels rolling along the
cobblestoned streets, eternal bickering and swearing, the discordant
efforts of Salvation Army bands, howling sirens of fire trucks, and the
paper boys' piercing calls: "Extra, Extra . . . read all about it." Peace and
quiet was understandably what many New Yorkers yearned for.

※

ALBON PLATT MAN, a lawyer with an office on Wall Street, worked
seven days a week, skipping breakfast so he could be in his office at sun-
rise and start the day's business before any of his employees had even
gotten out of bed. Despite being an incurable workaholic, Man spent
considerable time at his summer house in Lawrence, in Nassau County,
and it is said that when he rode his carriage to Lawrence, he rested his
horse at Richmond Hill, then farmland and wilderness. To Man it was
the prettiest area he had seen in such close proximity to the city. In 1868
he decided to found a small, upscale town in these beautiful surroundings. He was envisioning a suburb, then a relatively new phenomenon.
    In a joint venture with landscape architect Edward Richmond, who
had founded suburbs in Boston, he bought two farms and 681 acres of
land in the small village of Clarenceville near the coming Long Island
Railroad, still under construction. Man took on the role of developer,
dividing the land into plots and building elegant two- and three-story
houses, all large enough to house servants. The houses' signature features
were wraparound porches, tall gables, and small towers and turrets. The
size of the plots allowed for a generous garden and a spacious garage for
the family's horse-drawn carriage—most self-respecting families owned

carriages, which conferred status. All houses were set back at least twenty yards from the sidewalk, giving the neighborhood an air of secluded exclusivity. Richmond's town plan stipulated the planting of 4,000 oak trees, and within a few years these glorious oaks transformed the streets into grand boulevards. Man named the small town Richmond Hill, not after his partner but after a distinguished London neighborhood.

Richmond Hill became a success, attracting lawyers, bankers, stock-brokers, ministers, entrepreneurs, doctors, and actors and actresses. It did not take long before Richmond Hill had its own banks, several Protestant churches, schools, libraries, and clubs: a golf club, and Queens County Wheelman Club, for cyclists. In every respect Richmond Hill stood in stark contrast to the dark, stuffy city less than twenty-two miles away. The *Long Island Democrat*, the local paper, carried stories about stolen watermelons, a farmer being kicked by his horse, and the birth of one Jacob Hausewirth's calf.

Riis dreamed of moving out of the city to a place where he could leave behind the dirt and misery of the slums. "I have to be where there are trees and birds and green hills, and where the sky is blue above. So we built our nest in Brooklyn on the outskirts of the great park [Forest Park]," Riis wrote in his memoirs. Brooklyn was expanding rapidly, and as Riis's rent skyrocketed, he longed to escape.

One Sunday in the winter of 1884, he went for a long walk that led him to Queens and places he had never been. "I came upon Richmond Hill and thought it was the most beautiful spot I had ever seen," he noted in the memoirs. He hurried home and announced to his chil-dren—all sick in bed with scarlet fever—that they were moving.

The next day Riis went back and picked out a plot on Beech Street, which was lined with good-sized oak trees. With his small savings from the sale of the *South Brooklyn News* long gone, Riis financed the pur-chase of the land by taking a job writing insurance policies for a com-pany that sold insurance to Danes in the United States. He secured the position through a Danish friend, a retired general, General C. T. Christensen. The work brought him $200, and his old friend and part-ner from his days as an advertiser, Ed Wells, by then a prosperous phar-macist, lent him the remaining sum.

The Riises could not afford to have a house built on their new lot, but Riis borrowed what he needed from the manager of the Associated Press, agreeing to pay off the loan in monthly installments. The final phases of building coincided with the birth of the Riises' fourth child, Stephen Balthasar, in December 1885. In 1886, the family moved into their new two-story house, which had a lovely porch and green shutters. Behind the house was an enormous wild garden.

The idyllic suburban setting allowed Elisabeth to take full advantage of the social skills she had acquired in the upper-class milieu of Ribe. She quickly became part of a network of dynamic, cultured society women who managed perfect households and arranged spectacular dinner parties in their warm and inviting homes. Elisabeth also threw herself wholeheartedly into the work of the local women's group, the Twentieth Century Club, which advocated for the extension of women's voting rights by the turn of the century. The club collected money for the poor and were engaged in activities to help families in distress. Later, when Progressive ideas gained a strong foothold, Elisabeth helped organize summer outings for poor children from the city to Richmond Hill.

Like Elisabeth, Riis was soon an integral part of the local community. The family joined the Union Congregational Church, a few blocks from their house. Riis became curator and, according to church books, regularly gave talks to the congregation on his work as a journalist, revenues from his presentations—which in 1887 totaled $27—going to the church. Riis was a member of the Richmond Hill Club, which established a local library. Politics was the chief subject of discussion at club events. Most members were Republican, and disagreements on the issues of the day were rare. According to the Richmond Hill archives, Riis also became a member of the neighborhood's bicycle club.

Riis's life in Richmond Hill became the much-needed bulwark he had envisioned against the city. It was here that he slowly began to take a more active role in his children's lives.

In May 1886, shortly after the Riises had settled into their suburban home, tragedy struck when Stephen, only five months old, died. The first member of the Riis family to be buried in the hilly woodland of

Maple Grove Cemetery, his sudden and unexpected absence surely lent urgency to Riis's newfound involvement as a father.

※

IN EXCHANGE FOR Riis's having agreed to stay on as a police reporter, Shanks had agreed to put him on the day shift. Apart from giving him time with his family, the change allowed him to connect with the city's small but growing number of reformers. This window into their work was to become significant in altering the direction of Riis's own work in the following years. Meeting reformers helped effect his transition from a reporter who merely described the slums to a reporter who worked actively to change conditions. Finally Riis became, simply, a reformer himself.

"A new life began for me, with greatly enlarged opportunities," he wrote later. "I had been absorbing impressions up till then. I met men now in whose companionship they began to crystallize, to form into definite convictions; men of learning, of sympathy, and of power. My eggs hatched."

If Riis had felt alone in his concern with and outrage over the growing poverty problem in New York, he was soon to discover that he was far from the only one who was appalled. Reform movements were rising everywhere, and many of their leaders had a deeper understanding of the issues than Riis. These leaders recognized that poverty was not only unethical but a significant threat to democracy, paving the way to anarchy and unrest. They saw themselves as warriors, fighting for better living conditions for the poor. Riis was to become first one of them and then, eventually, one of their most effective spokesmen. In order to fully appreciate the development he underwent under their tutelage, as well as the significance of his later work, one must take a closer look at how poverty was perceived by Americans, and what the most visionary reformers believed needed to be done in order to combat the problem.

※

AMERICAN VIEWS on poverty were vastly different from those prevalent in Europe, where the condition was seen, within the larger context of hundreds of years of war, famine, market fluctuation, deadly epidemics, and poor crops, simply as part of the world order. The aristocracy tended to regard poverty both as inevitable—a disease the poor had brought upon themselves—and as the natural by-product of a class-divided society. This oddly contradictory position, however, did not translate into a laissez-faire attitude toward the poor but rather gave rise to well-intentioned, if flawed, legislation.

In England, the Elizabethan Poor Law of 1601 was founded on the belief that as poverty did indeed arise in large part due to class divisions, it was the moral responsibility of the upper classes to help the less fortunate. According to the Poor Law, local authorities in each parish were responsible for helping the poor in their area, procuring financial support for the unemployed, and assisting young men in getting apprenticeships, thus enabling them to learn a trade. They were also responsible for collecting the so-called poor rate, a tax placed on the wealthy. The flaws of this early, decentralized British welfare system were particularly evident in bigger cities. In London, where there was a huge concentration of the poor, relief was seriously insufficient. Still, the view that the wealthy were morally obligated to help the less fortunate was quite progressive. The Elizabethan Poor Law was also enforced in the British colonies and thus in America.

For many years the colonies experienced almost no poverty; by European standards the level of poverty was certainly infinitesimal. The colonies were sparsely populated and class distinctions of less consequence. As a result, the problem of large masses of poor people never entered into the equation of American life during this period. Moreover, there were no big cities; the colonies consisted mainly of small villages, where people felt naturally obligated to help their neighbors, such interdependence serving as insurance against starvation and poverty. Unemployment, which plagued Europe, was nonexistent, and in fact there was a pronounced shortage of manpower in America.

When the colonists declared their independence from Britain, they also broke, in many respects, with British sentiment and law. Among the legislation discarded was the Poor Law. The young country saw itself as a pioneer nation with vast, largely uninhabited areas to be explored and settled. The civilization of the West became a mission in itself during the 1840s, and the push for expansion, known as Manifest Destiny, would come to define the United States and its citizens. Accordingly, it was believed that work would always be plentiful and that anybody who was able and willing could stave off poverty. If people could not make it in the North, they could always go west.

Poverty came to be viewed as shameful and a mark of laziness and incompetence; if people could not make it in the land of endless opportunities, where in theory there were no class distinctions, they had only themselves to blame. Ironically, this mindset gained traction with the American public around the same time that great waves of immigrants began flooding the cities, bringing with them in their sheer number the seed of poverty. Cities on the East Coast, where the very poor clustered, quickly turned into social bottlenecks. Immigrants settled in poverty-striken neighborhoods, which soon became even poorer, feeding America's view of poverty as self-inflicted. Drunkenness, crime, and promiscuity flourished in such places, and—so contemporary thinking went—clearly their inhabitants were simply too lazy to work, a view that would become a self-fulfilling prophecy. Moreover, these people wore funny clothes and spoke strange languages and practiced weird religions. And they were dirty. The water supply was less than dependable in ill-served neighborhoods, and this subclass of people became known as "the great unwashed," a designation that was seen as yet another proof of their uncivilized character and general unworthiness.

It was this harsh view of poverty that prevailed when Riis arrived in 1870. Yet the precept "help thy neighbor" still informed American society. By the 1880s there were hundreds of charitable organizations, some publicly funded, others run by private foundations and churches—charities that offered shelter for the homeless and set up soup kitchens to feed the hungry. As the Gilded Age gained momentum, however, and the United States became industrialized, the relatively small publicly and privately funded charities were unable to help the growing number of poor. Laissez-faire capitalism and social Darwinism had taken hold of the political and business leadership in America, making it increasingly difficult for charity workers to wring money out of those whose pockets were lined with silk and who espoused the ethics of free-market capitalism.

Protestant virtues, the pillars of Victorian society, did not help the charities' cause either. According to Victorian thinking, those who did not live respectable lives, work hard, and keep clean and virtuous were considered "sinners." Collectively the poor, who were unclean and therefore impure, represented to contemporary Victorian citizens the frightening consequence of straying from Protestant practices.

※

IN THE FIRST DECADE of the Gilded Age there were 4,000 millionaires in the United States. With a sense of entitlement conferred by extreme sudden wealth, the nouveaux riches in particular began building mansions, many resembling small castles. It was a display that middle-class Americans found distasteful and immoral; the show of wealth offended Victorian sensibilities almost as much as the alleged shortcomings of the poor.

An event that came to represent this schism, as well as the divide between old and new wealth in America, was the 1883 costume ball orchestrated by Mrs. William Kissam Vanderbilt, born Alva Erskine Smith. When the Vanderbilts moved into their new chateau, as houses of castlelike proportions were called, at the corner of Fifth Avenue and Fifty-second Street, Alva Smith, as she was known, invited 1,200 to join her in celebrating the completion of the $3 million structure, modeled on French renaissance king François I's wing of the Château de Blois. Preparations for the ball were followed closely, and it was well known that Alva Smith had deliberately not invited Caroline Astor, widely considered the queen of New York high society. By this omission, she earned a social call from Caroline's mother—"*the* Mrs. Astor," Caroline Webster Schermerhorn Astor—and gained unstated entrée into the Astors' world of old money, made in real estate, shipping, and the fur trade. Caroline Astor was invited to the ball, and Alva Smith had successfully signaled a power shift. Her ball was like none New York had ever witnessed, with $155,730 spent on costumes alone. Other families soon followed suit, all vying for social power and sparing no expense. As their parties and their chateaus became more and more grand, and with three quarters of the city's population living in abject poverty a few blocks south of such unchecked ostentation, a reaction was inevitable.

※

AMONG THE LESS altruistic concerns of the reform movement was the frank realization, on the part of the old upper class and the middle class, that they were about to lose political power—that the lower classes posed a potential threat to the status quo in America, and that the poor would take the jobs of hardworking Americans and, with their foreign cultures, undermine the country's norms. One of the most important early reform initiatives took its theoretical and philosophical cues from a book published in 1873, *Progress and Poverty: An Inquiry into the Cause of Industrial Depression and of Increase of Want with Increase of Wealth*, written by the self-taught socioeconomic thinker Henry George. The initiative took hold around the time Riis became known on Mulberry Street as the Boss Reporter.

Henry George was a small, energetic man who grew up in Philadelphia and left school at the age of thirteen to work as an errand boy, later running off to sea and sailing around the world. When he returned to Philadelphia, the city was experiencing an economic downturn and he could not find a job. He tried his luck in California as a miner in the afterglow of the gold rush, but luck eluded him as it did thousands of other hopefuls. For a while he sold gold-mining equipment in Victoria, British Columbia; then, after giving gold mining a second try, he was forced to take up the life of a vagabond. In 1859 he secured an apprenticeship as a printer in San Francisco, but once he had served his apprenticeship, he found it difficult to get a steady job; most of the papers that hired him ended up going bankrupt, pushed out by fierce competition. George and a couple of fellow printers decided to launch their own paper, the *Evening Journal*, hoping to secure a living for themselves. Despite their strenuous efforts, the publication failed stupendously. Following this fiasco George earned a meager living as a reporter. It was as a writer that he became consumed, like Riis, with understand-

ing the mechanisms of the society he lived in. Why, he kept asking himself, did extreme wealth always go hand in hand with extreme poverty?
Was there an economic law that could explain why so many became
poor, when great wealth was concentrated in the hands of a few?

He found the answers to his questions while horseback riding outside
San Francisco. He had paused to inquire about rural property value and
learned, to his amazement, that a plot of land, even in this remote and
sparsely populated area, cost $1,000, a huge sum at the time. The infla-
tion was explained by the fact that the transcontinental railway would pass
through the area; developers were counting on a large influx of people.

Here was the correlation between advancing poverty and advancing
wealth. Economic disparity, George realized, began with land monopoly. In times of prosperity a country's relatively few landowners became
richer, because they could charge higher and higher rents. As the majority of wage earners did not own their homes but lived in rented quarters,
they were vulnerable to increasing rents. Once the rents became too
high, many were forced out of their homes and into poverty, whereas
the homeowners always came out on top, and the wealth continued
being concentrated in fewer and fewer hands. In order to level the disparity, George would argue, huge property taxes were the only solution.
He concluded that the topic warranted a book, but he found it hard
to find a publisher, and when he did, he was required to pay the cost
involved. When the book was finally published, it barely sold, and in
desperation George peddled it door to door. Following the financial crisis of 1873, people were ready to hear his message, as they had begun
asking the same questions he had. Why were so many people so poor
in a nation that was so rich? Perhaps the poor were not in fact stupid or
incompetent but the victims of larger forces. To George's own great surprise, his economic theories caught on with the American public. He
was to become an important political player in the mid-1880s.

※

THERE WAS GREAT UNREST in the labor market in the 1880s, not
unlike the turbulence during the period 1873–1877. The labor union
Knights of Labor rode successfully on the waves of discontent among

workers and launched many triumphant strikes between 1884 and 1885. In May 1886, however, things went badly wrong. The number of strikes across America had increased after May 1 demonstrations, bringing a significant boost to the labor movement, but on May 3, during violent rioting among demonstrators, the police, and the military, a bomb was detonated in Haymarket Square in Chicago. Seven officers and an untold number of civilians were killed and hundreds wounded in the explosion. The men who had thrown the bomb were anarchists, but the press blamed the Knights of Labor, and whatever sympathy the general public had had for the workers and the union vanished. Still, a growing number of people acknowledged that to avoid future strikes, riots, and outright anarchy, something had to be done to improve the conditions of the poor, who worked hard but earned little and had no prospect of escaping their plight. It was widely acknowledged that social reforms benefiting the poor were long overdue.

Though George was not a socialist, he was persuaded to run for mayor of New York as the Central Labor Union candidate in the election of 1886. He received more votes than the young Republican candidate, Theodore Roosevelt, but was defeated by Democrat Abraham S. Hewitt. His greatest success, however, was having forced social issues onto the political agenda. Both Hewitt and Roosevelt had campaigned, as had George, against land monopoly and poor housing. Hewitt, who had broken with the boss system of Tammany Hall, became one of the most reform-minded mayors in the history of New York City, although his tenure as mayor was also to make history as the city's shortest. Still, a breeze of change was sweeping through the streets and alleys of New York.

❊

KEY CHARITIES in New York included the Salvation Army, which arrived from England with great fanfare in 1880 and became an immediate success, the New York Association for Improving the Condition of the Poor, the Trinity Church Association, the State Charities Aid Association (SCAA), the Children's Aid Society (CAS), the Society for Prevention of Cruelty to Children, the Down-Town Relief Bureau, the Five Points Mission, the Committee on the Elevation of the Poor in Their Homes, and the Charity Organization Society (COS), an umbrella organization coordinating the profusion of minor charitable efforts. According to *King's Handbook of New York City*, from 1892 there were more than 500 charitable institutions in the city: 28 of them were publicly funded; 83 provided temporary relief; 51 offered special care; 26 helped primarily immigrants; 67 gave permanent help to the poor; 101 provided medical assistance; 16 aided those with what was known as defects; 16 focused on reforming the poor; and 116 provided miscellaneous help.

One reform leader stood out among those with whom Riis came into contact when he started working the daytime shift: Josephine Shaw Lowell. Shaw came from a politically involved upper-class family active in the abolition movement during the 1860s. The Shaws suffered great losses in the Civil War. Shaw's brother, Robert Gould Shaw, who commanded the first regiment of black troops, was killed in action, and her husband, Charles Russell Lowell, was killed, widowing Shaw at the age of twenty. She was to remain in mourning the rest of her life, devoting herself with fierce determination to charitable work. In Virginia, after the war, she worked for the Freedman's Relief Association, helping black children get an education. She continued her charity work in New York, volunteering at hospitals for the poor, including Bellevue, said to be no better than a slaughterhouse. As director of the SCAA, an institution whose goal was to find a solution to the vagabond problem in New York, she endeavored to place the 10,000 people living on the streets.

Shaw belonged to a school of hard-core reformers who despised the distribution of charity to the able-bodied without asking for something in return. Giving alms was corruptive, she argued; it made people lazy. Like the majority of contemporary reformers, and based on analyses of poverty she conducted for the SCAA, she concluded that vagabonds were "depraved" and their immoral behavior contagious, undermining the established order of society.

She attracted much attention during the Christmas season of 1876, when a story broke of an infant who had frozen to death in the arms of its mother while she begged on the streets. Most papers expressed outrage that this could have happened in New York; editorials rang with sympathy for the bereaved mother. Shaw had a different view: In an indignant article she put forth the opinion that it was not the death of the baby that was scandalous but the mother's conduct. The police, too, had failed. "It is important," Shaw stressed, "that we as society prevent the practice of begging."

Despite her hard edges, Shaw's priority was the well-being of the poor. Her thinking, however, was considered radical in some quarters: The poor should receive help, but only the kind of help that enabled them to help themselves. Also, the poor had to earn the privilege of welfare by going through a cleansing process. They had to prove to the authorities that they were worthy human beings—prostitutes should quit the profession, drunks stop drinking, and criminals cease criminal activities. Vagabonds should not receive help unless they were willing to work in return.

Shaw's self-help mantra so impressed New York Governor Samuel J. Tilden that he appointed her commissioner of the New York State Board of Charities. Shaw thus became the first woman to hold state office in New York. As commissioner she introduced a bill that required women who had conceived more than two children out of wedlock or committed minor crimes to be admitted to rehabilitation centers. During such stays these "fallen" and "weak" women were to learn "the joy of working."

In 1882 Shaw founded the COS, designed to insure that the hundreds of charities in the city did not overlap, resulting in unnecessary spending. As its director, she spoke out against "outdoor relief," such as food distribution at soup kitchens. Shaw was enraged by the concept of soup kitchens that allowed the poor simply to line up for food. How would they be moved to work, she asked, if they could get their food for free? The COS also tried to introduce a law that required homeless men to do manual work, like cutting wood, in exchange for shelter.

In response to Shaw's suggestions, the COS made comprehensive registers of all the families (27,400 households and 170,000 individuals) who received help. The registers were intended to prevent overdistribution, so that people did not get more than they needed. Shaw also organized a small army of volunteers, so-called friendly visitors, who were to visit poor families to help them improve their character. Before she sent her friendly visitors into the field, she instructed them: "All charity must tend to raise and elevate the moral nature, even if the process be as painful as plucking out an eye or cutting off a limb."

Though her approach to charity may seem, in retrospect, cold-hearted, Shaw was well respected in her time and considered enormously progressive. The basis of her philosophy was that with moral guidance almost all poor people—with the exception, perhaps, of vagabonds—could be transformed into upstanding, law-abiding citizens. In spite of her view of vagabonds as depraved, she did not see the non-homeless poor as inherently depraved.

By the time Riis became acquainted with Shaw, her views had softened somewhat. The COS had been sharply criticized by the church for being callous and for oppressing the poor. Shaw had taken the criticism to heart and resigned, devoting her time instead to the fight for better wages and working conditions for seamstresses—women who worked long, long hours in small, dingy, overcrowded workrooms for wages that could barely keep them alive. Shaw would later become one of the main forces in the Working Women's Society, a coalition that provided seamstresses a political voice.

Riis adopted Shaw's view of vagabonds but felt she was overly critical of the poor in the slums, for whom he had the greatest empathy. He acknowledged, however, that she had a strong voice and was an important reformer, and that it was imperative to listen to, learn from, and join forces with her. Riis and Shaw became warm friends as she became less rigorous during the 1890s, when he had earned recognition as a writer. The two of them at times met daily to coordinate long-term strategies as well as initiatives for emergency relief. One such initiative was set into motion during the Panic of 1893, when thousands became unemployed overnight and faced imminent starvation.

Another reformer whose thinking had a significant influence on Riis was Charles Loring Brace (1826–1890), a Methodist minister who devoted his life to the Children's Aid Society. CAS sent children from broken, poverty-stricken homes to families out west who would bring them up as their own. The thinking was that these neglected children would blossom and grow into well-functioning adults in healthy family environments and fresh country air. More than 200,000 children traveled on the so-called orphan trains to the West to take up new lives with new families under this program. The orphan trains stopped in 1930, but the foster care system, which Brace founded, has continued in other forms. Though a majority of Brace's children thrived, some were badly abused by their host families, who had only taken them in because they needed cheap labor.

Despite his reputation as a humanitarian, less than noble motives were behind Brace's program. Most of the children sent out west were Catholics, who had long made up the poorest segment of society and were, until the late nineteenth century, scorned by the Protestant elite. Under the guise of philanthropy, Catholic children were sent to Protestant families, who converted them. Notwithstanding such politics, Brace's main motive was to help children in need, and his success made him a respected and influential reformer. Riis never met Brace, who died in 1890, but he had a thorough knowledge of his work and thinking. Like Shaw, Brace was an old-school reformer who believed the poor were souls that had gone astray, as is evident from the title of his book *Dangerous Classes*. He believed, like Shaw, in "doing for oneself" and in work for help. At the same time Brace was an optimist who believed it was possible to eradicate poverty. If the young and the children from the slums were raised in a healthy environment, they would grow up to become model citizens, he declared. He did not believe that poverty was caused by inherent flaws in the moral fabric of the poor, but rather that they were a product of their circumstances. His solution was early intervention.

A reformer with a less moralistic bent to his thinking was the highly esteemed philosopher, social critic, and free-thinker Felix Adler. Adler had a modern and holistic outlook on the problem of poverty and influenced Riis personally on many specific issues. A well-known and well-liked public speaker, Adler is still regarded as one of the most visionary and compelling activists in American reform history. He saw poverty as a complex problem, rooted in the prevailing social order.

The son of a rabbi, Felix Adler was born in Germany in 1851. When he was six his family moved to New York and joined Temple Emanu-El. As a young man Adler studied at Columbia College (later Columbia University) and at the Hochschule für die Wissenschaft des Judenthums in Berlin, where he studied theology, philosophy, linguistics, economics—a discipline that incorporated social reform—and labor studies. His family had taken it for granted that he would follow in the footsteps of his father, Samuel Adler, and become a rabbi, but religious dogma was not for Adler. He chose instead to become a teacher of Hebrew and Oriental literature.

Bald and bearded, with a kind, direct gaze, Adler in middle age became increasingly dismayed by his countrymen's indiscriminate worship of religion and the set ideas and rituals upon which he felt they rested. He came to believe that a spiritual revolution was needed to free people from the straitjacket of established religion. He was skeptical of monotheism; instead of worshipping *a* God, he advocated that people convert their religious convictions into concrete action—into helping their neighbors. His motto was: "Deed not creed." In 1876 he founded the New York Society for Ethical Culture, and with this organization as his platform he became one of the city's most active reformers, focusing on improving the conditions in the slums. He was also among the pioneers behind the social gospel movement, a theological approach to social reform, whose members saw it as their mission to create a fairer society for all. Adler spoke out on issues of foreign politics and became one of the early critics of American imperialism and a spokesman for an international confederation in the form of a league of nations.

Riis met Adler for the first time in 1884. By then Adler was one of the main forces in the Tenement-House Committee (also known as the Drexel Committee, named after one of its members, banker Joseph William Drexel). The committee worked to get their proposals made into law, stipulating better housing for the poor and demolition of the worst tenements. It was founded at a time when the political atmosphere was receptive to its ideas, having been influenced by Henry George's thinking on land monopoly and housing speculation. Committee members met regularly at police headquarters offices on Mulberry Street, and because Riis now worked days he was able to attend the meetings. "I sat through all its sessions as a reporter and heard every word of testimony," Riis wrote in his memoirs, remarking also that not all members seemed to have their heart in it. "Mr. Ottendorfer [a philanthropist and editor of the *New-Yorker Staats-Zeitung*] and Mr. Drexel, the banker, often napped during meetings."

Of Felix Adler, Riis wrote:

His clear, incisive questions, cutting through the subterfuge and getting to the root of the problems, were at times like flashes of lightning on dark nights in which one quickly discovers the landscape far and near and we began to view the residents of the slums as souls, which was a big white milestone on a dreary road.

In Riis's words, it was primarily due to Adler that he and countless other New Yorkers were made aware that the people living in the tenements were "better than their houses."

✺

IN SPITE OF all the reformers and thinkers that Riis met, it was still the New York Health Department that, more than any one individual, informed Riis's views on poverty. Many of the department's inspectors were doctors who performed regular checks on the state of the tenements. In the summer, when the risk of epidemics was at its highest, an additional fifty inspectors were added to the staff. Thousands died every summer from contagious diseases, with epidemics always hitting the most densely populated areas. Nine out of ten who died from an epidemic disease in New York were from the tenements.

The Health Department tried to ward off epidemics by employing a host of preventive measures: enforcing sanitary regulations, particularly removal of waste on a regular basis, and making sure the laws against pig husbandry and the housing of people in dark, poorly ventilated basements were upheld. They kept detailed records of deaths and illnesses in the slums to see if there was a direct correlation between these occurrences and the development of epidemics.

Once an epidemic washed over the city, the Health Department worked tirelessly to try to contain it as well as tend to the ill, making sure that those who needed it were hospitalized and, if necessary, quarantined. Inspectors on Mott Street, where the suffering was most acute and epidemics took their greatest toll, were thus always on the front line. Although it had been of course understood by scientists and social scientists since the turn of the century that the coexistence of poverty, overcrowding, and poor sanitation caused disease and epidemics, until the late 1880s the public in general still believed that it was the very depravity of the poor that caused deadly epidemics. And while wherever these three elements coexisted epidemics posed a constant threat not just to the poor in the tenements but to the entire city—bacteria did not discriminate between the poor and the wealthy—the wealthy could leave the city in the summer, decreasing their chances of contracting potentially fatal diseases. Diseases and epidemics would continue to be a serious problem as long as housing speculators, or slumlords, continued to cram too many people into small, dingy, badly ventilated, and unhygienic apartments and as long as the municipal government continued to disregard waste removal and the malfunctioning sewer system was not improved. Thus long before Riis and other reformers started investigating the slums, health inspectors advocated improving the living conditions of the poor in the overcrowded tenements.

※

EPIDEMICS HAD PLAGUED the city long before tenements were built and before the onslaught of massive immigration. Through most of the 1600s, when Manhattan was the small, well-organized Dutch town of New Amsterdam, authorities had been reasonably successful at abating epidemics. The colony never suffered plagues of the scale seen in larger European cities. There seemed to have been two overriding reasons: The town was clean, and it was not overcrowded. The Dutch municipal government had provided much better sanitation services than would the British colonists, who took over in 1644.

Epidemic outbreaks became more common as the city grew, and from the late 1600s until the late 1700s, smallpox and yellow fever were recurring problems. During one of the city's worst epidemics more than 10 percent of the population died. The city did not have a health department at the time, but doctors and prominent citizens worked as ad hoc health inspectors, and several health committees were formed in the wake of the epidemic, prepared to take action if another outbreak occurred. As the number of epidemics increased and became more severe, a group of doctors began advocating for better hygiene and more efficient sewer systems.

John H. Griscom, one of the men behind the city's first sewer system, which had been put in place in 1820, vented his indignation over the deplorable conditions in the slums in an 1845 report titled *Sanitary Conditions of the Laboring Population of New York*, which may be seen as a forerunner of Riis's *How the Other Half Lives*. Riis read the report thoroughly and it became a source of inspiration for him in his work as a reformer. The health inspectors featured by Griscom had comprehensive knowledge of the poor and their living conditions. They realized that a sweeping reform of New York's housing situation was vital to the overall health of the city. Based on his findings, Griscom argued for the establishment of a corps of health inspectors—a health police, as he called it—whose task would be to prevent epidemics. The thinking was that preventive measures such as vaccination programs would be the best way of averting disaster.

Griscom inspired a generation of young reformers and became especially important to Riis. Clearly Riis took his cue from the first page of Griscom's report: "[I]t has often been said that 'one half does not know how the other half lives.'" Griscom delivered sharp criticism of the tenement housing system and bluntly blamed slumlords for coldly capitalizing on others' misery. The blatant cynicism they practiced, he argued, was possible only because slum housing was based on a system of subcontractors. The real estate barons hired men to let out apartments for them, thus avoiding the unpleasantness of having to come into direct contact with the unsavory aspects of their own business philosophy. His descriptions of the slums are characterized by tremendous attention to detail and color: "The poor are crammed together in closets," he wrote, "their [apartments] deserve no other name."

In these places, the filth is allowed to accumulate to an extent almost incredible. Hiring their room for short periods only, it is very common to find the poor tenants moving from place to place, every few weeks. By this practice they avoid the trouble of cleansing their rooms, as they can leave behind them the dirt which they have made. The same room, being occupied in rapid succession, by tenant after tenant, it will easily be seen how the walls and windows will become broken, the doors and floors become injured, the chimneys filled with soot, the whole premises populated thickly with vermin, the stairways, the common passage of several families, the receptacle for all things noxious, and whatever of self-respect the family might have had, be crushed under the pressure of the degrading circumstances by which they are surrounded.

Another very important particular in the arrangements of these tenements must here be noticed. By the mode in which the rooms are planned, ventilation is entirely prevented. . . . In this dark hole there is, of course, a concentrated accumulation of the effluvia of the bodies and breaths of the persons sleeping in it (frequently the whole family, several in number), and this accumulation goes on from night to night, without relief, until it can easily be believed that the smell becomes intolerable, and its atmosphere productive of the most offensive and malignant diseases. There is no exaggeration in this description.

Griscom's report had widespread appeal and was read with interest for decades. He was not successful, however, in creating the health squad he advocated. Wealthy New Yorkers were skeptical, fearing it would strain the city budget and necessitate tax increases. They soon came to regret their shortsighted self-interest, as the city was hit by an unprecedented health disaster in 1849: a cholera epidemic that killed 5,000. Many of its victims were from outside the tenements, and the city at large suddenly saw the prudence of Griscom's health squad proposal and vaccination programs. Still, it would take another fifteen years before a permanent health department was in place. In 1866, with the outbreak of another violent cholera epidemic, the Metropolitan Board of Health was hurriedly established on Mott Street. More than a thousand people died in the epidemic, but had it not been for the last-minute preventive measures initiated by the new Board of Health, the death toll would undoubtedly have been more extensive. The epidemic began downtown, and its spread uptown was controlled somewhat by herculean efforts to clean the streets. Gigantic trash heaps and enormous amounts of horse manure were removed. After the epidemic, politicians readily acknowledged the board's relative success and unanimously agreed to continue financing it.

Procuring funds never became easy. The Board of Health, in 1873 renamed the Health Department, was one of many city agencies vying for tax dollars. The department was therefore constantly underfunded, yet the city never hesitated to criticize its work. It came under fire not only because deadly diseases continued to plague the city but when corruption infiltrated its ranks, with health inspectors taking bribes from landlords and developers.

Notwithstanding its weakness, the Health Department employed many committed inspectors—those, like Griscom, who spent their days in the slums combating disease-causing conditions, or who spent long hours in the office preparing and analyzing vital statistics: data on life and death ranging from the number of infant deaths to the number of suicides. Many years after his first meeting with Riis, Roger Tracey, one of the department's prominent statisticians, wrote:

In 1881 there was an epidemic of smallpox in New York and of course a great deal of talk in the newspapers about vaccination. Happening in at the Office of the Health Board one morning I found a stranger probing Dr. Janes, the Assistant Sanitary Superintendent, about the risks of vaccination. Dr. Janes turned him over to me, and I was much impressed with the intelligence and pertinacity with which he conducted a sort of cross-examination with reference to the possibility of communicating other diseases through vaccination and was apparently satisfied after a while and went away. I asked Dr. Janes who he was and he said that he was a Tribune reporter and his name was Reese as I then understood it. I remarked that he had a slight foreign accent and did seem much like the ordinary reporter, the type with which we at the office were all familiar. Dr. Janes agreed with me in this. This was the first time I ever saw Jacob A. Riis with whom I became very intimate.

Numbers—mind-numbing numbers—were part of Riis's heaviest artillery in the fight against poverty. He befriended another outstanding statistician, John T. Nagle, who, after serving as a surgeon in the Confederate army during the Civil War, managed the Statistics Department on Mott Street. Riis was to base many of his stories on Nagle's research, including data contained in the latter's report *Suicides in New York City During the 11 Years Ending Dec. 31, 1880*. A tall man with perfect posture, black hair, a handlebar mustache, and large eyes, Nagle sat on various committees, working to increase the number of parks in New York. While working with him, Riis was introduced to what would become a new and revolutionary weapon in the fight against poverty: photography.

14

•◆•

Intruders

O NE MORNING during the fall of 1887, Riis was reading his paper at home in Richmond Hill when a four-line dispatch captured his attention. Two German chemists, Adolf Miethe and Johannes Gaedicke, had found a way "to take pictures by flashlight. The darkest corner might be photographed that way." As Riis wrote later, "I put [the paper] down with an outcry that startled my wife, sitting opposite. There it was, the thing I had been looking for all those years."

If this flashlight innovation—a powder made of magnesium and calcium chlorate—was capable of what the article claimed, it was the very tool Riis had been looking for. With the flash he would finally be able to show New Yorkers the dark side of the city. The flashlight could illuminate dark alleyways and penetrate filthy, poorly lit tenement garrets. It could expose basement dives and overcrowded five-cent lodging houses, show the trash heaps where tramps had dug caves to shield themselves from the elements. Riis could show his audience—the wealthier segments of society, policymakers and voters, whose actions could translate into social reform—what they had never seen before, places they could not even imagine, would not have wanted to imagine, existing in close proximity to their own homes. He could show his audiences images of raw, abject, and inexcusable poverty. Through photo documentation,

Riis would finally be able to show the public all that he had seen in the slums and tried to describe in his articles.

Riis never doubted that anyone who witnessed what he had seen could remain impassive. With the new photo technology, Riis felt sure, he would have a tool powerful enough to jolt the general public into active awareness. Working with reformers and health inspectors had taught him that it was possible to espouse change. But he also knew, like his colleagues, that it would require an awakening, a rude and shocking awakening, before he could expect respectable citizens to take up the fight against the cancer that was eating New York City from within.

"It was upon my midnight trips with the sanitary police that the wish kept cropping up in me that there were some way of putting before the people what I saw there," Riis wrote in his memoirs.

> A drawing might have done it, but I cannot draw, never could. . . . [A] drawing would not have been evidence of the kind I wanted. We used to go in the small hours of the morning into the worst tenements to count noses and see if the law against overcrowding was violated, and the sights I saw there gripped my heart until I felt that I must tell of them, or burst, or turn anarchist, or something. . . .
> I wrote [about it], but it seemed to make no impression.

Riis had no experience with photography, but he was abreast of the development of the technology, as were many people. Photography was an exciting innovation, shrouded in mystery: "To watch the picture come out upon the plate that was blank before, [it] is a new miracle every time. If I were a clergyman I would practice photography and preach about it."

News of photographers' clubs' meetings appeared in the press, and the release of photos showing hitherto never photographed images made headlines. When more light-sensitive emulsions were developed that allowed the photographer to use a shorter exposure time—from several minutes to thirty seconds—it was discussed enthusiastically by photographers and lay people alike. Attempts to photograph moving objects were followed with keen interest around the world. In 1882 a Briton

developed a "machinegun" camera with multiple lenses, each exposing a small part of the photo plate, thus increasing the photographer's
chance of capturing objects in motion, such as a ship. His monster-sized
camera was, however, never put into production, as it was cumbersome
and impractical.

Until the late 1870s photography was exclusively for professionals;
taking pictures was complex and involved. Emulsions had to be mixed
on location and poured evenly, without spilling, onto a wet plate, made
of glass. It was an unwieldy process requiring practitioners to handle
"highly flammable and noxious substances." The photographer had to
be something of an expert chemist. If he wanted to take photos outside
the studio, he had to bring with him a huge, horse-drawn darkroom.

The process became simpler in the early 1880s, with the introduction of the dry plate, whose great advantage was that it did not require
immediate development, presaging the modern film. Clubs for amateur
photographers quickly became ubiquitous, affluent citizens fiddling with
the fabulous and expensive new invention—especially in the United
States, where fascination with technological invention had always been
pronounced. In New York City two large clubs opened: the New York
Association of Amateur Photographers and the New York Camera Club.

Riis's friend John Nagle was a member of the New York Association
of Amateur Photographers. Immediately after reading the piece about
the flash powder, Riis had hurried off to the Health Department's offices
on Mott Street to discuss his revolutionary idea with Nagle. He out-
lined a plan to his friend: They were to walk the slums at night, when
conditions were the most sobering, and take pictures. It would provide
them with tangible evidence, Riis argued. Nagle was at once won over
to the idea.

⁂

THE QUESTION of how to take pictures in poorly lit locations was
an issue photographers had discussed since the advent of photography.
Optimal lighting was crucial. In the early days of photography, most
pictures were taken at midday, when the natural light source was most
intense. On overcast days, especially in the winter, when there was lit-

tle light and all was gray, photographers were unable to shoot pictures of people or moving objects. The need to find methods that would solve the problem of lighting was pressing.

One solution was a light-sensitive liquid, and by the end of the 1870s liquids had been developed that were so effective it was possible to reduce exposure time sufficiently to freeze a moving image. Photographer Eadweard Muybridge demonstrated the new technique with dramatic effect. Using a large battery of cameras with fast shutters, placed along a racecourse, Muybridge shot pictures of a trotting horse harnessed to a two-wheeled vehicle known as a sulky. His photos perfectly froze an image of the horse in motion. The photos, which were later published—as woodcuts, since it was still not possible to print photos—in *Scientific American*, drew worldwide attention. Not only had Muybridge been able to take a picture of a moving object, he had also proved beyond a doubt that there is a moment of suspension when a horse trots and no hooves touch the ground. Muybridge was hailed as a pioneer and inventor. His method, however, was neither simple nor inexpensive. Few people owned a whole battery of cameras, and there was still the problem of lighting; photographers were dependent on natural light.

Photographers were aware that if they could somehow generate strong artificial light, they would be able to shoot on overcast days and freeze even the fastest-moving objects. An electrical light source was tried in the mid-1800s, but it never worked well; it was difficult to generate a strong enough light with batteries. The electric flash therefore never caught on. By the late 1860s photographers were experimenting with magnesium solutions mixed with other substances that caused the powder to explode in a bright, clear light. The photographers saw much promise in the magnesium powder. When lighting the powder while simultaneously releasing the shutter, there would be enough light to expose the negative plate. The method had weaknesses: The light was harsh, and the exploding powder quickly turned into a thick fog of smoke. Still, it was the best solution yet. Belgian-born photographer Charles Waldack astonished the world in 1866 with his photos from the bottom of a Kentucky mineshaft.

Miethe and Gaedicke, whose invention was to have such a profound impact on Riis's career, were the first to create a magnesium powder mix that was less hazardous to the photographer than earlier mixes, and ignited with less fanfare. Photographers around the world immediately began experimenting with the new powder, including the amateur photographers in Nagle's club, who had, in fact, heard of it before Riis. A major article in the *American Journal of Photography* had, prior to the dispatch Riis read, described the method in great detail. The story had turned the Society of Photographers in Berlin upside-down, and the New York Association of Amateur Photographers had not wasted their time either. They were already busy experimenting with the invention when Riis and Nagle approached them with their idea.

The New York photographers found the German mix, or their version of it, a little too explosive, and hoped to developed a mix that was less dangerous. They soon did. One of Nagle's friends, dermatologist and chairman of the amateur photographers' club Henry G. Piffard, demonstrated his new version of the German powder to a stunned audience on October 11, 1887. Piffard told the audience and a large turnout of reporters that while the German mix of magnesium and potassium chlorate produced excellent light, "its very explosive quality made it a dangerous article to handle and have about." His own mix, which featured guncotton, lit into "a brilliant flash powerful enough to sufficiently expose the plate," wrote a reporter from the *New York Times*, in a dramatic piece headlined "GUNNING FOR PICTURES. PHOTOGRAPHS TAKEN BY A PISTOL FLASH." Dr. Piffard had also, he told his audience, experimented with a mix of magnesium and regular gunpowder, but the flash it produced was not "practical," which presumably meant that it exploded. The most sensational news of the evening was his revelation that magnesium mixed with gunpowder in a cartridge and fired from a gun produced a usable flashlight. Piffard proceeded to draw from his pockets a couple of cartridges, turn out the lights, remove the lens cover, pull out a gun, and fire a shot of a volunteer named Robert Roosevelt. "The light flashed in the darkness, and when some minutes later the developed plate appeared, an excellent negative of Mr. Roosevelt was the result," wrote the *New York Times* reporter.

❊

THE NEXT BIG QUESTION was of course where to go to test this
new invention's limits, while making use of it to capture some groundbreaking images. When Nagle presented Riis's idea of photographing
the slums to the members of the photographers' association, it immediately became clear that the police reporter on a mission and the
amateur photographers on the lookout for extraordinary in-the-dark
images shared a common goal. Riis could deliver dark and sinister
themes and the photographers could test the new technique. In turn,
the photographers could secure Riis photos that were bound to elicit
sympathetic responses from audiences, once he was ready to present
them. It was seemingly a perfect match.

A few days later a small party of men went on a night expedition
down the crooked alleys of Mulberry Bend. The group consisted of Riis,
as guide and leader; Henry Piffard; Richard Hoe Lawrence, a well-to-do
adventurer; and John Nagle. They brought along the fashionable detective camera, which was new and less clumsy than the earlier generations
of cameras. They also brought a pistol loaded with cartridges stuffed
with magnesium and gunpowder.

The four men, whom the press soon dubbed "the intruders," looked
quite daunting when they came marching with all their gear down the
narrow alleys. Crowds of people would gather around them to see the
strange spectacle that unfolded when they took a picture. Police officers
on duty were just as curious and often escorted them on their mysterious nightly expeditions in teams of two or four. When Riis found a shot
he wanted to capture, the small entourage would stop and set up the
camera, then one of them would pull the gun and fire. Startled onlookers thought they were being shot with live cartridges, but instead the
brief, crackling blue-white light of the flash appeared before their eyes
quickly followed by a billow of thick, gray smoke. At other times the
four men would barge in on people asleep in their beds, ignite the flash,
and shoot a picture. The whole affair was over so quickly that many
of their unwitting subjects never even registered what had happened;

some barely woke up before the slum photographers had vanished again into the darkness of the night.

The photo expeditions soon claimed the attention of reporters, among them those from prominent papers such as the *Sun* and the *Morning Journal*, who began accompanying the already large crowd following the photographers. The reporters had been granted permission to tag along, on the condition that they refrain from writing about the expeditions until the photographs themselves had been made public. The little band of photographers were keen on keeping their work a secret. They did not want their competition to know they were experimenting with the new flash light in the field. Riis, for his part, wanted the photographs to have maximum impact when they were brought to the public's attention for the first time.

Riis and the amateur photographers already had a plan for how they would present their slum photos. In addition to being fascinated by the possibilities held out by flash photography, the public closely followed magic lantern technology. When Riis had used the magic lantern to show ads, it was not technically advanced enough to show photographic slides. The technology had improved and Riis was certain that the new magic lantern was the perfect medium to show his pictures. Blown up on a huge screen, the sensational photographs of the slums would have a compelling effect. Riis wanted them to be the main attraction of lectures he planned to deliver on the slums.

The partnership between Riis and the amateur photographers was mutually beneficial. Riis was able to draw attention to social issues, while the photographers could demonstrate the advanced technique of flash powder and show what groundbreaking work the club was producing. Riis hoped the photos, which were blatant proof of miserable slum conditions, could be used to put pressure on the health authorities for new housing legislation.

※

IN FEBRUARY 1888, having been given the go-ahead by Riis and the amateur photographers to write about their now-frequent expeditions,

a journalist from the *Sun* described "FLASHES FROM THE SLUM. PICTURES
TAKEN IN DARK PLACES BY THE LIGHTENING PROCESS. SOME OF THE RESULTS
OF A JOURNEY THROUGH THE CITY WITH AN INSTANTANEOUS CAMERA":

> *With their way illuminated by spasmodic flashes, as bright and sharp and
> brief as those of the lightening itself, a mysterious party has been startling
> the town o' nights. Somnolent policemen on the street, denizens of the dives
> in dens, tramps and bummers in their so-called lodgings, and all the people
> of the wild and wonderful variety of New York night life have in their turn
> marveled at and been frightened by the phenomenon. What they saw was
> three or four figures in the gloom, a ghostly tripod, some weird and uncanny
> movements, the blinding flash, and then they heard the patter of retreat-
> ing footsteps, and the mysterious visitors were gone before they could collect
> their scattered thoughts and try to find out what it was all about. . . . The
> party consisted of members of the New York Association of Amateur Pho-
> tographers experimenting with the process of taking instantaneous pictures
> by an artificial flash light, and their guide and conductor, an energetic gentle-
> man who combines in his person . . . the two dignitaries of deacon in a Long
> Island church and a police reporter in New York.*

This New York police reporter and curate of his home congregation,
the article said, wanted to collect a series of lantern slides, "showing,
as no mere description could, the misery and vice that he had noticed
in his ten years of experience. Aside from its strong human interest,
he thought that this treatment of the topic would call attention to the
needs of the situation, and suggest the direction in which much good
might be done."

The *Sun* article and a similar story from the *Morning Journal* are
remarkable for several reasons. They show that Riis had the support of
fellow reporters. He was, as the articles stress, not the only journalist
who knew the slums intimately, nor was he the only one keen on making the public aware of their endemic misery and squalor. Riis was by no
means a singular activist but part of a reform movement.

In addition, these articles were extraordinary because they were
illustrated. Halftone photomechanical technology made it possible to

print photographs by rephotographing them through a mask, which then re-created the original picture in small black and white pixels. It was used for the first time in 1880 in the *New York Daily Graphic*, a trade magazine for photographers. However, the reproduction quality was poor and the halftone print was rarely used, never by newspapers. Skilled handmade woodcut illustrations based on photos were used by the most prestigious magazines, including *Harper's Weekly* and *Frank Leslie's Illustrated Newspaper*. Illustrations in newspapers, however, were relatively rare, and when they were used, it was in the form of pencil drawings. The decision by the *Sun* and the *Morning Journal* to illustrate their articles with woodcuts based on the photos is historically significant, the harbinger of twentieth-century press photography. The woodcut illustrations of the nightly expeditions were, as both papers informed their readers, published with Riis's permission. According to the *Journal*, Riis said permission had been granted as follows: "I am flattered by your request for copies of the pictures which I exhibit. . . . These pictures are not fancy sketches, but are taken from real life with 'detective' cameras, many of them at night by means of the newly invented pistol flash light that made it possible to photograph the darkest corners." The articles also mention the title Riis had chosen for his lecture: "How the Other Half Lives and Dies in New York." This was the first time Riis was to be associated with what became his signature phrase.

John Griscom's earlier use of the phrase notwithstanding, the inspiration for the title may have had an additional source. In 1887, an anonymous reader sent Riis a check for a dollar, with a note that read, "Here, give this money for your other half." The letter made a deep impression on Riis. It had been mailed from Tennessee, where Riis's articles for the Associated Press were also published.

Finally, the articles about the photo expedition are remarkable because they provide a unique perspective on how Riis operated as a reporter. It is apparent how far he was willing to go for his stories. Not even when he was escorted by his photographer friends did he hesitate to delve into the very worst of the dismal places he knew. On the contrary, he proceeded as if it were the most natural thing in the world. He led his team of photographers, the Morning Journal reported, with exquisite liveliness into the barracks on Roosevelt Street and Murphy's Alley, places the Journal described as particularly squalid and sinister.

Many of the photos later canonized as Riis's best, and which have found a place in the annals of photography history, were taken on these expeditions, among them the most famous: Bandit's Roost. These photographs, however, were most likely taken by Lawrence, Piffard, or, in some cases, Nagle. Yet none of the men questioned Riis's right to the photographs. It was Riis who had chosen the images, and they had just been there to test the new flash powder. In fact, Lawrence and Piffard were not interested in being associated with what they considered unaesthetic photographs.

According to the interview in the Journal, Riis stressed that the photographs were not art but rather crude sketches, not "real photos." It was maintained that real photos should exude the beauty of classical paintings. The motifs should not be offensive renderings of poor people but arresting landscapes, charming groupings of people in their finest clothes, imposing ships in powerful seascapes, or voluptuous park scenes with luscious bushes and silken lawns. Most important, real photos should be executed with great skill by a professional photographer. The images should be razor sharp, yet cast in a soft light and developed perfectly. None of Riis's photos met these criteria.

"I am downright sorry to confess here that I am no good at all as a photographer, for I would like to be," Riis writes in his memoirs. Nobody disagreed with him, and Riis was never referred to as a photographer, though he was making photographic history.

✸

THE AMATEUR PHOTOGRAPHERS soon tired of the nightly raids through the slums. It was exhausting work and, in winter, cold. The first few times they were out with Riis, Piffard and Lawrence had been excited by their wild adventure. They did not possess Riis's dogged perseverance, nor did they share his passion for social issues.

Riis's appetite, on the other hand, was whetted. After having seen the first finished photos, he felt sure that the magic lantern shows would be sensational. Still, he needed more photos. He wanted to show at least a hundred slides. Initial efforts to hire a professional photographer proved unsuccessful. Few photographers were interested in examining the slums, and the one photographer who did agree to assist him (his name is unknown) covertly and illicitly sold the negatives. When Riis found out, he fired the assistant immediately. It seemed there was nothing left for him to do but learn photography. He bought a camera and on January went to one of the most desolate places he knew in New York: potter's field on Hart Island.

Riis felt that photographs of the gravesites of the poor would be the best testimony to the appalling conditions under which many New Yorkers lived and died. Every year 4,000 people were buried at potter's field—10 percent of all burials in New York. Potter's field was, for Riis, the one place in the city that stood in starkest contrast to his hometown of Ribe—it was cold and empty of hope.

For a reformer like Riis, the ultimate goal was to help create a world in which nobody had to be buried in places like potter's field. The January day he chose was icy, and he was trying out his new camera for the first time. A winter-bare cityscape stood in the background, and the snow was rock-hard. Rays of sun slashed the Hudson River. He moved toward a huge, gaping, empty grave—a grave that eventually was to hold so many dead that the coffins had to placed side by side in long rows and on top of each other in several layers. Facing him, on the other side of the open pit, was a single wooden cross.

He set up his camera. He was nervous. He did not have much confidence in himself as a photographer. The glass plate had to be exposed for six seconds; Riis counted: one, two, three, four, five, six. No, it was impossible that an image would already be on the plate. Better be on the safe side and wait another six seconds before he closed the shutter. In his eagerness to do everything right, he accidentally placed the glass negative in the negative box, forgetting that twelve other unused glass plates were stacked in there. When he came home he could not remember which of the plates he had used and was forced to send them all to be developed.

The photo that emerged turned out to be too dark—it had been overexposed. But Riis liked it that way: "The very blackness of my picture proved later on, when I came to use it with a magic lantern, the taking feature of it. It added a gloom to the show more realistic than any the utmost art of professional skill might have attained." For the next few weeks he worked at a feverish pace. When he was not writing articles, he was out with his camera, continuing where Piffard, Lawrence, and Nagle had left off. Later he described how he had shot a photograph of "a particularly tattered vagabond" in a back alley. The vagabond was sitting on a ladder, leaning against a rickety shack, which was his home. He wore a misshapen hat pulled down over his eyes, layers and layers of shirts and sweaters, and a pair of pants with the fly open, and he had a pipe sticking out of his mouth. Rays of harsh sunlight shot through the back alley past rows of laundry. The vagabond stared at Riis as he set up his camera. Riis offered the man ten cents if he would let him take his picture. The vagabond agreed, put his pipe away, and waited. Riis felt it would be a better shot with the pipe, but had to raise the price to 25 cents for getting this prop in the picture.

He took photographs on the streets of Chinatown and in opium dens. He took photographs of vagabonds sleeping in rows of hammocks in lodging houses. He took photographs of the overflowing, stinking trash cans scattered along streets and alleys. He took pictures of pocket thieves and burglars. He took a photograph of gangsters gathering "like rats" under a wharf in New York's harbor from a police boat chasing river pirates, later describing how they lived like rats, too, on huge trash heaps of old cans, which even in winter let off a thick, nauseating smell.

The photographs not only documented how the other half lived and died but told an important story about the man behind the camera. Contrary to Riis's own assertion, his pictures reveal that he was in fact a gifted photographer. He had an eye for composition and the ability to tell a powerful story with his camera. Significantly, he also possessed the one talent essential to photographers: He was able to make most of his subjects relax and act naturally before a camera lens. Some do stare at the lens with blank expressions; a considerable number, however, smile and look comfortable. The latter clearly felt at ease with the photographer, who must have been able to win their confidence and speak their language.

Riis could also at times be so clumsy that he placed his subjects in danger. He did not have a flash gun but instead used a frying pan in which he ignited the flash powder. One night he barged into a small room at the top of a tenement in Blind Man's Alley, the home of six blind women. As always, the flash powder exploded with brilliant blue-white light, but it also set the room on fire. Riis, panic-stricken, escorted the women down the stairs and out of the building. Fortunately, the walls were covered in a layer of thick, grimy dirt that choked the fire. On another occasion Riis nearly blinded himself when a room caught fire and flash powder was blown into his face. Had he not been wearing glasses, he would probably have lost his eyesight.

On the night of January 26, 1888, Riis delivered his magic lantern lecture and slide show at the New York Association of Amateur Photographers. The show had been widely advertised with its full title: "The Other Half. How It Lives and Dies in New York. Illustrated with 100 Photographic Views."

The meeting room on Thirty-sixth Street was packed. A majority of the papers reviewed the show, and the photographs caused perhaps a greater stir than even Riis had imagined. It was the first time the public had seen the medium used to show not beauty but ugliness, dirt, and wretchedness. The New York Herald referred to the slides as "novel photographic views."

> The pictures were illustrative of tenement house life and its surroundings, and embraced not only the ordinary home life of tenement house dwellers, but also showed vividly many scenes in which vice and brutality reigned rampant. As each picture appeared on the screen Mr. Riis gave a brief and apt explanation of it.
>
> More than a hundred pictures were exhibited and when the exhibition was over it was unanimously agreed by the large and appreciative audience that the entertainment provided for them had proved most excellent.

The New Jersey News compared Riis's instinct for social realism to Émile Zola's and called his photos "shocking."

❋

PHOTOGRAPHY, since its inception, had been seen as a barometer of truth. As Ralph Waldo Emerson wrote: "No man quarrels with his shadow nor will he with his miniature when the sun was the painter. Here is no interference, and the distortions are not the blunders of an artist."

When fires raged, trains derailed, or hurricanes tore through the lands, professional photographers came to take pictures. The photographs, or rather the woodcuts based on them, were featured in magazines and published to a wide audience, who could see, with their own eyes, the horrors left behind. The practice of printing woodcuts became increasingly mainstream, but there was still no established tradition of photographic documentation. Cameras were still too large and cumbersome for photographers to grab them and race to the scene of an unfolding disaster. They were still dependent on the presence of strong natural light in order to shoot moving objects. Photographers could therefore in reality only document devastation after the fact.

As early as the mid-1800s photography had been used to document the horrors of war with the explicit purpose of shocking the beholder. During the Crimean War (1854–1856), Roger Fenton had taken photos from the battlefield. Mathew Brady, Alexander Gardner, and Timothy H. O'Sullivan took harrowing pictures of death and mayhem during the Civil War, photographs that have retained their ability to shock, though they did not reach a wide audience. People flocked to Gardner's studio to look at his war photographs, which were pasted into exquisite books, but he had never had any luck selling a lot of them. People were already too overwhelmed by the horrors of the war to render these photos commercially viable. Yet in the final stages of the war, magazines in New York added woodcut illustrations to their war stories. They were typically photos of starving Union soldiers in Southern prison camps meant not only to justify, but also to encourage readers to support, the war effort.

In Glasgow, Scotland, the slums had been documented in photographs that featured only buildings and were not intended to shock viewers into awareness but simply to preserve for posterity how such neighborhoods had looked before they were demolished. Before Riis, no one had photographed poverty with the express purpose of questioning the social order and shocking people into action. The spontaneity and uncensored nature of Riis's photographs was also in sharp contrast to the controlled character of studio portraits, in which subjects typically did not sit or stand in natural poses. The spontaneity was especially pronounced in the flash photos, where a small piece of living reality could be captured in seconds. Because of the relatively long shutter time, the photographs Riis took in daylight without a flash were more stilted. It is obvious that the people in many of them had been asked to pose "doing commonplace activities," such as stealing a wallet out of a drunken man's coat or sleeping in a stairwell. Despite their staged quality, even these photos broke new ground, deliberately capturing a squalid reality that otherwise would have remained in the dark. It is based on this work that Riis today is seen as the first de facto photojournalist.

15

• ◆ •

Flower Power

Saturday, March 10, 1888, was a mild day, with temperatures in the fifties; New Yorkers took off their coats, enjoying the warm breeze and the sweet smell of spring in the air. No one would have guessed that a blizzard was brewing that would paralyze the city over the course of the next few days. By afternoon, strong, gusty winds and heavy rains swept the East Coast. Still no one was prepared for what was coming. Shortly before midnight the temperature dropped dramatically to below freezing. The rain turned into snow and the snow turned into icy hail. The ensuing blizzard was one of the worst in U.S. history. More than three feet of snow fell that first night, and the wind drove the snow into snowdrifts up to thirty feet tall. Houses were buried, and three-story-high waves pummeled the coastal towns of Long Island, New Jersey, and Delaware. Trains, caught by the storm, were forced to stop between stations. Almost a hundred ships were destroyed, either crushed by gigantic waves at sea or smashed as gale-force winds hurled them ashore. More than 100 sailors and 300 people on land lost their lives. Several cities were completely shut down by the blizzard, with New York, the largest and busiest, especially incapacitated. The storm lasted almost three days, and it would take several more before New York got back on its feet.

Once stores and offices opened for business again, the papers were full of dramatic stories about the blizzard, many published in special editions devoted to the storm. A local weekly, the *Long Island Democrat*, covering Long Island City and surrounding areas including Richmond Hill, filled column after column with stories about what was soon to be known as the Great White Hurricane:

THE REMARKABLE STORM

The confusion resulting from the storm is quite beyond description. It extended from Washington north to New Hampshire but not far inland. Its greatest force was along the coast from Philadelphia to Boston and upon Long Island. It was not until the fourth day that trains could run from Philadelphia to New York, with all the efforts of the powerful Pennsylvania Railroad Company and the New York and New Haven Railroad . . .

There was great destitution of milk in New York. The electric light could not be used. Several banks could not get their reports to the clearing-house. No streetcars could be moved until Wednesday and Thursday. The news from Boston to New York, and vice versa, for several days was sent by cable via London. . . . All church services were omitted, and funerals were delayed. It is said that nearly 500 bodies await interment in New York and Brooklyn on Thursday. Many lives were lost in the snowdrifts especially in the rural districts.

In the same edition of the *Long Island Democrat* there were stories from the period immediately before the blizzard. The paper had simply been unable to publish them earlier due to the ferocious storm, which had made it impossible to print and distribute the news. Among these stories was the following article:

The lecture and exhibition of Mr. Jacob A. Riis of Richmond Hill, at the Town Hall on Wednesday evening last week, was very well attended and proved exceedingly interesting. Although Mr. Riis' German accent is very marked, yet he is a terse and graphic speaker, and pathos and mirth were mingled in a very pleasant manner, in his running comments on the scenes shown by calcium light on the canvas. He gave a startling exhibition of the abodes of poverty and vice in New York City, and his lecture is an excellent missionary sermon, and well calculated to draw the attention of well disposed persons to the condition of the poor and criminal classes in our great cities. He showed that some good work was being done in the way of alleviating the present sad condition of things there, but also demonstrated that the home field for charity and Christian benevolence is an ample one for philanthropic minds and willing hands. The entertainment netted a fair sum for the worthy object for which it was given, and the promoters of the affair are to be congratulated on their success.

The success Riis enjoyed after his first lecture at the amateur photography club catapulted him to an unprecedented level of activity. On February 28 he spoke at the Broadway Tabernacle, the following day he spoke at the Jamaica Town Hall and the Jamaica Opera House, and in the month of April he gave several lectures and slide shows in Manhattan. He gave talks at the Lexington Avenue Baptist Church and at Association Hall, among other places. The lectures were well received everywhere, the reviews essentially repeating what had been written in the *Long Island Democrat*. Use of the word "missionary" to describe his work was a personal triumph for Riis. Fifteen years earlier, he had been a shabby, starving tramp anxious to find a job. Though his situation had often been desperate, he had always felt he was meant to do great things with his life. One moment he had wanted to be a journalist, the next a missionary, and now he was both, having merged his two dreams.

This first rush of lectures preceded by just a few days the worst of the Great White Hurricane, the storm then forcing a brief lull in his schedule. It was during this enforced hiatus that he came up with a plan for getting his message across not just in New York City—not just to readers of the *Tribune* and the few hundreds or thousands who would attend his lectures—but to all Americans. He would write a book on the subject of poverty, which could be widely distributed.

When the storm had subsided Riis sent a letter to the U.S. Copyright Office applying for ownership of the phrase "The Other Half." He had composed a title page:

"One Half of the World does not know how the other Half Lives"

THE OTHER HALF,

HOW IT LIVES AND DIES IN NEW YORK

With One Hundred Illustrations, Photographs from Real Life
of the Haunts of Poverty and Vice in the Great City

—By—

JACOB A. RIIS

For many Years the Police Reporter of the New York Tribune
and the Associated Press at Police Headquarters

New York
1888

Within a few days he had received a reply, which included a reference number, 8239 T, and a declaration as formal and as simple as his own petition:

To wit: Be it remembered, That on the 19th day of March, anno 1888, Jacob A. Riis, of New York, had deposited in this Office the title of a Book the title or description of which is the following words, to wit: The Other Half: How it lives and dies in New York. With One Hundred Illustrations, Photographs from real life of the haunts of poverty and vice in the great City. By Jacob A. Riis.

In the New York publishing world, authors of books reigned supreme, though considerable prestige was also enjoyed by those who wrote for respected literary magazines: *Harper's Monthly*, the *Atlantic Monthly*, and *Scribner's Monthly*, which in 1881 was replaced by *The Century Magazine*. Reporters for daily newspapers were on the bottom rung, regarded as inferior writers by the literary establishment. "Real" writers who contributed to daily newspapers were accorded bylines and a deference rarely extended to reporters, who, as noted earlier, wrote anonymously.

Writing a book was thus an ambitious project for a reporter like Riis to undertake, and he was well aware that getting it published would be a challenge. Undeterred, he merely waited for time to begin the project.

It was a long winter, and it would be a chilly spring. Riis's children came down with scarlet fever again. As he wrote later:

There were three of them and they came down with it one by one, as it were, and it had all to be gone over again, all the anxiety, all the sleepless nights, so that, whereas the first had been stricken in Christmas week, it was almost Easter before the last sat up, pale and worn but safe, by the window and looked out on the storm-tossed world. None of us has ever forgotten that winter and its long hard cold.

Beneath the frozen ground lay a fertile seed waiting to bloom into the most spectacular summer of Riis's life. One cold morning early in the spring, Riis went outside for a breath of fresh air and noticed a plant with its roots pushed up through the ground by the water from the melted snow. He picked it up, carried it inside, and planted it in a flowerpot, which he placed on the windowsill of the children's room. The plant survived the transfer and on Easter Sunday burst into bloom—a bright yellow dandelion. Riis recalled:

The shout the children set up when they saw it, and the joyful commotion in that sick-room! It beat all the doctor's medicine, and, as if it knew, it grew more beautiful every day. . . . They watered and tended it and never thought it a bother, and the little flower repaid every kindness a hundred times. At night when I was home from the office and the doctor would let me, I sat in the sick-room and told them stories of the poor children I had seen that day, and their hard lives in the tenements, and the flower stood in our little circle and listened with the rest.

Riis's children never forgot the wonder of seeing the dandelion bloom. Two months later, when the weather finally grew warmer and they were playing in the meadow near their house on Beech Street, they came up with an idea. The flowers in the meadow reminded them of the dandelion their father had put in their sickroom and of how much it had cheered them. They thought that if they picked bunches of flowers for their father to bring to work, it might cheer up the children he saw in the slums. The next day Riis left for work, his arms laden with daisies, and somewhat to his surprise the faces of the children he encountered indeed lit up with joy when they saw the flowers; they practically tore them from his arms. In his memoirs, Riis noted that he was so overwhelmed by emotion that he sank down on the curb and wept. It was a redeeming moment after the grueling winter months. During that period of illness, sleepless nights, and long, demanding workdays, he had almost lost sight of hope altogether. Now his sense of hope had been rekindled, and it dawned on him that perhaps it would not after all require superhuman efforts to create decent living conditions for the poor in New York City—one just had to go about it in the right way.

The next morning, and the following morning, Riis brought bunches of flowers to the slums and every morning they were taken from his arms by eager children. Inspired by their obvious joy, Riis put an ad in the *New York Tribune* urging people to bring flowers to the poor:

FLOWERS FOR THE POOR

To the Editor of The Tribune.

Sir: The trains that carry a hundred thousand people to New-York's stores and offices from their homes in the country rush over fields these bright June mornings glorious with daisies and clover blossoms. There are too many sad little eyes in the crowded tenements, where the Summer sunshine means disease and death, not play or vacation, eyes that will close without having ever looked upon a field of daisies. If we cannot give them the fields, why not the flowers? If every man, woman, and child coming in should, on the way to the station, gather an armful of wild flowers to distribute in the tenements a mission work would be set on foot with which all the almsgiving of this wealthy city could not be compared.

Then why not do it? Ask your readers to try. The pleasure of giving the flowers to the urchins who will dog their steps in the street crying with hungry voices and hungrier hearts for a "posy" will more than pay for the trouble. It

will brighten the office, the store, or the schoolroom all through the day. Let them have no fear that their gift will not be appreciated because it costs nothing. Not alms, but the golden rule, is what is needed in the tenements of the poor. If those who have not the time or opportunity themselves will send their flowers to this office, 303 Mulberry Street, Police Headquarters, it will be done for them. The Summer doctors employed in July and August will gladly co-operate. Let us have the flowers.
Jacob A. Riis, Thursday, June 22, 1888.

On the day the ad ran, the weather suddenly changed, the temperature rising dramatically. An insufferable summer heat set in. The papers began publishing lists of people who had succumbed to the heat. On June 24 more than twenty people died of heat-related illnesses.

Yet people responded with overwhelming enthusiasm to Riis's ad. Flowers in bags, barrels, and boxes, load upon load, came in, donated by private citizens, companies, and organizations. They were sent to Riis's office on Mulberry Street in such quantity that he was unable to distribute them on his own. He called on his colleagues to assist; even his police friends became involved in the project. Some of the toughest officers left their nightsticks at the station for bags of flowers during those hot June days, going from apartment building to apartment building, door to door.

"Wherever we went," Riis wrote in his autobiography, "fretful babies stopped crying and smiled as the blooming message of love was laid against their wan cheeks."

Slovenly women curtsied and made way. . . . "The Lord bless you," I heard as I passed through a dark hall, "You are a good man. No such thing has come this way before."

Oh! The heartache of it, and yet the joy! The Italians in the Barracks stopped quarrelling to help keep order. The worst street became suddenly good and neighborly.

The well-known priest and poet John Tabb was inspired by Riis's assertion that "an armful of daisies kept better peace of a block that the policeman's club" to write the following poem:

Peacemakers ye, the daisies, from the soil
Upbreathing wordless messages of love,
Soothing of earth-born brethren the toil
And lifting e'en the lowliest above.

The *New York World*—Joseph Pulitzer's flagship, by far the city's largest daily—covered the story of the flowers, calling Riis a missionary reporter:

Last Sunday THE WORLD printed an appeal of Mr. Jacob A. Riis, a Police Headquarters reporter, who for many years made a study of the tenements, asking for wild flowers for the children of the tenements. They came yesterday in a flood, box or bundle, filled with white and yellow daises, buttercups, field violets and many other treasures of the fields and woods. Armfuls of these were taken by Mr. Riis and his friends to the Barracks on Mott Street and other bad tenements, and if old Santa Claus himself had dropped down with a bagful of dollars he would not have met a warmer welcome or caused greater delight. It may seem strange with Central Park blooming at our doors, but it is true that the reporter/missionary found little ones in Mott Street who had never seen daisies before. It costs money even to go to Central Park and money does not grow very fast in the Barracks or the Bend.

These were magic days for Riis, days that seemed to erase the memory of potter's field and the first pictures he took standing on the edge of a mass grave, documenting the miserable reality of the poor.

His project may be seen as impractical, sentimental, pandering— flowers do nothing to alleviate or rectify economic inequality. Undoubtedly, some well-to-do New Yorkers probably chose to send flowers because it was an easy way to appear charitable without exerting much effort. Seen in this light, the flowers seem a means of evading the real issues of poverty. Moreover, the idea of bringing a slice of nature to the poor was not new. It was widely believed that nature had a positive effect on human character. The Children's Aid Society had built greenhouses all over the city, and the *Tribune* had sponsored the Fresh Air Fund in sending city children on summer vacations in the country.

Riis's project stood out against these other initiatives, however, because it actively involved the city's citizens. Although perhaps indeed romantic in nature, it was a stroke of genius from a Progressive reform point of view. What usually made far-reaching reforms difficult was that "the poor" represented a faceless mass, believed by most to be degenerate and beyond saving.

By focusing on the children, whom even the staunchest cynic could not argue deserved their fate in the slums, Riis had put a human face on poverty. With his plea for flowers, he had managed to appeal to a deep-seated human instinct to help those in need. If he had solicited money instead, people would have been reluctant, thinking the money would end up in the pockets of a drunk parent. Asking for flowers for poor children brought out the best in people. And giving flowers was at least indirectly an acknowledgment of the fact that something was amiss. With the symbolic weight of his project's success, Riis and his children had helped to create awareness of the complex issues of poverty, issues that of course called for solutions other than flowers.

16

------------------ • ◆ • ------------------

The Manifesto

RIIS'S MAGIC SUMMER was followed by a gloomy fall. He had created a stir with his flower project and his lectures, but it became increasingly difficult for him to find new venues. Riis believed the issue of the slums was a Christian matter, and he saw his lecture as a kind of sermon, which naturally belonged in the house of God. He began actively pursuing churches as possible sites, having already given many talks—though still not his lecture "The Other Half"—in his own parish in Richmond Hill, at Union Congregational Church. If the churches were receptive to his cause, it would allow him to deliver his message to a wide audience. Initially Riis took it for granted that he would be welcome at the various congregations in the area, presupposing pastors and ministers would also see the church as a logical center of social reform. "In a church," Riis wrote in his memoirs, "one might, at all events, tell the truth unhindered. So I thought."

Shortly after his first lecture in New York in January 1888, Riis formed an alliance with three of the city's most radical Protestant church figures, Charles Parkhurst, Adolf Frederick Schauffler, and Josiah Strong, who, like Riis's friend Felix Adler, were adherents of social evangelism. Like Adler, they believed that the Christian message of loving thy neighbor was worthless if not translated into action.

Charles Parkhurst, of Madison Square Presbyterian Church, achieved fame for an 1892 sermon in which he accused New York police and politicians of thoroughgoing corruption. The substance of his accusations was evidence collected on night visits paid to bars and brothels in the company of journalists, an undertaking that led to the Lexow Hearings of 1894–1895, which disclosed pervasive police corruption in the city.

Adolf Frederick Schauffler was superintendent and later president of New York's Mission and Tract Society, and Josiah Strong, a Protestant clergyman, was a leader of the Progressive religious community and coeditor of the magazine *Kingdom*, the social evangelists' most important publication. He was also the author of *Our Country*, a book focusing on immigrants in bigger cities in the United States and on pervasive corruption in the political system and among the rich. Schauffler heard of Riis's slide show lectures in early 1888 and invited him to give a lecture at the Broadway Tabernacle. Parkhurst and Strong were in the audience, and both found his lecture impressive. By using their extensive network of influential friends they were able to arrange additional lecture engagements for Riis.

Perhaps because of his initial success and the company he now kept with the city's most radical social critics, Riis at times lost sight of the fact that the message he was delivering was profoundly shocking to most, as were many of his photographs, which some perceived as wantonly gruesome. Thus in spite of the intercession of Schauffler, Parkhurst, and Strong, church doors were slammed in his face throughout the fall and winter. When even his own Union Congregational Church would not invite him to deliver "The Other Half," he and his family quit the congregation and joined the Church of the Resurrection, also within walking distance of the house on Beech Street.

Frustrated and angered by the rejections, Riis approached the *New York Tribune* in the hope that they would cover the church's decision to turn a blind eye to his message of human suffering. He was now writing mainly for the Associated Press, which had ended its affiliation with the *Tribune*. On December 30, 1888, a *Tribune* reporter filed the following story:

Mr. Riis tells me that he has vainly knocked at the doors of church after church, and Sunday-school after Sunday-school, in this city and Brooklyn. Everywhere he met with indifference or jealous distrust until, out of pocket and tired of crying in the wilderness, he is almost ready to give up an effort that has taught some very practical, but to a Christian, very saddening facts.

The article noted that Riis felt he was being slighted by the clergy because of his "sordid" job as a reporter.

It cannot have been the best of times for the ambitious reporter from Mulberry Street, and to make matters worse it seemed none of the literary magazines were interested in publishing his photos and articles. The ultimate insult came from an editor who told Riis he wanted to buy his photographs but then intended to " 'find a man who could write' to tell the story."

✳

By March of 1889 Riis's luck had changed and he was on the road with his lecture and slide shows, traveling through Connecticut, New Jersey, and upstate New York. He had also continued to secure speaking engagements in New York City. Present in the audience at one of his lectures in the city was an editor from *Scribner's* magazine (founded in 1887), who approached Riis after his talk and asked if he would be interested in adapting "How the Other Half Lives" for publication.

The resulting piece, "How the Other Half Lives: Studies Among the Tenements of New York"—for which *Scribner's* paid $150, more than Riis earned in a month as a reporter—appeared in the Christmas issue of December 1889. Occupying no fewer than twenty pages, illustrated with elaborate woodcuts based on the slum photographs, the piece struck a decidedly more academic tone than the material Riis customarily delivered in his by now patented lectures: Included were statistical data, painstakingly amassed over the years from the Mott Street Health Department, arranged in charts and tables. Riis nonetheless told a gripping and direct story, taking his readers far into the city's tenements. Without the obvious space limitation imposed by a daily newspaper, he could finally write in depth about the complex issue of poverty, a subject that had consumed him for so long.

※

LITERARY MAGAZINES of the late nineteenth century had a pronounced global gloss, the educated classes' fascination with geography, ethnography, and anthropology being nearly insatiable. The world had been almost fully mapped, reporters could travel to the remotest destinations, and magazines fell in line in the race to outdo the competition. And while pieces sought unabashedly to provide moral justification for the practice of colonization, they were also usually well researched and rooted in genuine curiosity.

Riis's *Scribner's* piece took its place alongside such stories as "My Journey to Congo" (*The Century*) and "Jamaica, New and Old" (*Harper's*). Not entirely unlike the anthropologically minded travel writers in whose company he found himself, he took his readers into a world vastly different from their own. But Riis had not traveled thousands of miles to get his story, and his observations were of a people who lived right next door. It must be assumed that this dichotomy was not lost on his audience. The image of an unknown subculture in such close proximity to their own homes, its subjugation perhaps partially of their own doing, must have been powerful indeed to the *Scribner's* readership.

Turn but a dozen steps from the rush and roar of the Elevated Railroad, where it dives under the Brooklyn Bridge at Franklin Square, and with its din echoing yet in your ears you have turned the corner from prosperity to poverty. You stand upon the domain of the tenement. In the shadow of the great stone abutments, linger about the old houses the worst traditions of half a century. Down the winding slope of Cherry Street—proud and fashionable Cherry Hill that was—their broad steps, sloping roofs, and dormer windows (solid comfort stamped by the builder in every one of their generous lines) are easily made out; all the more easily for the contrast with the ugly barracks that elbow them right and left. These never had other design than to shelter, at as little outlay as possible, the greatest crowds out of which rent could be wrung.

The walk continued down Cherry Street, the severe overcrowding of once beautiful homes readily apparent. Houses once owned by the upper classes had preserved none of their former grandeur.

This one, with its shabby front and poorly patched roof, who shall tell what glowing firesides, what happy children it once owned? Heavy feet, often with unsteady step, for the pot-house is next door, have worn away the brownstone steps since; the broken columns at the door have rotted away at the base. Of the handsome cornice barely a trace is left. Dirt and desolation reign in the wide hallway, and danger lurks on the rickety stairs. Rough pine boards fence off the roomy fireplaces; where coal is bought by the pail at the rate of twelve dollars a ton these have no place. The old garden gate long since went to decay and fell from its hinges. The arched gateway is there still, but it leads no longer to a garden. In its place has come a dark and nameless alley, shut in by high brick walls.

From Cherry Street Riis proceeded down Blind Man's Alley, shrouded in darkness and the home of mostly blind beggars; then on to famous Gotham Court, bound by a few tall tenements that housed 142 families comprising a thousand individuals. He introduced his readers to Mulberry Bend, with its opium dens, bars, lodging houses, and back alleys, home to an untold number of tramps, and Bandits' Roost, near the Bend. He took them to the filthy slaughterhouses of Manhattan's West Side and finally north to Hell's Kitchen, where predominantly Irish immigrants had settled. The article gave the reader a tour of every ethnic group: Russian, Chinese, German, Italian, Spanish, French, Scandinavian. "The Arab who peddles 'holy earth' from the Battery as a direct importation from Jerusalem has his exclusive preserves at the lower end of Washington Street. The one thing you shall vainly ask for in the chief city of America is a distinctive American community. There is none; certainly not among the tenements."

As in most of his stories, Riis was able to put a face on the suffering of the poor—the slum dwellers are human beings, with feelings, worries, desires, and hopes. Readers were made to feel that these were people just like them. Perhaps of singular interest to the largely Protestant

readership of *Scribner's*, Riis cited a study conducted by the private charity The Association for the Improvement of the Condition of the Poor,
describing the life of a Protestant family in the slums.

> In the depth of winter, the attention of the Association was called to a Protes-
> tant family living in a garret in a miserable tenement on Cherry Street. The
> family's condition was most deplorable. The man, his wife, and three small
> children shivering in one room, through the roof of which the pitiless winds of
> winter whistled. The room was almost barren of furniture, the parents slept
> on the floor, the elder children in boxes, and the baby was swung in an old
> shawl attached to the rafters by cords by way of a hammock. The father, a
> seaman, had been obliged to give up that calling because he was in consump-
> tion, and was unable to provide either bread or fire for his little ones.

One of Riis's key messages was that the poor were not born incompetent. It was not genetics but rather circumstances that ruined so many.
It was crucial, he argued, that the situation be rectified; if nothing was
done, Riis believed, the slums would spread and eventually undermine
the very foundation of the country. "If New York's now 1.6 million poor
are not given help quickly, revolution and anarchy will spill over into
the rest of society."

✳

A FEW DAYS after publication of the *Scribner's* Christmas issue, Riis
returned from work and seated himself at the dinner table. Elisabeth,
serving dinner, was visibly distracted but refused to tell him what was
bothering her, saying only that they could talk after their meal. As they
settled in the living room later that evening, she got out a letter for Riis
whose content she already knew. It was from Jeannette Gilder, sister of
the *Century* editor Richard Watson Gilder. Jeannette Gilder, who edited
the magazine *The Critic*, was well respected in New York literary circles.
She had read Riis's article in *Scribner's* and wanted him to expand it into
a book. If he was interested, she wrote, she would like to help him set up
a meeting with the publisher Charles Scribner.

When, many years earlier, Riis had received Elisabeth's letter saying she would marry him, he had jumped for joy and danced in his tiny room. The letter he now held in his hand was almost as providential, yet it did not have a similar effect on him. Years of hard work had taught him that even a unique opportunity such as this one was never all good news. Writing a book would be exceptionally labor intensive. Elisabeth was wary of the prospect; throughout their marriage she had borne the brunt of his many work-related absences, often feeling alone and overwhelmed. The two of them sat silently together until Elisabeth leaned her head on his shoulder and quietly asked: "Are we going to lose you now?"

❊

IN FACT, for the most part the writing of what became *How the Other Half Lives: Studies of the Tenements of New York* was relatively effortless for Riis; he finished the manuscript in only ten months while still working full time. That he was able to write the book so quickly can be attributed partly to the fact that he had spent the last ten years of his life collecting impressions of, and data on, the slums, and thinking about the issue of poverty in America. Elisabeth kept the house quiet: When Riis returned home from the office, the children were not allowed to interrupt him and were asked to take their noisy games outside. On the rare occasions when they did interrupt him, he openly expressed his disapproval.

He sat up late at night writing long after the rest of the family had gone to bed. "It was my habit to light the lamps in all the rooms of the lower story and roam through them with my pipe, for I do most of my writing on my feet." The manuscript was begun in January 1890. Shortly afterward, Riis and the owner of the Associated Press had a serious disagreement. He decided to leave the bureau but continue to operate as a journalist. With typical energy and determination, he set out to scoop his fellow reporters, while at the same time staying up late at night working on his book. Later he wrote:

> I got up at five o'clock, three hours before any of my competitors, and sometimes they came down to the office to find my news hawked about the street in extras of their own papers. . . . How deadly tired I was in those days I do not think I myself knew until I went to Boston one evening to help discuss

*sweating at the Institute of Technology. I had an hour to spare, and went
around into Beacon Street to call upon a friend. I walked mechanically up
the stoop and rang the bell. My friend was not in, said the servant who came
to the door. Who should I say called? I stood and looked at her like a fool: I
had forgotten my name.*

Elisabeth became pregnant during this time, but the pregnancy
ended tragically. The baby was stillborn and became the second Riis
child to be buried in Maple Grove Cemetery.

Shortly after the funeral Riis's book was published. To his utter surprise it became a best-seller, its success giving the family a much-needed
boost, psychologically and financially.

※

HOW THE OTHER HALF LIVES begins with a dramatic manifesto
intended to unite readers in the fight against pervasive poverty in New
York City and other U.S. cities. Riis states his case succinctly, delin-
eating the causes of poverty, the extent of the problem, and how to
alleviate it. "Today three-fourths of [the urban population] live in the
tenements, and the nineteenth century drift . . . to the cities is sending
ever-increasing multitudes to crowd them. The fifteen thousand tenant houses that were the despair of the sanitarian in the past generation
have swelled into thirty-seven thousand, and more than twelve hundred thousand persons call them home."

The tenements "generate evil," Riis warns apocalyptically—epidemics,
crime, sin, and alcoholism originated there. Worse, the existence of
the slum environment is a direct threat to American values. Property
speculation creates the poverty problem, Riis concludes, arguing that
stricter housing legislation is the only way to curtail exploitative rent
practices.

※

APART FROM the fire-and-brimstone introduction, the book's message
is delivered relatively calmly. Riis's material is much better organized
than it was in *Scribner's*. The reader is taken back to seventeenth-century

New Amsterdam, when wealthy New Yorkers built their houses on the East River wharves. Riis points out that one of the most elegant streets in the city was then Cherry Street, where George Washington lived during the first six months of his presidency.

As the city grew, the rich began moving uptown, deserting their elegant homes. "It was the stir and bustle of trade, together with the tremendous immigration that followed upon the war of 1812 that dislodged them." When the rich moved north, the many neighborhoods they left behind, especially on the Lower East Side, fell into ruin. The old homes were bought by housing speculators, who divided them into apartments and filled them to the brim with immigrants. As the number of immigrants coming to New York continued to increase, two-story wooden buildings rose in the shadow of the old, increasingly dilapidated mansions.

> *Worse was to follow. It was soon perceived by estate owners and agents of property that a greater percentage of profits could be realized by the conversion of houses and blocks into barracks, and dividing their space into smaller proportions capable of containing human life within four walls. . . . Blocks were rented of real estate owners, or "purchased on time," or taken in charge at a percentage, and held for under-letting.*

With the appearance of the middleman came the era of tenement construction that turned out such blocks as Gotham Court, where, in one cholera epidemic, "the tenants died at the rate of one hundred and ninety-five to the thousand of population."

Ranging effortlessly through centuries and statistics, Riis shows that certain areas of New York were at the time the most densely populated in the world, the Lower East Side, with a population of 466,000 per square mile during the middle of the nineteenth century, rivaling the most densely populated area of London, which held 285,000 people per square mile. The crowding of people and animals continued to give rise to epidemics, and housing laws did little to solve the problem. "When another generation shall have doubled the census of our city, and to that vast army of workers, held captive by poverty, the very name of home shall be as a bitter mockery, what will the harvest be?" Riis asks.

Riis takes his readers on a tour of the slums, writing in a lively, at times dramatic feature-style overflowing with colorful details, his observations backed by statistics. In one chapter, the Dickensian influence evident, he addresses the reader directly, like a tour guide walking a few paces in front, describing the sights: "Be a little careful, please!"

> The hall is dark and you might stumble over the children pitching pennies back there. Not that it would hurt them; kicks and cuffs are their daily diet. They have little else. Here where the hall turns and dives into utter darkness is a step, and another, another. A flight of stairs. You can feel your way, if you cannot see it. Close? Yes! What would you have? All the fresh air that ever enters these stairs comes from the hall-door that is forever slamming, and from the windows of dark bedrooms that in turn receive from the stairs their sole supply of the elements God meant to be free, but man deals out with such niggardly hand.

Several of Riis's descriptions of immigrants later brought charges of narrow-mindedness and racism. Of Jews: "Money is their God. Life itself is of little value compared with even the leanest bank account." The Italian, "swarthy" and "hot-headed," "when he settles down to a game of cards lets loose all his bad passions." Germans are "heavy-witted," blacks lack "moral accountability" and are "superstitious." Riis held Chinese immigrants in lowest regard: "I state it in advance as my opinion, based on the steady observation of years, that all attempts to make an effective Christian of John Chinaman will remain abortive in this generation; of the next I have, if anything, less hope. Ages of senseless idolatry, a mere grub-worship, have left him without the essential qualities for appreciating the gentle teachings of a faith whose motive and unselfish spirit are alike beyond his grasp. There is nothing strong about him, except his passions when aroused."

Today, such cartoonlike, stereotypical descriptions seem at best naïve. In the 1970s, following the civil rights legislation of the 1960s, they were perceived as blatantly racist, leading to the disappearance of Riis's works from university curricula. Riis came to be seen as limited in outlook, caught, as it were, in a trap of his own biases. He was, of course, influenced by his time; people who were not Protestant, Anglo-Saxon,

Nine-year-old Katie in front of the Fifty-second Street Industrial School. When Riis asked her what kind of work she did, she replied: "I scrubs." Photograph by Riis

A "scrub" with her bed in the Eldridge Street Police Station. Photograph by Riis

Nisby's Alley, at 47½ Crosby Street. Photograph by Riis

Italian brothers. Photograph by Riis

An English coal-heaver's home in Poverty Gap. Photograph by Riis

Italian mother with swaddled baby on Jersey Street. Riis called this *Home of an Italian Ragpicker*. Photograph by Riis

Minding the Baby in Cherry Hill. Smaller children often looked after babies
while mothers went to work. Photograph by Riis

One of four peddlers who slept in a basement on Ludlow Street for four years. Photograph by Riis

The Tramp. Photograph by Riis

Under the dump at West Forty-seventh Street. Photograph by Riis

Three men in the Church Street lodging house where Riis's gold locket
was taken and his dog killed. Photograph by Riis

Not all was grim in the tenements. Four Cherokee Indians in a relatively well-kept apartment.
Photograph by Riis

A cobbler in a basement "apartment" on Ludlow Street. Photograph by Riis

Children in Mullin's Alley, one block from Gotham Court.
Photograph by Riis (and Henry Piffard and Richard Hoe Lawrence)

Mulberry Bend Park, today called Columbus Park. Photograph by Riis

Jacob, Elisabeth, and the children visiting aging Niels Edvard and Caroline Riis in Ribe, 1893.
Left to right: John, Ed, Niels Edvard, Caroline, Katie, Riis's sister Sofie, Jacob, Elisabeth, and Clara

or from northern European countries, he believed, existed on a lower rung of civilization. Moreover, Riis was a typical Victorian moralist who would never have dreamed of questioning the superiority of Christian values and who saw himself as superior to people of color. According to his world view, Christians in fact bore the burden, which they were morally obliged to take seriously, of acting as role models.

However, it has been lost on many of his later critics that Riis spent far more time painting positive portraits of the "other" than he did on making insupportable generalizations. No one worked harder than the Jews; Italians were "honest," "faithful," and "lighthearted"; the German "makes the most of his tenement, and it should be added that as soon as he can save up enough money, he gets out and never crosses the threshold of one again."

Riis clearly also despised slavery and revealed a deep sympathy for the plight of blacks, decrying the intense discrimination they suffered. Blacks littered the least in the slums, he noted, and were loyal to their government, reveling in their newly won status as citizens; they were well dressed and optimistic. Even the Chinese received kind words: "Rather than banish the Chinaman, I would have the door opened wider—for his wife; make it a condition of his coming or staying that he brings his wife with him. Then, at least, he might not be what he now is and remains, a homeless stranger among us."

The prudish ethics of the Victorian era marked Riis's approach to certain aspects of his topic. For instance, he avoided direct mention of all problems in the slums related to promiscuity. Instead, and only when absolutely necessary, he chose euphemisms like "immorality" and "vice." Prostitution was mentioned only in the context of its being widespread and in many respects one of the slums' defining characteristics— there was a brothel on almost every street corner. Conversely, Riis did not spare the reader any detail about such issues as alcoholism, lack of hygiene, and the harsh treatment—often serious abuse—of children.

Placing undue emphasis upon what may be seen as Riis's shortcomings and limitations would be to overlook the radical and progressive nature of his work. At the time of its publication, his book broke with many well-established ideas and beliefs. Riis's mission had been to abolish the abiding view of immigrants in the slums, and in this he succeeded as no one had before him. Throughout, he points out that immigrants may not look like "us," they may "behave" and "conduct" themselves differently, but if we take the trouble to see them, we will discover that they are not as different from us as we would like to think.

Riis's reformist message comes across with eloquent clarity in the middle and later chapters, as when he writes, in chapter 14, of another story to be told, "a story of thousands of devoted lives, laboring earnestly to make the most of their scant opportunities for good; of heroic men and women striving patiently against fearful odds and by their very courage coming off victors in the battle with the tenement."

The prospect of "victors," however, was still a long way off. Riis tells of starving mothers who killed their children because they could not feed them, and of a young Irish day laborer, his lungs destroyed by poisonous fumes emanating from the sewers where he worked, who went mad and would have killed his entire family if the police had not been there to prevent it. Unable to sleep at night, he paced the floor of his small apartment worrying, muttering to himself; fatigued and exhausted, it suddenly occurred to him, "it is better that I take care of it myself," and he got out his ax.

Riis related the story of a mother of six "with a husband sick to death, who to support the family made shirts, averaging an income of one dollar and twenty cents a week." He described the heartbreak of families evicted from their apartments by slumlords. The chapter reaches a powerful crescendo when Riis takes his readers to potter's field to see the final resting place of the poorest of the poor.

> One free excursion awaits young and old whom bitter poverty has denied the poor privilege of the choice of home in death they were denied in life, the ride up the Sound to the Potter's Field, charitably styled the City Cemetery. But even there they do not escape their fate. In the common trench of the Poor Burying Ground they lie packed three stories deep, shoulder to shoulder, crowded in death as they were in life, to "save space"; for even on that desert island the ground is not for the exclusive possession of those who cannot afford to pay for it.

✳

RICHLY ILLUSTRATED, *How the Other Half Lives* is not a photography book, as many have later been led to believe. Of its 44 illustrations half are woodcuts—the same woodcuts originally printed in *Scribner's*—based on Riis's photographs. There are a number of architectural blueprints of tenements, and finally 15 of Riis's original photos reprinted using the new halftone technique that had made such reproduction in books and magazines possible. The technique, still in its infancy, made the photos look gray, muddy, and out of focus.

The publisher presumably chose to use halftone reprints because it was less costly and much faster than for a graphic artist to make additional woodcuts. Apparently neither the publisher nor Riis deemed it particularly revolutionary that any photographs were reprinted; on the contrary, they were probably nervous that the photographs would detract from the overall quality of the work.

The book's sources, and sources of inspiration, were many. In the sections criticizing housing speculation, the voice of Henry George can be heard; in the introduction, Felix Adler's influence is strong. In its focus on the plight of the children in the slums, the ideas of Charles Loring Brace shine through. The vast statistical material and the many warnings that the overcrowded slums are breeding grounds for contagious and deadly diseases originated in the Health Department and with the ideas of John Griscom, in whose work, as we have seen, Riis read the phrase "how the other half lives."

In Riis's critical treatment of vagabonds one sees the influence of Josephine Shaw Lowell, and in his romantic, at times sentimental, tone one hears Hans Christian Andersen. The book's somewhat sensationalist approach was of course colored by the aggressive yellow journalism of the day and all its stylistic trappings. Riis later acknowledged that the portrait of the slums he had painted in his book was much darker than the reality warranted. But he had felt justified in order to get his message across: New York was facing a poverty crisis and something had to be done—now.

Riis wove these voices into a beautifully unified tapestry that impressed his readers even as it chastened them. Shortly before the book was launched, the British founder of the Salvation Army, William Booth, had published a similar book on London's poverty problems called *In Darkest England and the Way Out*, in which he urged immediate action. Booth's book was read widely in the United States, and it was with the utmost curiosity that the public received Riis's work. It could not have been published at a better time.

The book received largely favorable reviews. The *Silver Cross* wrote: "A great many books come to the table of an editor. Some of them never ought to be noticed at all; some of them deserve much severer notice than they get, and some do not get as good notice as they deserve. It is rare that a book comes of which, all in all, from the first page to the last, the editor feels like saying: Read it, and do not omit a line; turn back to the beginning and read it over again." A reviewer in the magazine *Epoch* wrote that *How the Other Half Lives* "is a volume that the political economist, philanthropist, the preacher, the novelist and the journalist will find inevitable, because of the great mass of facts it contains about the poor, because of its information about the different parts of the city inhabited by various nationalities and because of its vivid pictures of the lives of the toilers."

According to a lengthy review in the *New York Times*, Riis had "written a powerful book, which deserves careful and thorough reading." *The Dial* said that "such a study has never before been made with anything approaching the thoroughness and insight with which Mr. Riis has conducted his investigations. The value of the book is that having revealed the evil, he is ready with a plan of remedy."

How the Other Half Lives also received critical reviews, however. Its detractors found it devoid of literary grace, calling it crude, offensive, and almost vulgar in tone. "His book," wrote the reviewer in *The Critic*, "is literally a photograph and as such has its value and lesson, but also its serious limitations. There is a lack of broad and penetrative vision . . . and a roughness amounting almost to brutality." Others pointed out that the book's scientific foundation was questionable compared to that of Booth's *Darkest England*.

Sales of the book provided Riis with a level of financial security he had never enjoyed before, while also firmly establishing him as one of the nineteenth century's great troubadours of social reform. *How the Other Half Lives* became a rallying cry for reformers of all stripes poised, at the dawn of the Progressive Era, to effect sweeping change.

The book also transformed the life of its author, taking him into a new era of his life. Now that he was famous, Riis was able to form alliances with those within the existing power structure who were highly influential and who could help him get to work on improving the conditions of the other half. Among the most significant of these was a man on a political fast track toward the White House, Theodore Roosevelt.

17

Brothers

I N AN ARTICLE Riis wrote in 1884 on corruption, he had pointed out that the young politician Theodore Roosevelt was the one reformer who could clean up the police force as well as the Health Department, where management, according to Riis, was corrupt. In turn, after reading *How the Other Half Lives*, Roosevelt realized that Riis was a significant ally in the battle against poverty and a mentor of sorts, providing valuable insight into the slums. As Roosevelt wrote to Riis many years later, in 1897, looking back on their work together:

> *When I joined the Police Department it was on your book that I had built, and it was on your behalf that I continued to build. Whatever I did there was done because I was trying, with much stumbling and ill success, but with genuine effort, to put into practice the principles you had set forth, and to live up the standard you had established.*

Born into one of New York's oldest and wealthiest families, Roosevelt traced his ancestry to the city's early history as a Dutch colony. He was born on October 27, 1858, a frail baby who developed asthma. The family lived in a brownstone on Twentieth Street before moving uptown. Physically weak and forced to stay indoors much of the time, Roosevelt became an avid reader, amassing impressive knowledge of such subjects as history, biology, zoology, botany, and geology. His father, anxious that his son not succumb to lifelong illness, instituted an arduous regimen of exercise, weight lifting, and boxing. The workouts, which became part of Roosevelt's daily routine, turned the weak boy into a strong, muscular young man with significant stamina. The training also helped Roosevelt overcome his asthma.

However, Roosevelt never lost his love of books and studying. He read extensively throughout his life, and it is perhaps in this one regard that his friendship with Riis was a union of opposites. Roosevelt, erudite and broad-minded, embraced many causes and interests during his life, while Riis remained passionately focused on the slums and, while highly knowledgeable on this subject, remained somewhat simplistic in his outlook on other topics and on the world in general.

Roosevelt became police commissioner of New York City in 1895, by which time he had already published several well-researched books on American history, including *The Naval War of 1812*, a book on the city's early history, and a history of America's westward expansion in four volumes bearing the triumphant title *The Winning of the West* (1889).

Roosevelt's scholarly aptitudes were evident early on. As a young boy he wrote a small book on zoology. He graduated magna cum laude from Harvard. The intelligent young man was eager to pursue an academic career, but his father was against the idea, primarily because the financial rewards were limited. When Theodore Roosevelt Sr. died in 1878, Roosevelt was only nineteen, and he inherited a considerable fortune. Yet even with his new and improved circumstances, he set aside his academic aspirations out of respect for his deceased father and enrolled at Columbia Law School.

When Roosevelt was at Harvard, Riis was living as a tramp on the streets of New York. Still, Riis's years of living in poverty did not define his character, and he and Roosevelt were remarkably alike in outlook as well as appearance: Both were rather short, hyperactive men who wore glasses, and their high level of energy affected all who came in contact with them. Roosevelt was known for his broad smile and excited outbursts, as was Riis, and both men were exceptionally enterprising—

neither had any respect for people who were all talk and no action. Both had a tendency to moralize.

Roosevelt later wrote in his memoirs: "He and I looked at life and its problems from substantially the same standpoint. Our ideals and principles and purposes, and our beliefs as to the methods necessary to realize them, were alike." Both men worked ridiculous hours, often to the point of debilitating exhaustion. Even their early experiences with love were similar: Roosevelt fell in love with Alice Hathaway Lee when he was about the same age as Riis had been when he became infatuated with Elisabeth. Both men remained true to these first loves, though Roosevelt did not propose in vain, and he was spared the pain of unrequited love.

Both men also possessed tremendous willpower, Roosevelt demonstrating his as a child, by improving his physique in order to conquer his asthmatic condition. Finally, both seemed capable of doing the impossible. Against all odds, Riis married Elisabeth. In an adopted culture, he became a well-respected author, journalist, and reformer. Roosevelt surprised his supporters and constituents by not following the traditional Republican path when he entered politics. In the New York State Assembly he allied himself, as expected, with the party leadership in opposing pay raises for city officials; he later worked closely with Democratic Governor Grover Cleveland, and as head of the State Assembly City Affairs Committee he became an avid reformer, examining and exposing the corruption of the departments within city government.

Roosevelt's political career came to a sudden, temporary halt on February 14, 1884, when both his young wife Alice and his mother died within a few hours of each other, Alice in childbirth and his mother of acute typhoid fever. Consumed with grief, and nearing the end of his term, he decided to quit politics for a while and move out west to the Dakota Territory. He hoped a life full of physical activity could help him overcome his grief, as it had once helped him conquer his asthma. He settled in the West, living a comparably simple life among cowboys for the better part of two years. Roosevelt spent his days hunting down cattle thieves and sleeping outdoors, roughing it with the best of them. In 1886 he returned to the city and to politics, feeling renewed and invigorated. That year he ran for mayor of New York City but lost, coming in a poor third. Undaunted by this defeat, he continued to pursue a political career, winning appointments to a number of prestigious positions. From 1889 to 1895 he served as a member of the Civil Service Commission in Washington, appointed by President Benjamin Harrison. In 1895 New York City Mayor William Strong offered him the position of police commissioner. The city had four police commissioners, all theoretically of the same rank, but Roosevelt, 37, quickly made it clear that he would be supervising the work of the others, Frederick D. Grant, Avery D. Andrews, and Andrew Parker. Thus Roosevelt paved the way for his eventual appointment as head of the Board of Commissioners.

The commissioners were based at police headquarters, on Mulberry Street, across the street from Riis. Earlier in the year, when rumors of Roosevelt's imminent appointment had reached Riis, he had exclaimed, "'Theodore Roosevelt is the man for president of the police board, and God will attend to this appointment. That's all I want to know. I don't care who the other commissioners are. T.R. is enough.'" Riis considered Roosevelt capable of cleaning up the police force and improving conditions in the slums of New York City almost single-handedly. Roosevelt did indeed create a whirlwind of activity from the minute he arrived on Mulberry Street, on May 6, 1895. In the morning, after a swearing-in at City Hall, Roosevelt, Grant, Andrews, and Parker walked in procession to their new offices, where Riis and the other reporters, who had only just heard the news of the appointments, awaited them. When Roosevelt spotted Riis, he broke into a run, according to Lincoln Steffens, then a reporter for the *New York Evening Post*, and shouted:

"Hello, Jake," to Riis, and running up the stairs to the front door of police headquarters, he waved us reporters to follow. We did. With the police officials standing around watching, the new board went up to the second story, where the old commissioners were waiting in their offices. T.R. seized Riis, who introduced me, and still running, he asked questions: "Where are our offices? Where is the board room? What do we do first?"

After the board's first meeting that day, Roosevelt asked Steffens and Riis to his office, where he began briefing them about what he hoped to achieve as police commissioner. According to Steffens, Roosevelt treated them as if they were his newly appointed personal advisors, which to some degree they did become. "Now, then, what'll we do?" he asked. Throughout his tenure as commissioner, he constantly consulted with his friends on issues relating to the slums. Roosevelt used to lean out of his window and shout, "Hi yi yi," signaling his friends to cross the street and meet him at his office for an impromptu meeting. "For two years we were to be together all the day," Riis recalled, "and quite often most of the night, in the environment in which I had spent twenty years of my life. And these two were the happiest by far of them all. Then was life really worth living, and I have a pretty robust enjoyment of it at all times."

The following years were brutally hectic for the police force. The Lexow Hearings were under way, brought about by the investigative work of Riis's friend the Rev. Charles Parkhurst. The sensational nature of Parkhurst's report on widespread corruption within the police force inflamed the public, and the open hearings became a press circus. The disclosure of how readily officers had taken bribes from brothel madams to keep quiet was perhaps rivaled only by the revelation that a majority achieved promotions merely by buying their titles. Each title cost a certain amount; the higher the rank an officer desired, the higher the price. For most officers it was a worthwhile investment, as a high rank automatically carried with it larger bribes.

One of Roosevelt's first acts as commissioner was to fire Clubber Williams, who admitted during the Lexow Hearings to "of course taking bribes." In addition, Roosevelt succeeded in getting rid of Thomas Byrnes, despite Byrnes's brash declaration soon after Roosevelt's appointment that he would continue to reign supreme in Mulberry Street: "It will break you. You will yield. You are but human." Byrnes was allowed to resign, but everybody knew he had been shown the door by the new commissioner. Riis, though aware of the corruption during Byrnes's reign, was saddened by his departure. For all his obvious flaws, Byrnes had been an old-school cop, colorful and efficient in his way, and although his means had been questionable, he had managed to keep crime under control in the city. His resignation heralded the end of an era in the history of New York City's police, and it also closed a chapter in the life of Jacob Riis. During the years when Riis had struggled to cement his career as a police reporter, Clubber Williams and Police Chief Byrnes had been an important part of his everyday life. Both Williams and Byrnes went on to profitable careers outside the force: Williams founded an insurance company and made a fortune, and Byrnes formed a successful detective agency on Wall Street.

Next on the agenda for Roosevelt was an overhaul of the remaining officers on the force and, if necessary, a weeding out of exceptionally bad seeds. Like Riis, Roosevelt firmly believed that the majority of the patrolmen and officers were essentially good men who had simply been misled. Roosevelt was convinced that, with guidance, most of them would turn out to be fine policemen. But he realized it was crucial for him to win their respect, and he set out to do so by introducing a simple new policy: Any officer caught violating the rules of police conduct would be fired immediately. Roosevelt's campaign against corruption came as a shock to the force because of its unorthodox execution, in which Riis played a central role.

※

AT 2:00 AM ON June 7, 1895, a man wearing a soft bowler hat pulled down over his eyes and a long black coat with the collar turned up left the Union League Club on Fifth Avenue. He slid into the warm dark summer night and was soon joined by another man, in equally inappropriate attire and green tinted glasses. The two mysterious personages moved quickly down Third Avenue—a top-secret mission was under way.

The man in the bowler hat was Roosevelt; the man with the green glasses was Riis.

Roosevelt had wanted to see for himself, without being recognized, how his patrolmen conducted themselves on the job. The two men would walk the streets of the Lower East Side and other high-crime areas, inspecting the performance and behavior of officers on duty. It was Riis who had mapped the evening's route, and he was to plan many similar night trips.

After two decades Riis had a profound knowledge of the world that unfolded in the slums at night, and he knew which patrolmen walked the different districts. According to Riis, Roosevelt's worst expectations were confirmed the first night out: Only one patrolman was on his post, the others having been found chatting in groups on the street, drinking in bars, or engaging prostitutes, none terribly concerned with patrolling the city.

Roosevelt and Riis stayed out until dawn and were in high spirits upon returning to headquarters, considering the mission a great success. Roosevelt had made his identity known and believed word would spread through the force. After an hour's nap he called in six of the offenders for a meeting. He could easily have fired them all, but he was so exhilarated by his triumph that he let them go with a warning, stressing, however, that if they were caught again it would cost them their jobs. The object of the expedition had been achieved: The men were terrified.

Riis gave a detailed account of the night's events to his fellow reporters at 301 Mulberry Street and, as intended, it was a huge story in the papers the following day. News of the commissioner's mission spread quickly within the force, and by the next raid Riis and Roosevelt found the patrolmen not only on their posts but on their toes. Looking at the records from the time, however, it seems Riis and Roosevelt in fact caught only one patrolman straying from his post that first night.

From this point on Roosevelt and Riis, the two brothers of the slums, regularly conducted night raids. Six months after their first expedition Riis showed Roosevelt the police lodging house on Church Street where his dog had been killed, the event still a bitter memory some twenty-five years later:

It was raining outside. The light flickered, cold and cheerless, in the green lamps as we went up the stone steps. Involuntarily I looked in the corner for my little dog; but it was not there, or any one who remembered it. The sergeant glanced over his blotter grimly; I had almost to pinch myself to make sure I was not shivering in a linen duster, wet to the skin. Down the cellar steps to the men's lodging-room I led the President of the Police Board. It was unchanged—just as it was the day I slept there. Three men lay stretched at full length on the dirty planks, two of them young lads from the country.

*Standing there, I told Mr. Roosevelt my own story. He turned alternately
red and white with anger as he heard it.*

*"Did they do that to you?" he asked when I had ended. For an answer I
pointed to the young lads then asleep before him.*

"I was like this one," I said.

He struck his clenched fists together. "I will smash them to-morrow."

Early in his career as a reporter Riis had promised himself he would
do everything in his power to effect the closing of police lodging houses.
Based on his own experience and what he later witnessed as a reporter,
he believed other institutions, not the police, should make provisions
for homeless men. The mix of rough cops and homeless men was always
bound to result in abuse and violence. Having risen through the ranks
at 301 Mulberry Street, Riis was tempted to use his power to get the officer who had abused him fired. It would have been easy for him to find
out who the officer was; he had free access to the police records and
could look up who was on duty that night in October 1870. In the end
he resisted the temptation, realizing that in the bigger scheme of things
going after one officer would change nothing. It was not the individual
officer who was the problem, it was the entire system, and it was in that
direction that Riis needed to focus his efforts.

In the early 1890s Riis joined the Committee on Vagrancy of the
Conference of Charities of New York City, which worked toward finding better ways to help the homeless—or "the shiftless and floating city
population," as they were referred to in an 1897 piece in the *Annals of
the American Academy of Political and Social Science*. Riis had already tried
unsuccessfully to convince the authorities to shut down the police lodging houses. In 1893 he had cautioned that the city was at risk of a major
cholera epidemic if the lodging houses were not immediately closed. As
Riis predicted, a cholera epidemic broke out. To support his claim Riis
had taken a series of photos of tramps huddling together on the wooden
floorboards in the cramped rooms of the lodging houses and had brought
them to the Academy of Medicine, which had promised to look into the
matter but never did, to the great detriment of the city's health.

Roosevelt, however, made good on the promise made to Riis while touring the Church Street lodging house: All the police lodging houses in the city were closed the following day, February 16, 1896—an act that, although well intentioned, was not the most humane solution for the hundreds of tramps thus left without shelter in the middle of winter; it would take months before any charity organization could build and open new shelters. Riis could not but see the closings as an important first victory in the battle against what he called the slum's core of evil.

Riis had another important score to settle with the city of New York, namely Mulberry Bend. The area was completely ignored by the authorities despite the fact that it was a cauldron of crime, vice, and misery. Again Riis's outrage was colored by personal experience: Mulberry Bend was of course where he had been staying when he had contemplated suicide during his first few months in the United States. The most densely populated slum in the world, it clearly was unfit for human habitation. For years Riis had reiterated his point about the Bend's being beyond redemption to anyone who cared to listen. In Roosevelt he was finally to find someone who would take action against this particular blight.

Roosevelt began inspecting the tenements with Riis early in his tenure as commissioner. They went through some of the worst in the city, and Roosevelt was appalled. "Roosevelt wanted to know the city by night, and the true inwardness of some of the problems he was struggling with. . . . One might hear of overcrowding in tenements for years and not grasp the subject as he could by a single midnight inspection with the sanitary police. He wanted to understand it all, the smallest with the greatest," Riis later wrote.

"I used to visit the different tenement-house regions, usually in company with Riis, to see for myself what the conditions were," Roosevelt wrote. "It was largely this personal experience that enabled me while on the Health Board [in his capacity as police commissioner] to struggle not only zealously, but with reasonable efficiency and success, to improve conditions. We did our share in making forward strides in the matter of housing the working people of the city with some regard to decency and comfort."

Riis and Roosevelt's first goal was to set in motion the demolition of all tenements deemed beyond rehabilitation. Riis had in fact already made strides toward achieving this goal, but with Roosevelt as commissioner the last important phase of what would become a massive cleanup of the slums proceeded. In 1885 the Tenement-House Committee had been established under the leadership of Felix Adler, and Riis had been working through its auspices with other reformers and the Health Department to convince city authorities to demolish the entire area. Since 1888, when he was able to show photo documentation of the horrendous conditions in the Bend, he had had some success in convincing the authorities that something needed to be done. Several influential politicians had gone on record condemning the conditions in Mulberry Bend and had recommended that it be turned into a park. It would, however, be many years before this was accomplished.

By 1894 plans to demolish the Bend were set in motion, and the City Council set aside $1.5 million as compensation for the landlords. Between the time that the city took over the area and it actually began tearing down the tenements, the city simply took over the landlords' role collecting rents from those who could afford to pay. The lag made Riis furious, and he launched a campaign against the authorities in the papers, pressuring them to act on their word. Finally, by the end of 1895 most of the Bend had been razed.

There were a number of tenements near the Bend that also needed to be torn down, and it was when Riis began focusing on these rookeries that Roosevelt came into the picture. Roosevelt was given a list, written up by Riis, of the sixteen worst slum areas in the city. As police commissioner Roosevelt worked closely with the Health Board, presenting the list to the health inspectors, long Riis's allies. The Health Board was the city body that legislated on housing and thus had the power to initiate further demolition. After careful consideration the board decided to act on Roosevelt and Riis's recommendations, which included tearing down Gotham Court and the Mott Street Barracks. It was not an easy plan to execute. The landlords responded by suing both Roosevelt and the Health Board. The lawsuits, while slowing down the process, could not stop the wave of demolitions that had been set in motion before litigation was initiated. By 1897, more of the city's worst tenements had been demolished.

"Directly or indirectly, I had a hand in destroying seven whole blocks of them as I count it up. I wish it had been seventy," Riis wrote later.

❈

RIIS AND HIS FELLOW reformers' efforts to clean up the slums were, as he admitted in his memoirs, only the first step in a long journey toward a complete reform of housing conditions in the city of New York, a journey that would take many years. According to several present-day housing experts the journey is far from over; miserable living conditions and homelessness are of course still problems in New York City today. Still, Riis accomplished so much more than he ever imagined he would, and he could hardly believe it when he saw the huge crater left by the demolition of the tenements in Mulberry Bend. Tragically, it was not until a young child had fallen in and died that this iniquitous reminder of the city's past was filled in with dirt, fully a year after the destruction of the houses themselves. Grass seed and, later, trees and bushes were planted, transforming the infested elbow-shaped street, which had once held the city in a sickening embrace, into a park. It was christened Mulberry Bend Park (today Columbus Park) and opened on June 15, 1897.

Thousands of New Yorkers attended the opening that warm summer night. A band played, speeches were made, and food was consumed in an atmosphere of general merriment. Riis and Lincoln Steffens stood at some distance from the crowd, listening intently. The last speaker was Riis's friend Captain George Waring, a main force behind the improved sanitation system in the city, including the establishment of a regular street sweeping program, also in 1897. Waring praised Riis for his tireless efforts to improve the conditions of the poor. "Without Riis," he roared, "this park would not be here today." He concluded by sending up a loud cheer for Riis, and the exalted crowd joined him.

The orchestra began playing people's requests for contemporary pop tunes like "Sweet Rosie O'Grady" and "The Sunshine of Paradise Alley." It was almost as if Mulberry Bend had never existed.

18

⸺⸺⸺ •◆• ⸺⸺⸺

The Golden Years

I N HIS OWN WORDS, the 1890s were "golden years" for Riis. A
central figure in New York's reformist circles, every initiative he set
forth succeeded. He noted in his memoirs that good luck seemed to
come in streaks.

Riis was not the first to achieve star-journalist status in the United
States; that distinction belongs to Henry Morton Stanley. Nellie Bly,
of the *New York World*, also preceded Riis, achieving renown in 1889
when she traveled the world in seventy-two days in a successful attempt
to trump the fictional hero of Jules Verne's *Around the World in 80
Days*, Phileas Fogg. However, Riis was the first investigative reporter to
become widely celebrated for social documentation.

Heading into the 1890s, Riis could, if he had known the term, have
called himself the first American muckraker. Ironically, it was Roosevelt,
then president, who, in coining the term "muckraking"—only latterly
applied to Riis and other investigative journalists—also to some extent
disparaged its practice. In "The Treason in the Senate," a 1906 speech
made following a *Cosmopolitan* series by investigative reporter David
Graham Phillips that took aim at Roosevelt's Senate allies, the president damned investigative journalists with faint praise, acknowledg-
ing their service to society but invoking *Pilgrim's Progress* (1678): John

Bunyan's "man with a muck-rake" was, said Roosevelt, "the man who
could look no way but downward . . . who was offered a celestial crown
for his muck-rake, but would neither look up nor regard the crown he
was offered, but continued to rake to himself the filth of the floor." The
term had been rehabilitated by the time of its application to Riis and
others. But Roosevelt, said an enraged Lincoln Steffens the day after the
president's speech, had put an end to a legacy of good work—a legacy on
which the president himself had built his reputation.

※

BORN INTO PRIVILEGE in San Francisco on April 6, 1866, Steffens's
own reputation was cemented in 1906 with an exposé of state politics, *The Struggle for Self-Government*, and the cofounding, with fellow
investigative journalists Ida Tarbell and Ray Stannard Baker, of the
American Magazine; two years before, he had brought out a collection
of his McClure's articles, *The Shame of the Cities*. An interview in Russia
with Lenin in 1919 yielded his signature line, "I have been over into
the future, and it works," although his infatuation with Communism
was relatively short-lived, fading by the publication, in 1931, of his
Autobiography.

Steffens was the son of a millionaire businessman. He studied in
Heidelberg, Leipzig, Paris, London, and at the University of California
at Berkeley before arriving in New York in the early 1890s with dreams
of making a living as a writer. "By now you must know about all there is
to know of the theory of life, but there's a practical side as well," wrote
his father. "It's worth knowing. I suggest that you learn it, and the way
to study it, I think, is to stay in New York and hustle.

"Enclosed please find one hundred dollars, which should keep you
till you can find a job and support yourself."

In short order Steffens sold an article to *Harper's* magazine for $50.
Later, with the help of his father, he secured an interview with the
editor of the *New York Evening Post*, a paper that preceded the *Wall
Street Journal* in covering finance and the stock market. When Steffens
showed up for the interview, impeccably dressed and filled with anxious
anticipation, the editor refused to offer him a job. He was told to come

back the following week and to take a seat on the bench in the front
office, where other hopeful reporters sat, like day laborers, waiting for an
assignment. If the paper needed extra writers, the editor told Steffens, he
would be willing to give him a chance. Full of faith in himself, Steffens
showed up day after day and sat on the bench, a long vigil that gave him
a feel for a reporter's day: "I was awed by the way they would, upon a few
words from the city editor, dart or loaf out of the room, be gone an hour
or so, come in, report briefly, and then sit down, write, turn in their copy
carelessly, and lie back and read, idly read, newspapers," he remembered
years later.

Finally Steffens's patience paid off. He was the only one sitting on
the bench once when an editor needed someone to cover the mysterious disappearance of a stockbroker. Steffens interviewed a few of the
man's colleagues and was able to report that the stockbroker had disappeared with the company's fortune. His story was a hit and Steffens's
scoop was praised by the editor, who hired him.

Steffens started out covering Wall Street and in 1893 became the
paper's police reporter, a beat he had not expected to be given but with
which he was thrilled. The *Evening Post* had long seen itself as above
reporting police matters, but with the increasing number of stories about
police corruption, notably the crusade against the force run by the radical Reverend Charles Parkhurst, then making headlines, the paper felt
it could no longer ignore the goings-on on Mulberry Street.

Steffens managed to insult both Clubber Williams and Thomas
Byrnes on his first day. However, he also met Riis, his idol. Steffens had
noticed a small, disheveled man screaming at the top of his voice—
"Maaaaax, Maaax"—on the street in front of the police reporters' office.
He asked a colleague who the man was and was told it was Riis, calling
for his assistant, Max Fischel.

"So! That was Jacob A. Riis, the author of *How the Other Half Lives*,
and not only a famous police reporter, but a well-known character in
one half of the life of New York. I liked his looks."

Riis immediately took to the young, enthusiastic reporter with the
goatee and glasses. He invited him upstairs to his office and they began
talking:

"Glad you've come," [Riis] said. "The Post *can help a lot up here, and you've begun well."*

"Begun well!" I exclaimed. "I haven't begun yet."

Riis roared his great laugh. "Oh, yes, you have. Max [Fischel] says you banged Alec Williams one and disappointed the old man himself."

He meant that I had failed with Superintendent Byrnes! I was about to protest, but Riis was shouting through that open window.

"That's the way to handle them! Knock 'em down, then you can pick them up and be the good Samaritan. It's their own way with us reporters. They put the fear of God into us, then they are kind to us—if we'll let them. Not me. They are afraid of me, not I of them, and so with you. You have started off on top. Stay there."

With these words Riis initiated Steffens into police reporting and a lifelong mentorship.

Among other great muckrakers to follow in Riis's footsteps was Steffens's colleague Ida Tarbell, who exposed Standard Oil's business dealings and illegal monopoly in the pages of *McClure's*. Riis's journalism also inspired fiction writers such as Stephen Crane, whose novel *Maggie: A Girl of the Streets* painted a harsh, undiluted portrait of New York's underworld, and Upton Sinclair, who shocked the country in 1905 with *The Jungle*, describing conditions in Chicago's slaughterhouses. That Sinclair's novel effected new, radical legislation was a mark of these writers' debt to Riis and *How the Other Half Lives*, the first journalistic writing that became a catalyst for social reform.

When *How the Other Half Lives* was published, Riis was overwhelmed by the tremendous backing suddenly offered him, and he briefly considered resigning as a journalist in order to devote himself full time to reform work by giving lectures and writing books. The number of reform organizations had mushroomed in response to the five-year-long depression set in motion by the financial panic of 1893. Unemployment skyrocketed; in New York alone it was estimated that up to 100,000 lost their jobs. Most of the unemployed became homeless, unable to pay rent on their apartments or rooms because they had no savings. The panic of 1893 was the worst economic crisis the country had faced, and both private citizens and politicians joined forces to offer emergency relief for its victims, setting up soup kitchens and procuring temporary shelters for the homeless. The crisis underlined how vulnerable the poor were, and a majority of the political elite began realizing that social reform was essential, giving momentum to what would become known as the good government movement.

The mayoral election of 1894 brought reform-minded Republican businessman and millionaire William L. Strong into office. With his victory Tammany Hall, which had regained power in the 1880s under Hugh John Grant, was again forced onto the sidelines. Strong and others became leading forces within the reform movement, forming, during the mayoral campaign, the Committee of Seventy, which campaigned successfully against Tammany Hall. Following the election they established twenty-four so-called Good Government Clubs, which were to examine the workings of local government and help develop community service programs. Each club was given a specific area to oversee and develop, one handling street sweeping and renovation (almost nonexistent in large areas of the city), another looking at the Health Department and disease prevention. Yet another probed the tenements, examining the possibilities of improving the living conditions of the city's poor.

Riis played a significant role in several Good Government Clubs. In 1894 he was made informal advisor of the Tenement Club, chaired by Richard Watson Gilder, editor of *The Century*, to which Riis had become a regular contributor since publication of *How the Other Half Lives*. A couple of years later Riis was made chair of a club that worked to create more parks and playgrounds for the city's children.

Since the success of the flower project, he had made a habit of putting an ad in the paper every spring, imploring people to bring in or send flowers to the children of the slums. From the first year Riis had noticed a remarkable number of boxes with the initials IHN—a private charity organization, Riis learned: The Circle of the King's Daughters; IHN was an acronym for In His Name, which appealed to Riis, who had always been strong in his faith. Riis contacted the organization, gave his lecture to its members, and a lifelong working relationship followed. The organization made Riis's mission their own.

In the summer of 1890, Riis secured a temporary office for the King's Daughters in the basement of the Mariner's Temple on the Lower East Side near the Bowery and Chinatown. Initially, the King's Daughters focused their efforts on helping the corps of doctors that inspected the slums every summer. The organization hired a nurse to follow up on the work done by the various medical teams. Later the King's Daughters moved into 48 and 50 Henry Street, on the Lower East Side, their two houses eventually becoming known as the King's Daughters Settlement House. Settlement houses became a stronghold of reform work in the slums, providing community services to people in need.

The King's Daughters was part of a settlement house movement that had started in London with the founding of Toynbee Hall in the poverty-stricken East End in 1884. Toynbee Hall was run by a group of well-educated reformers who had settled in the East End with the express purpose of improving the living conditions of the poor. The settlement house movement was intended to build a bridge between the poor and the middle and upper classes. Well-educated reformers were to teach the poor and because they lived among them they were able to inspire them by their own example. The houses also functioned as safe meeting places for the poor, where they could socialize with friends and become better acquainted with the reformers who were trying to help them. The arrangement was advantageous for the reformers as it gave them an opportunity to get to know the poor, acquiring an in-depth understanding of their problems and sincere and personal empathy for their plight.

The concept was picked up in the United States, where the first settlement house, the Neighborhood Guild, was founded in 1886 on Forsyth Street by a young, well-educated idealist named Stanton Coit. Coit had lived for a while at Toynbee in London and was strongly influenced by Felix Adler's belief that actions speak louder than words. Coit's settlement house was initially called the Lily Pleasure Club and its focus was to have been poor men. A year after it opened, however, women and children in need were also welcomed and the house was renamed the Neighborhood Guild (later it became the University Guild). More settlement houses soon followed, primarily on the Lower East Side.

In 1889, Jean Fine and Jane E. Robbins founded a settlement house exclusively for women. Fine and Robbins planned to educate the women of the slums. Riis and the King's Daughters were greatly influenced by the work of these settlement house pioneers, whose efforts inspired an entire movement. Settlement houses opened in all large U.S. cities, providing platforms for dynamic, influential, and innovative female reformers including Jane Addams, who founded Chicago's famous Hull House, and the New York nurse Lillian Wald, who established the Henry Street Settlement House, a few blocks from the King's Daughters. Both Addams and Wald became close friends of Riis's and formed long, rewarding working relationships with him.

Riis ultimately decided against quitting his career as a journalist. Most of his reform work, except his chairmanship of the Good Government Club, which lasted a year, was on a voluntary basis, and Riis was not confident that book revenues and lecture fees would earn him enough money to support his family. As he told Watson Gilder, "The deadly certainty of salary makes cowards of us all." Riis did, however, decide to close what had become his own news bureau, as running it was simply not compatible with his many other activities.

He had plenty of job opportunities. The *Evening Sun* and the *New York Sun* offered him the best deal, and he became their police reporter. While delivering stories to both papers, he could, according to a stipulation in his contract, freelance elsewhere. None other than the grand old man of the news business, Charles A. Dana, known as "the Old Chief," had recruited him. Dana was owner and editor in chief, and being hired by him was a symbolically weighted triumph for Riis. It was Dana to whom Riis had come for help in 1870, hoping he could somehow facilitate his enlistment in the French army. Riis's salary was $50 a week, twice as much as what he had earned when he was first hired by the *Tribune*.

Still, it was not nearly enough to support a family living in Richmond Hill. Maintaining a comfortable middle-class lifestyle—keeping up with the Joneses, as it were—required much more than $50 a week. Riis supplemented his income by freelancing for *The Critic*, *The Outlook*, and *The Century*; magazines that had once been a closed world to Riis now eagerly invited him in. Articles brought up to $200, and Riis grew increasingly dependent on this source of income. All the same, money still seemed to disappear, and the family somehow never seemed to be able to get ahead.

Lincoln Steffens noted that Riis, despite intermittent efforts to account for every penny spent and earned, could be careless with his money, apparently living by the creed that something would turn up when the till was empty. While this assessment seems unduly harsh, as Riis was in fact always worried about money and being able to support his family, Steffens's point that Riis had very little sense of the value of money was accurate. Riis never had great dreams of becoming independently wealthy. The press of children's piano lessons, servant's salary, school tuition, magazine and newspaper subscriptions, pipe tobacco, dinner parties and dinner cigars, clothes and shoes, Christmas presents, church dues, and insurance policies precluded that possibility.

※

RIIS, WHO MOSTLY voted Republican, was not in political sync with the Democratic *New York Sun*, and the editorial staff did not share Riis's strong reformist views. Still, Dana did not shy away from publishing articles written by reporters with opposing political views, and he was determined to keep Riis on his staff. Riis was treated extremely well by the paper, permitted to choose his own story topics and given an assistant to help him gather and report the news, which allowed him to focus on assembling the news and writing his characteristically colorful commentaries. Max Fischel, in his mid-twenties, was the son of Jewish immigrants from Prague. Fischel had been four years old when he arrived with his parents in the United States. He grew up in New York's tenements and had an insider's understanding of this world—in fact, in many ways he knew it better than Riis. Fischel started working for Riis in 1891 and the two soon became inseparable, Riis relying heavily on the young man's help. The loud roars of Riis shouting for his assistant could be heard down Mulberry Street throughout the day.

Fischel started work at 4:00 AM and summaries of the night's events would be ready for Riis on his desk by seven, when he arrived at the office. Riis could commence writing immediately; could meet the early deadline for the morning papers hours before the other papers, with only one reporter assigned to the beat, were ready to file their articles.

Middle-aged, with graying hair and a few extra pounds around his waist, Riis was as active and agile as ever and still preferred walking at a quick pace, almost a jog. With his booming laughter and upbeat, tireless storytelling, he was the undisputed king of Mulberry Street. Elisabeth ironed and starched his shirts and pressed his pants and jackets, but by the time he got to Mulberry Street he always looked scruffy, a dishabille that only added to his charm.

Because he now had an assistant, Riis floated above and beyond basic reporting and was not as close to his subject matter as when he had prowled the slums at all times of the day looking for stories. He had become an institution and had acquired a signature style that was popular among readers. In effect, he worked like the old painting masters who had young artists do the initial rough work, the artist himself then coming in and adding a few finishing touches. Eventually Riis let Fischel write most of his stories. He would edit them and add personal touches here and there. Since it was these touches that made the articles unique, Fischel in fact could not have written the stories without Riis. Riis also had the contacts, the access to important sources—relationships it had taken him years to establish. He knew people in top positions on Mulberry Street who had long since realized that it was futile to try to keep anything from this experienced and resourceful journalist.

Even though Riis had assigned much of his work to Fischel and no longer worked the long, grueling hours he used to, on occasion he wrote an article from the ground up. It was while working for the *Sun* that he wrote one of his most important series of stories, exposing unsafe drinking water.

One day in August 1891 Riis visited the Health Department and learned that a new report had been published, revealing that small amounts of nitrate had been found in the city's drinking water. The source of the city's drinking water was the Croton Reservoir. Health inspectors believed the elevated nitrate levels were caused by leaking sewers along the Croton River. If true, a cholera epidemic could be imminent. Alarmed, Riis set to work, first simply reporting the Health Department's findings, in a piece entitled "Sewage in Croton Water." Armed with his camera and a notebook, he followed up by traveling along the Croton River for a full week. He observed that many of the smaller towns dumped their sewage directly into the river. Riis shot revealing photos and took them to the Health Department for use as documentation. He then wrote yet another story, this time richly illustrated with drawings based on his photos. "SOME THINGS WE DRINK," ran the headline, and in the article Riis explained that New Yorkers were drinking contaminated water.

The article brought outrage; the City Council eventually earmarked several million dollars, a tremendous amount of money in the 1890s, to purchase land along the Croton River, the only means by which the authorities could ensure that waste was no longer dumped. Riis considered the story his biggest to date. As he later wrote, "It cost millions of dollars, but the cost was the merest trifle to what a cholera epidemic would have meant to New York in loss of commercial prestige, let alone human lives."

✳

AT HOME ON Beech Street, the family—Elisabeth, the four children, Ed, Clara, and John, almost teenagers, and the youngest, Katie—enjoyed more time with Riis. Though he still worked hard and sometimes was felled by exhaustion, the pressure was no longer as intense, and he had more energy to engage himself in family activities. He and Elisabeth could finally spend some long-deferred time together. In the evenings, after the children had fallen asleep and the dishes were washed and put away, they sat together in the living room, treasuring these quiet moments. Riis wrote and Elisabeth sewed. Often Riis read out loud to her from articles or book chapters he was working on.

He even took time off for summer vacations, which he had rarely done before. Every summer, he and Elisabeth went to the Berkshires alone. "Our life is like a romance. . . . God is to be thanked for all this," he confided to his cousin Emma Reinsholm in Ribe.

Their first summer romance, in 1894, when Riis was forty-five, produced a child, born Billy and nicknamed Vivi. Riis, who had not had much of an opportunity to enjoy his other children when they were small, was completely engrossed in the care of the new baby, often finding it difficult to leave him when he had to go to work in the morning.

Riis loved his other children as much as he did Billy, but with them there simply had not been enough time in the day for the kind of nurturing he now gave to his youngest child. In a letter to Emma Reinsholm, he admitted that he was finding it difficult to concentrate on his articles and that they would have to wait until Billy had gotten his first teeth.

Spending time with the children inspired Riis to write a book about them. Their games, sense of logic, and conversations fascinated him, and he took pleasure in documenting them. One day Katie said to her father: "You had better not be so sassy, you don't own this house alone." John replied: "Oh, yes he does." Katie: "No, he don't. God owns it too."

Riis also loved telling stories to his children. "I used to listen, in rapt attention," Katie remembered, "as he drew the stories out of his imagination and continued them from evening to evening. As they progressed, they grew more and more remarkable and fantastic. They were usually about animals, some of them weird creatures of his imagination, and others, just the animals we know but who did the most unheard of things."

Everyone in the Riis family loved animals, and Riis was concerned about the welfare of their large menagerie. He had always been incapable of killing animals while hunting with friends, even the fish he caught on fishing trips. Long gone was the time when, as a matter of course, he had shot sparrows in Ribe. The family kept a cow named Olivia; a cat, Jim; a dog, Bruno; yet another cat, with a broken tail, which came to the house during a blizzard; a calf that was being bottle-fed; eleven chickens and a rooster; twelve pigeons and "one pigeon, which thinks it is a hen and therefore could be found brooding with the other hens in the hencoop." Finally there were some rabbits that later ran away, and a canary, which Riis referred to as a South American bird.

The Riises were both influenced by childhood Christmases in Ribe, celebrated for weeks in accordance with age-old tradition. Katie remembered her childhood Christmases:

> The Yule was always a glorious time in our house. . . . There was always
> the Christmas Eve dinner with roast goose, stuffed with apples and prunes,
> the delicious Danish "apple-cake" my Mother made, covered with whipped

cream and dotted over with currant jelly and the risingröd, the traditional Danish dish that is made of rice cooked in milk, and seasoned well with butter, salt and cinnamon sticks. Somewhere in that bowl of risingröd, lay buried one, just one, almond. Lucky indeed was the one person who got the coveted almond in his portion, for he got a prize!

Following the pudding the family gathered around the Christmas tree to sing, accompanied by Elisabeth on the piano. Katie remembered her father on Christmas Eve:

A little box of some Danish candy had been sent from the old country, and Father, who delighted in sweets, sat reading beneath the tree, occasionally taking a piece of candy. Suddenly he awoke to the realization that he had eaten it all, and then his conscience began to prick. Sheepishly he turned the box over to see just whom the candy had been sent to, anyhow, and great was his relief when he found it was addressed to himself! It was for long a source of amusement in the family.

Riis had long been saving for a trip to Denmark, and in 1893 the family finally decided to go. It had been seventeen years since he and Elisabeth had left for the United States. Riis had waited because of a promise he had made to himself: He would not return to Denmark until he had made it in America.

That Riis achieved this triumph is eminently clear from the family's attire in the photo of the family reunion taken in Niels Edvard and Caroline's backyard in Ribe. The "American" part of the family are dressed in expensive suits and gowns: Elisabeth in a long, elegant black dress with a high collar adorned with a lovely cameo and the girls in frilly polka-dot and checkered dresses, little John in fashionable knickers and a fine coat with shiny buttons, Ed in a suit and tie. Even the customarily rumpled Riis is elegantly dressed in a suit, high collar, bow tie, and shiny shoes.

Riis paid a visit to The Castle with his cousin Emma. The Giørtzes no longer lived there, having vacated the house after their bankruptcy in the 1880s. Giørtz, the strict father and former business owner, had long since died in abject poverty in Copenhagen. Riis and Emma entered The Castle, which had been transformed into an art museum, and walked through the room where Giørtz had put forth his unkind ultimatum. As Riis retold the story to Emma, he seethed with anger. Riis had never forgiven his father-in-law for placing Elisabeth in such a humiliating situation. "It is either him or us!"—words Riis never forgot. Elisabeth, on the other hand, had completely divorced herself from the past. In fact, she had submerged herself so completely in her life in America that she was reluctant to go home for a visit. All her homesickness had vanished, and she was curious as to why Riis was so anxious to go back. Unlike Riis, she looked back at their departure from Denmark as an escape from something shameful and sad, which she never wanted to revisit. For Riis, leaving Denmark with his beloved bride had been a victory.

Despite Elisabeth's reservations, the visit to Denmark was a success for the whole family. For Riis perhaps the best part was the change in his relationship with his father, who seemed to have mellowed with age. They had no conflicts during the visit, and the retired schoolteacher seemed to have become a mild-mannered old gentleman. Niels Edvard embraced his son with love and did something he had never done before: He praised him, telling him how proud he was of all his accomplishments. Father and son spoke at length about Riis's publications—by this time Riis had published *The Battle with the Slum*, a sequel to *How the Other Half Lives*—and about his reform work in New York. It became clear to Riis that his father, though harsh and stern, had been concerned solely for his son's well-being. The only way he had known how to express this was through harsh criticism.

Now that Niels Edvard was assured that his son was well settled, he was ready to acknowledge his success, even to admit that Riis had far exceeded his high expectations. Riis's strongest memory from his trip to Denmark was an image of his father sitting in a chair with a smile on his face and one of Riis's books in his lap.

He never saw his father again. Six months later, Niels Edvard died at the age of seventy-eight.

19

The Making of an
American

R IIS HAD a lifelong proclivity for unlikely alliances, and out of
each of these alliances—with Elisabeth, with Theodore Roosevelt,
and, ultimately, with America—came his most unexpected, enduring,
and significant accomplishments.

The opening of Mulberry Bend Park constituted the culmination of
Riis's career as a reformer, and it would have been understandable if his
association with Roosevelt had ended there. That their friendship instead
deepened, surviving the vicissitudes of politics and, later, geographical dis-
placement, is a testament both to Riis's singular appeal and to the frisson
of urgency—the relentless insistence—that he brought to almost every
one of his important relationships. It was an urgency that, in Roosevelt's
case, was repaid in kind, even after he reached the White House.

After two years as police commissioner Roosevelt accepted an
appointment as assistant secretary of the navy, a position that required
him to move back to Washington, D.C. The job in New York had
earned him many political enemies, especially among German immigrants who opposed his enforcement of the Sunday Closing Act, ban-
ning sale of alcohol on the Christian Sabbath. In the following years
Roosevelt's journey to the presidency proceeded with unprecedented
speed. During the Spanish-American War he stepped down from his

navy post to lead the Rough Riders, returning home a decorated war
hero. Elected governor of New York, he moved on, in March 1901, to
the vice presidency of the United States under William McKinley. Six
months later, the assassination of McKinley catapulted Roosevelt, 42,
into the highest office in the land, and he became the youngest president in the nation's history.

Despite the hectic life he led, Roosevelt worked actively to maintain
his ties with Riis. The two years they had spent working together on
Mulberry Street had been formative for him, and he felt deeply indebted
to Riis for his insights into the slums and the issues of poverty. Though
the two men clearly no longer traveled in the same circles, their bond
was reinforced by the friendship that arose between Elisabeth Riis and
Roosevelt's second wife, Edith. The two couples met often for dinner.

When the two "slum warriors" made plans to reunite after being
apart for long periods of time, they addressed one another familiarly
and exuberantly, like brothers who had endured an extended period of
separation. "Dear Jake—You blessed old trump, I want to see you so
much. If you are in New York on Monday wont you come to the Union
League and lunch with me at one P.M.?" wrote Governor Roosevelt on
November 8, 1900. "When are you going to be in Washington?" he
asked the following year. "I really must see you here in the White House
not too long hence. I am getting homesick for you!"

When Roosevelt was governor, Riis acted as an informal advisor to
him on Lower East Side labor issues. The two men even went slumming
together again, as in the old days, inspecting sweatshops to make sure
employers treated their workers in accordance with existing labor laws.
"I should like to go over the different sweatshops with you. . . . we might
be in a condition to put things on a new basis, just as they were put on a
new basis in the police department after you and I began our midnight
tours," Roosevelt wrote. As president, he toyed with the idea of appoint-
ing Riis governor of the Danish West Indies (now the Virgin Islands),
then being sold to the United States. "I would like to be able to call you
Governor hereafter, and I should be awfully proud at being able to give
you the appointment; while I believe it to be a thoroughly wholesome
thing, from the standpoint of American citizenship, to let people see

what a self-sacrificing and disinterested career like yours may have in the way of at least partial acknowledgement," Roosevelt wrote to Riis on March 18, 1902. Riis was flattered, and even though he had never aimed for a political post, he briefly considered accepting Roosevelt's offer. He never had to make up his mind, as the sale of the islands did not go through until 1917.

Riis never hesitated to ask Roosevelt for the kind of favors one typically asks of close friends, such as helping Danes who were having problems with American authorities, and guiding his wayward son into the navy. John Riis was a young version of his father: rebellious, adventurous, and fed up with school. He ran away from home, making headlines when he was found in Atlantic City, about to run away to sea. Roosevelt wrote the navy command, but John was nearsighted and unable to meet the physical requirements of the navy. Not even Roosevelt could solve this problem.

When Riis in 1900 visited Denmark without his family to write a couple of travel pieces for *The Century* and visit his mother, who was in poor health, he brought with him a document from Roosevelt, declaring, "Jacob Riis is New York's most useful citizen." During his election campaign in 1903 Roosevelt created a stir in Richmond Hill when he visited with Riis. The president had traveled from Syracuse and sailed to Long Island, where he and his entourage of advisors and security staff boarded a special train to take him home to Sagamore Hill in Oyster Bay. Riis was traveling with the president on the train, and Roosevelt had promised to make a stop in Richmond Hill. The train arrived at nine o'clock in the morning on September 8, 1903. It was the first time in Richmond Hill's history that an American president had paid a visit. Hundreds of flags waved, and 2,000 people gathered at the station to greet Roosevelt. "The crowd felt closer to Mr. Roosevelt than they otherwise would," according to the *Brooklyn Daily Eagle*, "because of his warm personal relations with their neighbor, Mr. Riis." Katie Riis, 17, presented a bouquet of flowers to Roosevelt, who delivered a speech honoring Riis: "You know I am very fond of Mr. Riis, and the reason why is because when I preach about decent citizenship I can turn to him and think he has practiced just what I have been preaching." Noticeably moved, Riis joined his family on the platform, and as the train slowly pulled out of the station, he stood waving good-bye to his friend with the other citizens of Richmond Hill.

Riis's *Theodore the Citizen*, published in installments in 1904, hewed to a time-honored tradition of fulsome campaign biographies filled with unqualified praise:

> *Dear Jake:*
>
> *I feel ashamed on reading your biography of me, for I feel as though I ought to be dead in order to justify it! But I am very glad you have written it. I like the chapter that is just out the best of any, for it tells of our work together.*

One of the last times Riis communicated with his mother was in the company of Roosevelt. On December 18, 1902, he and Elisabeth were attending a dinner party at the White House. The following morning, while the two couples were breakfasting, Riis was talking about Ribe, his old friends, and his mother, who was seriously ill. According to Riis's, Edith Roosevelt was moved to tears.

"Let us send her a telegram and tell her we are thinking of her," she suggested, though she had never met Caroline Riis. A waiter appeared with pen and paper. While they drank their coffee, a telegram was dispatched to Riis's mother in Denmark, where the skies were already darkening and the day was waning, as was Caroline Riis's life.

> *The White House*
> *Mrs. Riis, Ribe, Denmark*
> *Your son is breakfasting with us. We send you our love and sympathy.*
> *Theodore and Edith Roosevelt*

The telegraph office in Ribe was new and telegrams rare, especially from as far away as America. When a delivery boy handed the bedridden Caroline a telegram, she was convinced a mistake had been made and insisted he return it to the office. Furthermore, Caroline did not know anyone named Edith or Theodore Roosevelt, so surely it could not be for her. Fortunately, both the delivery boy and Caroline Riis's neighbors understood, and made sure Caroline read her telegram from the White House.

The petite woman with the full face and kind eyes had been a loving and caring mother to all her children and an anchor for Riis in his childhood. Her children had been her life, and she never stopped caring about them. She had always sent Riis and his family in America loving letters, addressed to "My Dear Children."

On February 21, 1903, a few months before her eightieth birthday, Caroline's heart gave out. When Riis received the telegram from Elisabeth bearing the sad news, he was on a lecture tour between Colorado and California. At first he wanted to go home immediately to attend his mother's funeral, but he changed his mind, realizing that the trip would be too strenuous for him and that even if he left right away, he would not be able to make it home in time. Instead, he lavished Elisabeth with loving letters throughout the rest of his tour, beginning each with "Dearest Lamb" or "Sweet Lamb" and closing with "Your very own Muslingeskal [sea shell], who will always love you" or some variation. Riis clearly felt the shadow of death moving closer and missed being near his wife.

❋

A FEW YEARS EARLIER, in 1900, Riis had felt the breath of death upon his own body. He had been ill most of the year with chest pains and difficulty breathing. His condition was exacerbated by stress in connection with the extensive preparations for Kate's wedding. The house on Beech Street had been a frenzy of activity for months, and Riis, who did not care for the lavish and ostentatious event it was promising to become, wrote to a friend, "Isn't our style, I think it is vulgar." Hundreds of guest were invited to the wedding, including Vice President Theodore Roosevelt and family.

Riis collapsed shortly after the wedding. His doctors later determined that he suffered from angina pectoris and an enlarged heart muscle. His treatment was bed rest and no smoking, which forced Riis to give up his treasured cigars. It was a depressing time, and he was in low spirits. He wrote to his doctor that he really was not finished with life yet. But his condition was serious and he was bedridden for several weeks, convinced he was dying. Roosevelt shared his fear and took time off to spend entire days with his "brother" Jake. Riis's condition improved slowly, and after two months of vacation in Canada, he felt able to resume a normal life, though even he recognized that going back to being a daily reporter would be far too stressful. Instead he focused his energy on magazine articles, lectures, and books, working mostly at home. He had not forgotten his carpentering skills and built himself an office in the back yard where he could work undisturbed. Riis wrote three books during the 1890s: *The Children of the Poor, Out of Mulberry Street*, and *A Ten Years' War*. They received fine reviews but did not sell nearly as well as his first book. One journey through the slums with Riis had apparently been enough for most readers.

But Riis was to make his mark as a writer again with his autobiography. The humor, drama, and endearing love story of *The Making of an American*, published in 1901, riveted readers, and the book became a best seller. The flavor of the Riises' marriage is encapsulated in the book's seventh chapter, told in Elisabeth's voice—or Riis's approximation of it. Riis finds his conceit for the marriage midway through the chapter when, with the newsman's eye for the "real" story, he abruptly takes back the reins of authorship, in a passage describing his letters to Elisabeth following the death of her fiancé Raymond Baumann:

> *Strange to say, Jacob's mother had never sent the letter in which I refused him a second time. Perhaps she thought his constancy and great love would at last touch my heart, longing as it was for somebody to cling to. So that he got my last letter first. . . . he came [to Ribe] in a few weeks. . . .*
>
> *And now, after twenty-five years—*ELISABETH
>
> *I cut the rest of it off, because I am the editor and want to begin again here myself, and what is the use of being an editor unless you can cut "copy"? Also, it is not good for woman to allow her to say too much. She has already said too much about that letter. I have got it in my pocket, and I guess I ought to know.*

Elisabeth, who had lived a relatively anonymous existence, suddenly became a celebrity. Readers from New York to California fell in love with her just as Riis had. *The Making of an American* was reprinted several times, proceeds from the sale of the book enabling Riis to do something he had never been able to do before: save money for their retirement. In a single year he set aside $30,000.

On March 5, 1901, the Riises celebrated their twenty-fifth wedding anniversary. The day began with a reception at the King's Daughters Settlement House on Henry Street attended by Bishop Henry Codman Potter and a large number of well-known reformers and reporters, including Charles Dana, his son Paul, Felix Adler, and Josephine Shaw Lowell. Riis was praised for his great humanity and compassion, without which, it was said, the settlement house would not be the success it was. It had been decided, during a secret board meeting, to rename the settlement house after Riis, and this announcement was made by Bishop Potter. When Riis rose to thank Bishop Potter and the other board members, he had to stifle sobs. Both Riis and Elisabeth, who was active in the settlement house and had organized outings to Richmond Hill for the children, were made honorary vice presidents of the newly christened Jacob A. Riis Neighborhood Settlement House.

In the evening the Riises gave a lavish party at their house in Richmond Hill, attended by dozens of prominent New Yorkers. The *Brooklyn Daily Eagle*, which covered the event, referred to the house on Beech Street as the "Little White House" and to Riis as "Sir Jacob." Riis had recently been knighted by the Danish king. A photo of the Riises taken that day shows them seated on a bench studying the cover of a magazine, perhaps featuring one of Riis's articles. On their faces one clearly sees evidence of the inner peace and quiet satisfaction emanating from two people who have shared a rich life of public service as well as the fruits of their private successes.

❈

IN THE SUMMER OF 1904, during a visit to Denmark—the second time Riis and his family had gone back—Elisabeth fell ill. Riis had a long lecture tour scheduled upon their return to the United States, and though he had qualms about leaving Elisabeth, he carried through with his plans. While he was away, Elisabeth was diagnosed with a type of rheumatism that affected her muscles. At times she was incapable of standing. By March 1905 she was forced to remain in bed. On March 10, she wrote to their son John. Her handwriting, feeble and difficult to read, attested to her weakness. It had always been neat, even elegant, but here it was, in places, barely legible. Her chief concern was to assure her son that she would get better and that they would see each other again.

"Darling John!" she began, and proceeded to tell him that she had been bedridden since his father had attended the inauguration of President Roosevelt.

> *Am now lying on my back, but feel much better. Hope to be O.K. in a few days. Will then tell you all about [the] inauguration. Thanks for your letters. Father is in Bridgeport today. He says and I say you must do what you think best about staying on the ranch or going to Denver. Father thinks Denver is best. But whatever you do, promise me to come home for Christmas! I am not as strong as I was and I might never see you. Though, I do hope to live a good many years yet. But I am looking forward to next Christmas in the hope of having all of us here together . . .*

In early May she contracted pneumonia. Riis cut his tour short and returned home to care for her, writing to his friends in the Jacob A. Riis Settlement House: "O pray for us, all of you, that she may stay with us for we cannot think of life without her. Every hour our hearts are broken as she lies struggling with death." On May 18, Riis wrote two sentences in his notebook: "The lamb is dead. God help us." On the same day, he noted in their family Bible that Elisabeth had been 52 years, 11 months, and 13 days old when she died.

Roosevelt, who had been sending letters to Riis daily, wrote on the day of Elisabeth's death:

> *Beloved Friend:*
>
> *In the terrible elemental grief, no one, no matter how close, can give any real comfort. All I can say is what you know, my dear friend with the bruised and aching heart. You know how my wife and I loved the dear, dear one who has gone before you, you know how we love you, how we think of you, how*

we feel for your crushing calamity. The life of you two was an ideal life. Later, though not now, you will be able to realize what a wealth of precious memories are left you. You and I, friend, are now in range of the rifle pits; and if we live, sorrows like this must befall us. May the UNSEEN *powers be with you as you now walk in the shadow.*

> *Ever Your Friend,*
> *Theodore Roosevelt*

Elisabeth was buried in her wedding dress and laid to rest in Maple Grove Cemetery next to their two children. Atop her gravestone balanced the small marble figure of a lamb.

With only Billy now on Beech Street, Riis fell into a profound depression, regretting the time he had spent away from home and losing faith, he said, both in God and in the value of his life's work.

"This was probably the most difficult time of his life," wrote John Riis Owre, Riis's grandson. It seemed everything went wrong. John, working as a national park ranger, was restless and had marital problems. Ed, the Riises' eldest son, was also in an unhappy marriage and, like John, seemed incapable of settling down. Clara and her husband had financial problems and were dependent on Riis for support. In addition to helping Clara, Riis still had tuition for his two youngest children to worry about, but he felt incapable of getting back to work touring the country. And he could not bring himself to write.

Riis had many close friends to help him through his grief, and, despite his misgivings, he was soon working again, fundraising for a children's hospital. He managed to raise a significant sum, and the success seemed to bring him back to life. With most of the family scattered all over the country, he went back on tour. It had been his great wish that the family would come to Beech Street for Christmas in 1906, but he never managed to get everyone together and instead went off to a health resort, the St. Joseph's Sanatorium in Michigan, where he spent Christmas alone. It was the first time he had spent a holiday on his own since he was the editor of the *South Brooklyn News* thirty years earlier.

Riis hated being alone and knew his youngest son, just thirteen when Elisabeth died, needed a mother figure in his life. To his children's great surprise, Riis remarried only two years after Elisabeth's death. His new wife, Mary Phillips, was young, intelligent, well-educated, elegant, and loving. She was thirty years old—twenty-eight years younger than Riis—and had become Riis's secretary after Elisabeth's death. One of Riis's friends, Roger Tracey, later said that "he would have to marry again. He could not get along without a woman to look after him, nor could he live a contented life without a woman's companionship. The only question was whether he would ever be lucky enough to meet a congenial mate. He did."

Mary Phillips had met Riis at one of his lectures a few years earlier and was a great admirer of his work. Both acknowledged later that theirs was not at first a marriage of passion. As Mary told John Riis Owre:

> I really did not love your grandfather when I married him. I admired him enormously—I was fascinated by him—he was the most exciting man I had ever met—but I did not love him. It was not until several years later, when I realized that I really loved him. He came into the room and I saw the tilt of his head under the light, and I said to myself "I love him, I love him . . ."

To Katie, Riis wrote: ". . . friendship between man and wife is that which abides. Don't you know it is for that reason I chose Mary to go the rest of the way with me—we are such friends. No, I do not suppose you can understand yet, but you will."

Though they started out as friends, in later years there was nothing platonic about their marriage, their letters suggesting both ardor and comfort. While traveling Riis wrote: "I myself long for your soft arms, dear, and your soft bosom to lay my head on. . . . Isn't it good to think of home? Beloved one, I think of you early and late . . . and thank God who sent you to comfort me when the world was dark, I know she loves you too." The *she* refers of course to Elisabeth, to whom Riis referred frequently in their letters.

In 1909 Mary became pregnant but gave birth to a stillborn child. The child was buried next to Elisabeth and her two children in Maple Grove Cemetery.

✳

THE BIOGRAPHER risks romanticizing the life of a subject who him-self was prone to the same pitfall as a writer. Still, one may venture that Riis's life is primarily a story of love—a story in which Mary Phillips is an important chapter. Riis's great love for Elisabeth was of course the greatest influence on his story; his love for her drove him to leave Denmark and immigrate to the United States. His once unconditional love for his hometown, Ribe, inspired his philanthropic work and his compassion for others. His childhood had in most respects been won-derful, and though he acknowledged his tendency to romanticize it, he also recognized that, especially when compared to the children in the slums, he had been blessed with a privileged childhood. Riis believed all children in the world, regardless of class and ethnicity, deserved a simi-larly good start in life—a goal he presupposed all could agree on work-ing toward realizing.

Unfortunately, Riis's great love for his hometown—which he had shared with the world in his 1909 tribute to Ribe, *The Old Town*—was not reciprocated. On the contrary, the citizens of Ribe were skeptical of Riis and cold-shouldered him on many occasions. It would take years before Riis understood and accepted that he was not welcome in Ribe.

Why did Ripensers turn their back on someone like Riis, who by all rights should have made them exceedingly proud? Ribe is, as we have seen, situated in the western part of Denmark In this relatively poor part of the country, people were reserved and withdrawn. There was no room in their hearts and minds for someone like Riis, who had achieved so much, had by their standards become so rich, and who, to them, was loud, boisterous, and something of a braggart. Perhaps Ripensers did not understand or could not acknowledge that Riis's loud enthusiasm was fueled by his love for them and for his town.

It was during the summer of 1904 that Riis discovered how much he was disliked in Ribe. He had traveled to Denmark with his family for the reopening of Ribe Cathedral, which had undergone a major restora-tion. When they docked in Copenhagen harbor, they received an invitation to lunch from the crown prince of Denmark. Riis had achieved considerable fame in Denmark for his reform work in the United States, but the recognition he enjoyed in Copenhagen he did not obtain in Ribe. The *Ribe Stiftstidende* carried only a small notice of Riis's arrival: "Mr. Jacob Riis and wife arrive in Ribe today for an extended visit." He was not invited to the gala dinner held in honor of the reopening of the cathedral until Christian IX, who was attending the event, requested his presence. To the great consternation of most Ripensers, the king praised Riis in a speech at the dinner.

That Riis was baffled by the animosity he encountered in Ribe reflects his naïveté about his hometown. Riis had left Ribe when he was young, too young to have developed a mature understanding of its culture and too young, in the eyes of those who remained, to call himself a true Ripenser. Growing up in Ribe, he had, and accurately so, perceived it as a place with wonderful opportunities for children, who could roam freely in a spectacular natural environment. But because he left at such a young age, he never realized that once the children of Ribe grew up, the town transformed from a vast universe full of opportunities to a remarkably small place. It was therefore understandably hard, if not impossible, for adult Ripensers to recognize and appreciate a man who had had many opportunities and much success in his life.

One could have wished that Riis had not taken quite so long to discover the true nature of Ribe's citizens; it would have saved him much grief. After Elisabeth's death, Riis wrote the Church Council, offering to donate two candlesticks and a beautifully colored triptych church window, showing the Good Shepherd, his sheep, and their lamb—the lamb symbolizing, of course, Elisabeth—to the cathedral in his first wife's memory. He also wrote to the local museum, Elisabeth's childhood home, offering to contribute a painting of her to their collection. He envisioned it hanging in the room where they had celebrated their wedding. The museum responded coolly, expressing concern that the painting would be too primitive for their collection of accomplished Danish artists.

When the Church Council, after several months, finally answered Riis's letter, their tone was even chillier than the museum's. They turned down the windows because, as they said, the style Riis had suggested was unsuitable for the old cathedral, although Riis had plainly assured the council that they were free to choose the style they deemed appropriate.

Riis was astounded. Never had he imagined that he would be scorned by his hometown. Ribe died for him in that moment. In 1913, the last year of his life, he wrote to Emma Reinsholm:

> I sincerely doubt I will ever return to Europe. I no longer feel drawn to the place like I used to. Ever since Mother [Elisabeth] during the dinner at the reopening of the Cathedral said to me: Come let us go back home. We do not belong here anymore, I've felt thus and this sentiment has become stronger over the years. For the sake of the ideal, it would be better to let the Old Town remain but a childhood memory.

The triptych was instead donated to the Church of the Resurrection in Richmond Hill, where it can still be seen today.

❀

IN HIS OLD AGE Riis may be said to have founded his own little Ribe, or at least tried to create a country paradise in its image. He and Mary had long talked about moving out of the city, away from the noise and stress of city life. In 1911 they bought Pine Brook Farm, with thirty-two acres of land. Founded in the seventeenth century, Barre was in some sense a New England version of Ribe, with its charming square and its houses surrounded by white picket fences. The farm required considerable renovation and its fields had been badly neglected. It cost $3,500, and the Riises expected to carry out renovations for about the same amount. Their estimate proved far off the mark, and they ended up spending almost all of their savings on repairs. To their great dismay, they also discovered that the land was too poor for crops and could only be used for cattle and hay production, which was not very lucrative. Riis soon realized that farm work was exceedingly exhausting and did not give them enough to live on. What proved to be harder for Riis, however, was the social isolation. He had grown accustomed to a busy life through his work and social connections.

He spent the summer making a pond, where he would later set out trout, and removing rocks from the property's stony fields. He had imagined he would spend much of his time fishing and hunting, but although he had a fishing rod and a gun waiting for him in a shed, he somehow never got around to it. Riis's romantic dream of living in the country was exactly that, a dream. The reality of country life had turned out to involve considerably more backbreaking work than he had anticipated.

In 1912 Riis picked up where he had left off before they bought the farm. They still had the house in Richmond Hill (it was not sold until 1913), and with that as home base, Riis began touring the country again. He also once again supported Roosevelt, when his friend decided to run as an independent presidential candidate on the Progressive Party ticket, then known as the Bull Moose Party. Riis threw himself wholeheartedly into the campaign, though he realized that Roosevelt had no chance of winning. He traveled to all the larger cities on the East Coast and in the Midwest, including Chicago, campaigning for Roosevelt.

The years 1911 and 1912 were for the most part good ones for Riis. Successful with his lectures, he was happy to be working with issues of poverty again. His marriage to Mary had brought new meaning to his life. He had hired people to work the farm, which allowed him time to enjoy the place when he was there, and there was much to enjoy: The area had a magisterial beauty, with its pine forests, gurgling creeks, fresh air, and rolling hills. There was a spectacular view from his front porch, and he often sat there at night taking in the sunset. From the porch he could glimpse Riverside Cemetery, where he knew he would one day be buried; the thought filled him with peace. He was making a considerable amount of money, and knowing that he would be able to save up enough money for Mary to live on after his death provided him with a feeling of reassurance.

But toward the end of 1912 Riis's optimism began to evaporate. Once again financial problems loomed. He was burdened not only by the expenses of the farm but by his children, who continued to depend on him for support. The worst blow to his equanimity, however, was the diagnosis of coronary heart disease. He had begun to experience digestive and breathing problems, apparently caused by his heart condition.

During 1913 his health deteriorated, and he was forced to acknowledge that he probably did not have long to live. Worried about Mary, who would have very little to live on if he died soon, and despite doctors' warnings, he continued to tour the country with his lectures, driven by the need to earn money. He was hoping that he could beat the odds, as he had done so many times before. But even his strong will was no match for his heart condition.

※

RIIS WAS BURIED on the afternoon of May 28, 1914. His funeral was small and simple, as he had requested. The service was held in the room where he died, conducted by one of his old friends from New York, the Rev. Endicott Peabody, founder of the Groton School. Present were a few of his closest friends from the Settlement House, Mary, Ed, Billy, and Katie. Clara, who lived in California, was not able to make it home in time.

After a short service, the members of Groton's boys' choir sang two of Riis's favorite hymns, "Abide with Me" and "Hark! Hark, My Soul!"

> *Rest comes at length: though life be long and dreary,*
> *The day must dawn, and darksome night be past;*
> *Faith's journeys end in welcome to the weary,*
> *And Heaven, the heart's true home, will come at last.*

After the last notes of the hymn had sounded, local farm workers carried Riis's casket to Riverside Cemetery, where he was laid to rest in a small, secluded corner. He had not wanted a traditional tombstone but had requested a simple granite stone with no inscription. Riis had further asked that no flowers be sent. The family had put a notice in the papers on his behalf inviting people instead to donate money to charities helping the children of the slums.

EPILOGUE

TEN YEARS AFTER Riis's death, a twenty-one-year-old Russian immigrant named Alexander Alland arrived in New York City. Born in Sevastopol, Crimea, he had fled with his parents to Turkey during the Russian civil war before arriving alone in the United States.

Had it not been for Alland, Riis might very well have been forgotten. Said to have built a camera out of cardboard when he was twelve years old, Alland took on a string of menial jobs in New York but remained passionate about photography. Within a few years he was able to support himself as a freelance photographer, and by the 1930s he had become a sought-after instructor of photography.

Alland's preferred subjects were representatives of the many different ethnic groups in New York City, and in 1941, a reviewer compared his muckraking instincts to Riis's. Alland had heard of Riis and knew that there were similarities in their personal histories, but he did not know much about Riis's work as a police reporter and writer. Like many others, he was also not aware of the significant body of photographs Riis had produced. Although the photographs taken for *How the Other Half Lives* were an important tool in Riis's reform work, they were viewed as secondary to his books and articles. When Riis died, none of the obituaries mentioned his photographs.

Riis was of course a photographer for only a brief period; it was assumed

286

that he had stopped shooting pictures in 1898 or perhaps even earlier. His photographs were also mainly intended for his slideshows. In later years, Riis bought other people's photographs to illustrate his books rather than take his own. Thus when he asserted in his memoirs that he really was not a photographer, he was to a certain extent speaking the truth.

When Alland read *The Making of an American*, he was surprised to learn that Riis had taken photos of the poor. He was further astounded when he saw some of the reproductions in *How the Other Half Lives*. Where were all these photographs? he wondered. He went to museums, photo archives, and libraries, but nobody knew.

In the early 1940s Alland contacted Mary Riis, who, according to Alland's book about Riis, *Jacob A. Riis: Photographer & Citizen* (1974), did not show any great interest in helping him find the photographs. She referred him to Riis's son Billy, who agreed to help but never quite got around to it. Frustrated by the family's lack of interest, Alland next sought the help of a photo curator at the Museum of the City of New York, Grace Mayer, asking her to write a letter to the family. Alland felt that if the museum showed an interest in the photographs, the family might be more interested in helping him locate them.

Grace Mayer sent a letter to the family in 1945, and as Alland had suspected, her request proved effective. Billy went up to the old farm in Massachusetts and found a box of lantern slides. They were in poor shape, but Alland managed to restore them, rephotographing them and touching them up.

But his great reward came a year later, when the house on Beech Street was deemed in such poor condition that it had to be torn down.

During a cleanup preceding the demolition, the family who lived in the house found a box of Riis's original photographs: 412 glass plates, 161 slides, and 193 paper photos. The owner of the house looked up Billy, who lived in Manhattan, and as he was not home at the time, the man simply placed the box of photographs on his doorstep.

If it had rained, or the box had been stolen or moved by accident— it could easily have been taken for trash—we would know almost nothing of Riis's legacy as a photographer. We may never even have heard about Riis, as he had been all but forgotten by the larger public.

Billy Riis handed the box over to Alland, who immediately set to work restoring the photographs. Himself a superb photographer, Alland was also a bit of a magician in a darkroom. What emerged from his developer fluid was as much his work as it was Riis's. He used all of his expertise and technical skill—something Riis had never had—to crop and resize the photos, making them even more powerful.

Alland showed the finished photographs to Grace Mayer, who admitted that they deserved a heavily publicized exhibit at the Museum of the City of New York. "Special Exhibition, 'The Battle with the Slum' 1887–1897. Fifty Prints by Alexander Alland from the original negatives by Jacob A. Riis" was shown in the spring of 1947. The exhibit was a great success, the photographs so popular that they became a traveling exhibit, touring all over the United States and abroad.

The Alland/Riis photos were soon the Museum of the City of New York's most sought-after works, making their way into history books, photography books, and books on the slums. Eventually they came to define America's, as well as the rest of the world's, view of New York during the great waves of immigration.

The photographs are still widely used as educational material, and most people today are familiar with Riis through his photographs even if they have never heard his name. The photographs tell stories that are as moving and powerful as Riis's articles and books once were. In Alland's masterful rendering, they have inspired generations of historians to read Riis's books, in particular *How the Other Half Lives*, required reading since the 1960s for all American university students of journalism, history, and photography.

Thus Riis not only formed his contemporaries' view of the slums but will, thanks to Alland's work, do the same for generations to come. The prologue to Alland's book on Riis was written by none other than world-renowned photographer Ansel Adams, helping to ensure Riis a prominent place in the history of photography nearly fifty years after his death. Since the mid-1950s Riis has been identified as the inventor of modern photojournalism. That he would one day be more famous for his photographs than his books would have surprised Riis tremendously, for he considered these haunting images but a small part of his life's work.

≈ NOTES ≈

Documents from the followüng archives have been used:

Barre Historical Society
The Danish Emigration Archives, Aalborg
The Danish Royal Library
    The Newspaper Collection
Harvard University Library
    The Theodore Roosevelt Collection
Historical Archives of Ribe
Library of Congress
    Papers of Jacob A. Riis
    The Theodore Roosevelt Papers
The Library of Kathedralskolen, Ribe
National Archives, New York
New York City Municipal Records
New York Public Library
    Genealogy and Local History
    Jacob A. Riis Collection (Manuscripts and Rare Books Collection)
    Map Division
    Microfilm Collection / U.S. Newspapers
Richmond Hill Historical Society

PART ONE: RESTLESSNESS

PROLOGUE: "THE IDEAL AMERICAN"

1   It was 1:47 AM: *Worcester Gazette*, May 15, 1914.
1   the etched lines: letter from Ed Riis to John Riis, May 31, 1914. Papers of Jacob A. Riis, Library of Congress.
1   collapsed in New Orleans: *New York Times*, April 18, 1914.

1   Yet even though: Mary Philips to Theodore Roosevelt, September 3, 1913. Papers of Jacob
     A. Riis, Library of Congress.

2   He was considered: *New York Times*, May 26, 1914.

3   "in a more serious": *New York Times*, April 19, 1914.

3   The three companions: *Worcester Gazette*, May 15, 1914. J. Riis Owre, Epilogue, in Jacob
     Riis, *The Making of an American. A New Edition with an Epilogue by His Grandson, J. Riis
     Owre* (New York: Macmillan, 1979), 335.

3   where his fishing rod: letter from Ed Riis to John Riis, May 31, 1914. Papers of Jacob A. Riis,
     Library of Congress.

4   Shortly after his: *New York Times*, May 11, 1914.

4   "We are pleased:" *Worcester Gazette*, May 22, 1914.

4   Once, many years ago: Riis, *The Making of an American* (New York: Macmillan, 1901), 287.
     All quotations except those identified as being from the J. Riis Owre/1979 edition are taken
     from this source.

4   "dirty, little, ragged": Riis, *Silver Cross*, August 1889.

6   a staggering one thousand: According to a contract with the *Chicago Tribune* Business
     Department, May 8, 1900. Papers of Jacob A. Riis, Library of Congress.

6   Christian IX, knighted him: Riis, *The Making of an American*, 425.

6   Sir Jacob: *Brooklyn Eagle* March 2, 1901.

6   returned to his home in Brooklyn: It is known that Ed lived in Brooklyn because his address
     is listed in Riis's notebook, 1914. Papers of Jacob A. Riis, Library of Congress.

6   "magnificent": letter from Ed Riis to John Riis, May 31, 1914. Papers of Jacob A. Riis, Library
     of Congress.

7   "In common with other New York papers": *New York Times*, May 21, 1914.

7   "Jacob Riis Is Dying": *New York Times*, May 25, 1914.

7   He arrived in Barre: letter from Ed Riis to John Riis, May 31, 1914. Papers of Jacob A. Riis,
     Library of Congress.

7   "We Loved Him": *Worcester Gazette*, June 15, 1914.

8   "I am grieved more than I can express": telegram, June 8, 1914. Jacob A. Riis Papers, New
     York Public Library.

8   "Read your book": Riis, *Theodore Roosevelt: The Citizen* (New York: Macmillan, 1904), 131;
     Theodore Roosevelt, *An Autobiography* (New York: Macmillan, 1913), 174.

9   "distinguished man": handwritten letter from Roosevelt to Riis, December 29, 1897. Theo-
     dore Roosevelt Papers, Library of Congress.

1: THE OLD TOWN

13   "as if fallen": Jørgen Bukdahl, *Den gamle Bys Drøm* (København: Hagerup, 1921), 20–21.

13   Ribe was a prosperous: Most literature on the early history of Ribe is written in the Dan-
     ish except for a chapter in Riis, *The Old Town* (New York: Macmillan, 1909), 169ff. For a
     brief Danish introduction to Ribe's history, see Mogens Bencard, *Ribe i tusind år* (Ribe: Bygd,
     1978). A more detailed historical work is J. Kinch, *Ribe bys historie og beskrivelse*. Repografisk
     genudgivelse af Jysk Selskab for Historie (Århus: Universitetsforlaget i Århus, 1985).

14   The last woman: J. Kinch, *Ribe bys historie og beskrivelse*, 624. David Grønlund, *Historiske
     efterretninger om de i Ribe Bye for Hexerie forfulgte og brændte Mennesker* (Ribe: Historisk Sam-
     fund for Ribe Amt, 1973).

15   culture of conservatism: Susanne Benthien, "Ribe i guldalderen," unpublished manuscript.
     Historical Archives of Ribe.

15   "When a man's time": Riis, *The Old Town*, 8ff., and Riis, *The Making of an American*, 12ff.
15   "take an evening stroll": Aage Jacobsen, *Ribe. En kortfattet historie og en vejledning for en 2½ times rundvisning gennem byen* (Ribe: Dansk Hjemstavns Forlag, 1954), 30.
15   annual flood season: Ib Gram-Jensen, *Stormfloder*, Scientific Report 91-1, 1991, Danish Meteorological Institute, Copenhagen.
16   "The town is small": H. V. Clausen, *Jylland. Enkle billeder* (København: Gyldendal, 1935), 1.
16   "When I remember": Mathilde Cold, *Minder fra 80'ernes jul i Ribe* (Ribe: Bentzons boghandel, 1965), 39ff.
16   It was said of one boy: Roy Lobove, Introduction, in Riis, *The Making of an American* (New York: Harper Torchbooks, 1966), xvi–xviii. Riis himself writes: ". . . perhaps it was the open, the woods, the freedom of my Danish fields I loved, the contrast that was hateful. I hate darkness and dirt anywhere, and naturally want to let in the light. I will have no dark corners in my own cellar" (*The Making of an American*, 435).

2: THE EARLY YEARS

19   Ribe was at the center: The best book on Ribe and the war is Torsten Friis, *Forsvaret af Ribe og togtet mod Tønder* (Ribe: Liljebjerget, 1998).
20   quite "civilized": *Ribe Stiftstidende*, May 18, 1848.
20   Niels Edvard stayed: Riis, *The Old Town*, 26ff. His account of the war is lively, but many details are inaccurate.
21   "The only thing": H. Stemann, *Minder fra Biskop Hertz's Tid: efter hans Datters (Lucie Elise Hertz's) Optegnelser* (Ribe Amt: Særtryk, 1906), 17.
21   A young scholar: Peter Adler, *Peter Adlers Breve* (Ribe: Eget Forlag, 1937), 14–15.
21   travelers were known: Riis, "A Christmas Story," *South Brooklyn News*, Christmas Edition, 1884. In this story about traveling to Ribe in the winter, Riis claims that almost every year people would vanish on the moors.
22   In 1850 Russia: Friis, *Forsvaret af Ribe og togtet mod Tønder*, 58.
22   four of whom: "Statement of Jacob A. Riis, 1895." In this statement to his family doctor, Riis relates the medical history of his family. Papers of Jacob A. Riis, Library of Congress.
22   "He was talked out of": Riis, *The Making of an American*, 22.
22   Riis was particularly: As adults, Riis and Reinsholm wrote numerous letters to each that reflect their great friendship. The letters are on file at the Danish Emigration Archives, Aalborg, Denmark.
22   His relationship: Emma Reinsholm to Katie Riis, February 22, 1922. Papers of Jacob A. Riis, Library of Congress.
22   at least one maid: author's interview with Angla Kuhlman, August 2003. Kuhlman is the grandchild of Sophie Tarp, Riis's youngest sister.
23   once a thriving: Riis, *The Old Town*, 51.
23   bottle-message: ibid., 139.
23   "I tried" and "As a means": ibid., 137.
24   "I defy anyone": ibid., 131.
24   The mess in front: Riis, *The Making of an American*, 8.
24   Riis noted: ibid., 22.
25   "amuse with conversation": Susanne Benthien, ". . . at samles her som brødre og som Venner. Foreningen Klubbens oprettelse og første år," in *By, marsk og geest* (1997): 9.
25   Ribe County budget: J. P. Trap, *Statistisk-topografisk beskrivelse af Kongeriget Danmark*, vol. 2 (København: Gad, 1858), 93.

25   Jacob the Delver: Riis, *The Making of an American*, 8.

25   "This box is for starlings": Riis, *The Old Town*, 4.

26   The first larger animal: ibid., 146–47.

26   "Drop your bait": ibid.

26   In fact, Ribe: *Ribe Politikorps 1855–1990*, booklet, Historical Archives of Ribe; Riis, *The Old Town*, 35.

27   "We boys caught": Riis, *The Making of an American*, 18.

27   "The two-foot-high": *Petrea Müllers Dagbog 1832–35*, booklet. Historical Archives of Ribe.

27   On July 6, 1860: *Ribe Dom og Kirkebøger*, 1853–1865, C589-17.

27   "He has departed!": author's interview with Angla Kuhlman, August 2003.

27   For years she kept: Louise Ware, *Jacob A. Riis: Police Reporter, Reformer, Useful Citizen* (New York, London: D. Appleton-Century, 1938), 9.

28   "it became but a shadow": Emma Reinsholm to Katie Riis, December 28, 1922. Papers of Jacob A. Riis, Library of Congress.

28   "a poisoned old house": "Statement of Jacob A. Riis, 1895."

28   A chronological list: Ware, *Jacob A. Riis*, 5.

28   "was known to be" and "it harmed": Bjørn Kornerup, *Ribe Katedralskoles historie*, vol 2 (København: Gyldendal, 1952), 368.

29   "a small, elegant": Emma Reinsholm, "Family history," unpublished document. Papers of Jacob A. Riis, Library of Congress.

29   "One morning he": ibid.

30   "Clement's Love": Jacob A. Riis Papers, New York Public Library (box 6).

30   so utterly alone: Recollections of Judge Petersen, one of Niels Edvard's former students, in *Ripenserbladet*, June 1923.

30   "Of all my sons": Emma Reinsholm to Katie Riis, October 9, 1917. Jacob A. Riis Papers, Library of Congress.

30   An avid reader: Riis, *The Making of an American*, 4.

30   "I helped Father": Riis to Reinsholm, March 18, 1906. Jacob A. Riis Papers, Library of Congress.

31   "Disciples must arrive": *Ribe Katedral Skoles Skoleprogrammer* and *Disciplinariske Bestemmelser*, available in the school library of the Ribe Katedralskole.

31   "It is merely harking back to": Riis, The Old Town, 191.

32   "I do not know": Emma Reinsholm to Katie Riis, October 9, 1917. Jacob A. Riis Papers, Library of Congress.

32   "I think his father": ibid.

32   Niels Edvard's only response: Niels Edvard to Riis, November 29, 1875. Jacob A. Riis Papers, Library of Congress.

32   "I've only found two misprints": Niels Edvard to Riis, December 3, 1890. Jacob A. Riis Papers, Library of Congress.

32   Riis's relationship with his mother: How much Caroline cared for Riis is evident from the many letters she sent to the Riis family in New York. The letters are in the Jacob A. Riis Papers, New York Public Library.

32   Born in 1823: Reinsholm: "Family history."

3: HEARTACHE

35   economic boom: *Betænkning fra den af Ministeriet for offentlige Arbejder nedsatte Kommission angaaende Ribe Bys økonomiske Forhold*, København, 1906. A public survey assessing Ribe's economic strengths and weaknesses in the latter part of the nineteenth century.

35   The most successful: Benthien "Ribe i guldalderen."

35   Designed by: William Gelius, *Ribe Kunstmuseum 100 år* (Ribe: Ribe Kunstmuseum, 1991).

36   Among those who worked: Riis, *The Making of an American*, 23.

36   "[German troops] ravaged": *Ribe Stiftstidende*, May 2, 1864.

37   Catholic Mass: Riis, *The Old Town*, 61.

37   Like many of his peers: Riis, *The Making of an American*, 25.

37   Still just fifteen: ibid., 23.

37   Born in the Jutland: Delilah Stokes Foster, *Gustav Waldemar Nelson: His Family in America and Denmark* (Baltimore: Gateway Press, 1998), 196ff.

38   "I am so happy": Riis, *The Making of an American*, 152–53.

38   "On the outskirts": ibid., 1.

39   Had he been strikingly: Riis's height and build estimated by his grandchild Martha (Mimi) Moore Riis. Interview with the author, February 2003.

39   ". . . how I could do such a thing": Riis, *The Making of an American*, 25.

40   Copenhagen was the most: Kristian Hvidt, *Politikens og Gyldendals Danmarkshistorie, 1850–1900* (København: Gyldendal og Politikens Forlag, 1990), 172ff.

40   three days after his arrival: Riis, *The Making of an American*, 28.

41   an elderly Hans Christian Andersen: ibid.

41   not particularly welcoming: Hvidt, *Politikens og Gyldendals Danmarkshistorie, 1850–1900*, 172.

41   "A real sailor": The details about Elisabeth's stay in Copenhagen and the quotes from her letters on the following pages are from her correspondence with her girlfriend from Ribe, Christine Bendtsen. Historical Archives of Ribe.

42   A conscientious student: Susanne Benthien: "En kærlighedshistorie," unpublished manuscript. Historical Archives of Ribe.

42   "[she] has always shown": ibid.

42   His obsession: Riis, *The Making of an American*, 31.

43   "I don't have to tell you": ibid., 154.

43   "bruised my heart": letter from Riis to a childhood friend in Ribe, Malfriede Øgmundsen, October 17, 1871. Jacob A. Riis Papers, The National Danish Media Museum, Odense.

43   "I will never be": Riis, diary, October 17, 1871. Jacob A. Riis Papers, New York Public Library.

44   Riis's parents: Ware, *Jacob A. Riis*, 12.

44   local tavern: Riis in a letter to his friends, May 4, 1870. Danish Emigration Archives, Aalborg.

44   There was a mantel clock: Riis, "The Boy," unpublished autobiographical sketch. Papers of Jacob A. Riis, Library of Congress.

4: "A TERRIBLE HOMESICKNESS"

49   500,000 Danes: For the latest and the most thorough research on Scandinavian immigration to the United States, see Torben Grøngaard Jeppesen, *Danske i USA 1850–2000—en demografisk, social og kulturgeografisk undersøgelse af de danske immigranter og deres efterkommere* (Odense: Odense Bys Museer, 2005).

49   "He never asked me": Riis, *The Making of an American*, 32.

50   Among his belongings: Riis, *The Making of an American*, 32 and 154.

50   40 American dollars: ibid., 34.

50   "The first thing": Georg B. Hesse, *Amerikanske Forhold. Raad og Oplysninger for Emigranter* (København, 1871).

50   "It is probably": Riis in a letter to his friends Scholl, Thun, Bruun, and H. Ferslev, May 4, 1870. Danish Emigration Archives, Aalborg.

51   passage on the *Rising Star*: In his letter to his friends Riis mentioned a steamer that was sailing directly to New York from Copenhagen; this steamer was totally booked. According to travel schedules in Danish newspapers in early May, this ship was the *Rising Star*.

51   The *Iowa* was: Information on the Iowa can be found at http://www.theshipslist.com/ships/descriptions/ShipsI-J.html. Passenger lists with information on nationality are available in the National Archives, New York.

51   broad-shouldered German: Riis, *The Making of an American*, 40.

51   had contrived a new identity: The police records of immigrants are available in the Danish Emigration Archives, Aalborg, and can be retrieved online at http://www.emiarch.dk/search.php3?l=da.

51   "I was tired of hammer": Riis, *The Making of an American*, 36.

52   more than 95 percent: Maldwyn A. Jones, "Transatlantic Steerage Conditions. From Sail to Steam, 1819–1920," in Birgit Flemming Larsen, ed., *On Distant Shores* (Aalborg: Danish World Wide Archives, 1993), 363.

52   The first few days of June: weather report, *New York Tribune*, June 6, 1870.

52   "It was a beautiful": Riis, *The Making of an American*, 35.

52   its 60,000 to 70,000 buildings: James McCabe, *Lights and Shadows of New York Life; or, the Sights and Sensations of the Great City* (Philadelphia, Chicago: National Publishing Company, 1872), 55.

52   New York in 1870: ibid., 51.

52   number of inhabitants doubled: Kenneth Jackson, ed., *The Encyclopedia of New York* (New Haven, CT: Yale University Press, 1995), 923.

53   the city quintupled: Ric Burns and James Sanders, *New York: An Illustrated History* (New York: Alfred A. Knopf, 1999), 153.

53   20,000 inhabitants: J. Owen Grundy, *History of Jersey City, 1609–1976* (Jersey City: W. E. Knight, 1976), 41.

53   $106 million: Isaac Newton Phelps-Stokes, *The Iconography of Manhattan Island* (New York: Robert H. Dodd, 1915–1928), 1936.

54   notoriously filthy Immigration Station: George J. Svejda, *Castle Garden as an Immigrant Depot, 1855–1890*. Division of History, Office of Archeological Preservation (Washington, D.C., 1968), 134.

54   "We [in Denmark] discerned": Riis, *The Making of an American*, 38.

54   15,000 vehicles passed through Broadway: Burns and Sanders, *New York: An Illustrated History*, 132.

54   For a brief period in 1865: membership card to the local gun club, 1868. Jacob A. Riis Papers (box 6), New York Public Library.

54   Riis wandered: Riis, *The Making of an American*, 38.

55   "Smoke, smoke, smoke": James Barton, "Pittsburgh," *Atlantic Monthly*, January 1868.

56   700 houses, several schools: Robert Walter Smith, *History of Armstrong County* (Chicago: Waterman, Watkins & Co., 1883), 569.

56   "The Letter That Never": Riis, *The Making of an American*, 42.

56   "I climbed the hills": ibid., 42.

56   After a few weeks: ibid., 44.

57   While it is undoubtedly: Riis to Malfriede Øgmundsen, July 25, 1870, and October 1, 1870, Jacob A. Riis Papers, The Danish National Media Museum, Odense; Riis, *The Making of an American*, 46–47.

57   It was letters like these: Niels Peter Stilling, "The Emigrant Letter as a Stimulus to Emigration," in Larsen, *On Distant Shores*, 363.

57   There were no Frenchmen: Riis to Malfriede Øgmundsen, July 25, 1870, Jacob A. Riis Papers, The Danish National Media Museum, Odense; Riis, *The Making of an American*, 50ff.

59   "There, go and": Riis, *The Making of an American*, 56.

59   his daydreaming got him: ibid., 61–62.

60   "It was the last straw": ibid., 65. Riis's attempts to get to France on a French ship are also vividly recorded in his letter to Malfriede Øgmundsen, October 1, 1870. Jacob A. Riis Papers, The Danish National Media Museum, Odense.

5: THE FAST MARCH TO BUFFALO

63   Every fall: Edwin Burrows and Mike Wallace, *Gotham* (New York: Oxford University Press, 1999), 1030.

63   "I joined the great army": Riis, *The Making of an American*, 66.

64   "Strangers coming to New York": McCabe, *Lights and Shadows of New York Life*, 57.

64   In fact, as: Burrows and Wallace, *Gotham*, 967.

64   at least 500 existed: Timothy Gifoyle, *City of Eros* (New York: W. W. Norton, 1992), 126.

64   7,000 bars: Warren Sloat, *A Battle for the Soul of New York* (New York: Cooper Square Press, 2002), 11.

64   As a reporter Riis: Jacob Riis, *How the Other Half Lives* (New York: Charles Scribner's Sons, 1890), 210.

65   The most notorious: Tyler Anbinder, *Five Points: The New York City Neighborhood That Invented Tap Dance, Stole Elections, and Became the World's Most Notorious Slum* (New York: Free Press, 2001), 337ff. For conditions in the slums, see also New York State Assembly, *The Tenement House Problem in New York. For the Information of the Commission Legislation Affecting Tenement and Lodging Houses, Provided for in Chapter 84, Laws of 1887, December 14, 1887* (New York: W. P. Mitchell, 1887). Report issued by the Health Department.

65   "This is the place": Charles Dickens, *American Notes* (New York: Harper, 1842), 107–8.

66   According to Board of Health: John Duffy, *A History of Public Health, 1866–1966* (New York: Russell Sage Foundation, 1974), 758.

66   Not until 1881 did New York: Burrows and Wallace, *Gotham*, 948.

66   "A tour around": *New York Times*, March 6, 1871.

67   Below street level: Anbinder, *Five Points*, 337 ff; Richard Plunz, *A History of Housing in New York* (New York: Columbia University Press, 1990), 33.

67   According to an 1873 study: *The Sanitarian: A Monthly Journal*, May 1873.

68   Delmonico's menu: Michael and Ariane Batterberry, *On the Town in New York: The Landmark History of Eating, Drinking, and Entertainments from the American Revolution to the Food Revolution* (New York: Routledge, 1999), 72.

68   magnificent dining rooms': "Dinner at Delmonico's in the Evening," *New York Times*, April 16, 1871.

68   "Get up there!": Riis, *The Making of an American*, 69.

68   19,000 flickering gas lights: McCabe, *Lights and Shadows of New York Life*, 52.

69   "How should he": Riis, *The Making of an American*, 75.

69   "For the first time": Riis, *The Making of an American*, 76.

70   The counsul: ibid., 77.

70   British journalist B. P. Barry: B. P. Barry: *Over the Atlantic and Great Western Railway* (London: Sampson Low, Son, and Marston, 1866).

70 "energetic kissing games": Riis, *The Making of an American*, 80.
71 Twice a week: ibid., 84.
72 His chores included: ibid., 90.
72 "The news changed": Riis's diary, October 2, 1871. Jacob A. Riis Papers, New York Public Library. All subsequent references to "Riis's diary" are to the diaries in the New York Public Library.
73 Buffalo was at: *A Complete Pocket Guide to the City of Buffalo, N.Y.* (Buffalo: Jno. Laughlin, 1892).
73 After five weeks: Riis's diary, October 2, 1871.

6: "MY LOVELY DREAM"

75 "Vol. II": The diaries are kept in the Jacob A. Riis Papers, New York Public Library. They are mostly written in Danish. All quotes on the following pages are translations.
76 "[It] only paid": Riis's diary, October 14, 1871.
77 "I am so unhappy": Riis's diary, October 22, 1871.
77 "Now I must interrupt": ibid., November 7, 1871.
77 "Rønne's friendship": ibid., November 25, 1871.
78 "no letter": ibid., December 26, 1871.
78 "The other day": ibid., February 11, 1872.
79 "What are you?" Riis, *The Making of an American*, 99. In his diary, Riis does not mention the meetings with the editors. Maybe he made up these details in his autobiography in order to write a more lively account.
80 "in a foreign, heathen": Riis's diary, March 21, 1872.
80 "I am 333 miles": Riis's diary, April 12, 1872.
81 "looked just like": Riis's diary, May 17, 1872.
81 then a prestigious job: Edwin Gabler, *The American Telegrapher: A Social History, 1860–1900* (New Brunswick: Rutgers University Press, 1988), 40 and 57ff.
81 "my lovely dream": ibid. and June 15, 1872.
82 ad for a job: Riis, *The Making of an American*, 107.
82 Most women had more: Esther S. Berney: *A Collectors' Guide to Pressing Irons and Trivets* (New York: Crown, 1977).
82 "Work, work, work" and "I'm all business now": Riis's diary, September 15, 1872.
82 "I'm not sleeping well": ibid., November 3, 1872.
83 "Dunkirk, Dunkirk! Dunkirk": ibid., July 21, 1872.
83 "Somehow, I will sell these irons": ibid., August 12, 1872.
83 "Which was probably a good thing": ibid., August 31, 1872.
83 in his memoirs: Riis, *The Making of an American*, 111.
84 "The air is": Riis's diary, October 20, 1872.

7: "TRUE LOVE CAN NEVER DIE"

88 To lead the cavalry: N. C. Esman: *Det Aarøske Strejfkorps* (København: Bianco Lunos Kgl. Bogtrykkeri, 1884), 2ff.
88 "handsome, strong": Oberstløjtnant Bjergager, "Kaptajn Aarøes Strejfkorps i Marts og April. Beretning til Krigsministeriet," unpublished report to the Danish Ministry of War, 1891. Det Kongelige Bibliotek (The Danish Royal Library).
89 "Alles in Ordnung": Esman: *Det Aarøske Strejfkorps*, 20.

89 "The officers flew": Quoted in Susanne Benthien, "En kjærlighedshistorie—Jacob A. Riis og Elisabeth Nielsen," *Ripenser-Bladet*, January 1992, vol. 11, no. 5.

89 Baumann moved: ibid.

90 "the one I favor": Elisabeth Giørtz's letters to Christine Bendtsen, 1868–1875, are kept in the Historical Archives of Ribe.

90 "must be tall": ibid.

90 "so different": Elisabeth Giørtz to Christine Bendtsen, June 14, 1872.

90 "Never did the sun": Riis, *The Making of an American*, 155.

91 "Two ladies": Riis's diary, February 15, 1873.

91 "It is so much easier": Riis's diary, January 26, 1873.

91 "Everything is big in America": Niels Edvard and Caroline Riis to Jacob A. Riis March 26, 1873. Papers of Jacob A. Riis, Library of Congress.

91 "I have always had": Riis's diary, February 15, 1873.

91 During the first half: For details about Chicago in 1873, see David Lowe, *The Great Chicago Fire: In Eyewitness Accounts and 70 Contemporary Photographs* (New York: Dover, 1979).

93 "Chicago is such an ugly city": Riis's diary, April 6, 1873.

93 "Everyone seems to have": ibid., March 19, 1873.

94 "People started talking": Niels Edvard and Caroline Riis to Jacob A. Riis, March 26, 1873. Papers of Jacob A. Riis, Library of Congress.

94 "I will not": ibid.

94 "All is hopeless": Riis's diary, May 18, 1873.

94 "In the name": Riis's diary, June 5, 1873.

8: "THE STILL CENTRE OF A CYCLONE"

97 "How many liaisons": Riis to Malfriede Øgmundsen, June 6, 1873. Jacob A. Riis Papers, The Danish National Media Museum, Odense.

98 "One does not": Riis, *The Making of an American*, 115.

98 He imagined: ibid., 116, and Riis's diary, July 27, 1873.

98 He established a routine: Riis's diary, October 18, 1873.

98 He applied for a job: ibid.

99 "nowhere to nowhere": Burrows and Wallace, *Gotham*, 1021.

99 "Why, what are you": Riis, *The Making of an American*, 122; Riis's diary, November 29, 1873.

100 Thompson sent a letter: Riis, *The Making of an American*, 123–25.

100 "the still centre": ibid., 125.

101 "You will do": ibid.

101 "The pay is not great": Riis's diary, November 29, 1873.

101 "This business is a strange": ibid.

102 "The position we occupy": *New York Tribune*, November 29, 1873.

102 was approached by: Riis's diary, June 14, 1874; Riis, *The Making of an American*, 129.

103 "I think," he wrote: Riis's diary, June 14, 1874.

103 One evening shortly: Riis's diary, December 24, 1874.

9: A SECOND PROPOSAL

105 Their summer wedding: Benthien, "En kælighedshistorie."

106 "It is so strange": Elisabeth Giørtz to Christine Bendtsen, April 21, 1874.

107 "he is so, so tired": ibid.

107 "Good morning": Elisabeth Giørtz to Christine Bendtsen, November 11, 1874.

107 "tough guys on their": Riis's diary, June 14, 1874.

108 "Imagine, on": Riis's diary, December 24, 1874.

108 "My dear Jacob": Niels Edvard to Jacob Riis, November 29, 1874. Papers of Jacob A. Riis, Library of Congress.

109 "It is a sad letter": Riis's diary, December 24, 1874.

109 "I lay down": ibid.

110 "No, no, Jacob": Riis, The Making of an American, 135.

110 "I kept two printers busy": Riis, The Making of an American, 132.

111 "I will definitely": Riis's diary, August 17, 1875.

111 "The three shots": Elisabeth Giørtz to Christine Bendtsen, November 11, 1874.

111 "seriously unintelligent": ibid.

112 "a pale, anemic": Elisabeth Giørtz to Christine Bendtsen, January 16, 1875.

112 "to be loved": ibid.

113 "Dear Jacob": Elisabeth Giørtz to Jacob Riis, October 6, 1875. Papers of Jacob A. Riis, Library of Congress.

114 "I came in late": Riis's diary, November 7, 1875.

115 "Wish you joy": Riis, The Making of an American, 150.

PART TWO: RIIS AND THE OTHER HALF
10: "FAT AND STRONG"

119 On a rainy afternoon: Riis, The Making of an American, 167ff.

120 "This way": ibid., 169.

120 "Bless my soul": ibid., 170.

121 As the young men had lain dying: Emma Reinsholm to Katie Riis, October 9, 1917. Papers of Jacob A. Riis, Library of Congress.

122 It was dark: Riis, The Making of an American, 167ff.

122 according to a letter: Emma Reinsholm to Katie Riis, April 29, 1920. Papers of Jacob A. Riis, Library of Congress.

123 church register: Historical Archives of Ribe.

123 townspeople filled: Riis, The Making of an American, 179.

123 "fat and strong, whereas": ibid.

124 Of 250,000: The City of Brooklyn (New York: H. and C. M. Goodsend, 1871), 18ff.

124 Elisabeth was almost immediately: Riis, The Making of an American, 175ff.

124 Fortunately, she spoke: ibid.

125 "I mind": Riis, The Making of an American, 177.

125 According to a letter Riis wrote: quoted in Ware, Jacob A. Riis, 34–35.

125 "My darling Musling": Elisabeth Riis to Jacob Riis, August 27, 1879. Papers of Jacob A. Riis, Library of Congress.

126 "A chief reason why": Riis, The Making of an American, 184.

126 He had a magic lantern: ibid.

128 The railroad industry: Robert Bruce, The Year of Violence (Indianapolis: Bobbs-Merrill, 1959), 28ff.

129 Entire neighborhoods in Pittsburgh: Stefan Lorant, Pittsburgh: The Story of an American City (Pittsburgh: Esselmont Books, 1999), 171.

129 "Pittsburg[h] at the Mercy": *New York Times*, July 23, 1877.

129 Riis and Wells arrived in Elmira: Riis, *The Making of an American*, 178.

130 "In all my life": Riis, *The Making of an American*, 190.

11: POLICE REPORTER

133 Shanks lived: Shanks obituary, *New York Times*, February 24, 1905. See also www.famous americans.net/williamfranklingoreshanks.

133 The most important paper: Frank Luther Mott, *American Journalism: A History of Newspapers in the United States Through 260 Years, 1690–1950* (New York: Macmillan, 1950), 418ff.

133 sent reporter Henry Morton Stanley on: For a well-written account of the Stanley expedition see Martin Dugard, *Into Africa: The Epic Adventures of Stanley & Livingstone* (New York: Doubleday, 2003).

134 Born in 1811: Richard Kluger, *The Paper: The Life and Death of the New York Herald Tribune* (New York: Alfred A. Knopf, 1986), 19ff.

135 The worst blow, however: ibid., 126f.

136 Whitelaw Reid, ambitious: Bingham Duncan, *Whitelaw Reid: Journalist, Politician, Diplomat* (Athens: University of Georgia Press, 1975), 56ff; Mott, *American Journalism*, 422–24; Kluger, *The Paper*, 132.

136 Shanks himself was: Shanks obituary, *New York Times*, February 24, 1905.

137 Because it had become: Mott, *American Journalism*, 414.

138 Under Whitelaw Reid's: Duncan, *Whitelaw Reid*, 55. Kluger, *The Paper*, 138.

138 Initially, Riis's work: Riis, *The Making of an American*, 193–94.

139 "SEVEN LIVES LOST": *New York Tribune*, February 2, 1878.

140 "Is that the way": Riis, *The Making of an American*, 196.

140 " 'Mr. Riis' ": ibid.

140 "And with this": Riis, The Making of an American, 195–97.

141 Alexander T. Stewart, the so-called: David B. Sicilia, "A. T. Stewart" in Jackson, *The Encyclopedia of New York City*, 327.

141 On the night: George W. Walling, *Recollections of a New York Chief of Police* (New York: Caxton Book Concern, 1887), 224.

141 When the body: *New York Times*, November 8 and November 9, 1878.

142 "GRAVE-ROBBERS UNCAUGHT": *New York Tribune*, November 11, 1878.

142 "I slept little or none": Riis, *The Making of an American*, 221.

142 "the *Tribune* police": ibid., 222.

143 "Got staff appointment": ibid., 199.

143 Marble Palace: *Morning Journal*, March 20, 1883.

143 "it was my task to cover": *Riis, The Making of an American*, 203.

143 the Dutchman: Riis, *The Making of an American*, 221.

145 "the only renown": ibid., 202.

145 Mulberry Street had: Frank Marshall White, "The Passing of '300 Mulberry Street,' " *Harper's Weekly*, 1908, and "Inspector Byrnes and the 'Third Degree,' " *Harper's Weekly*, June 18, 1910.

146 chamber of horrors: Jacob Riis in the *Morning Journal* (unknown date). Papers of Jacob A. Riis, Library of Congress.

146 song of the nightstick: Jacob Riis, "Ominous Signals," *Morning Journal*, December 30, 1883. Papers of Jacob A. Riis, Library of Congress.

146 A gong was also: ibid.

147 Three thousand men: Moses King, *King's Handbook of New York City: An Outline, History, and Description of the Great Metropolis* (Boston, 1892), 481ff.

147 "Clubber" Williams loved: Marylinn Johnson, *Street Justice: A History of Police Violence* (Boston: Beacon Press, 2003), 41ff; *New York Times*, "Farewell to Williams," May 25, 1895.

147 Thomas F. Byrnes, born: Wright, "Inspector Byrnes"; "Ex-Chief Byrnes Dies of Cancer," *New York Times*, May 8, 1910; "Chief Byrnes's Record. He Completes Twenty-Five Years of Service To-Morrow," *New York Times*, December 9, 1888.

148 In a remarkably: Riis, *Sunday Mercury*, March 23, 1884. Newspaper clippings in his scrapbook. Papers of Jacob A. Riis, Library of Congress.

149 "The department reporter": Riis, *The Making of an American*, 215.

149 "TALENT ON THE FORCE": Riis, *Mail & Express*, January 14, 1886.

150 "an old man": Riis, *Evening Sun*, November 19, 1889.

150 "I went along as a kind": Riis, *How the Other Half Lives*, 71.

12: ANATOMY OF THE SLUMS

155 On June 13, 1871: The story about Rasmus Andersen is based on his diaries, available at the Danish Seamen's Church, Brooklyn.

157 "a small man": Victor Bancke, *40 Aar i Amerika. Oplevelser og Hændelser* (København: A. Rasmussens Bogtrykkeri, 1935), 27.

158 "He was a loving and good father": Ware, *Jacob A. Riis*, 61.

159 With a weekly: For incomes of the lower classes, see Riis, *How the Other Half Lives*, 173. See also Riis, "How the Other Half Lives," *Scribner's*, December 1889.

159 "An argument against": Riis, *Aftenposten*, undated, newspaper clipping in Riis's scrapbook. Papers of Jacob A. Riis, Library of Congress.

160 "Secretary of the Treasury": ibid.

160 "I telephoned the office": Riis to Mr. Bigony, April 20, 1886. Papers of Jacob A. Riis, Library of Congress.

161 The slums were at their worst: Riis, "Pestilence Nurseries. Summer Sufferings of Dwellers in Tenement Houses," *New York World*, June 11, 1883.

161 tens of thousands: "Life in Tenement Houses," *New York Times*, October 24, 1884.

161 "We are all just": Riis, *The Poor in Great Cities: Their Problems and What Is Done to Solve Them* (New York: Charles Scribner's Sons, 1895), 80.

161 "The father's hands": Riis, *How the Other Half Lives*, 168ff.

162 It was Riis who coined: Anbinder, *Five Points*, 357.

163 "The degree to which": Riis, "Visiting Tenement-Houses," *New York Tribune*, July 18, 1881.

163 "The halls in nearly": William T. Elsing, "Life in New York Tenement Houses," *Scribner's*, June 1892.

163 Ironically, the construction: Anbinder, *Five Points*, 347–48.

164 stood at 15,000: Riis, *How the Other Half Lives*, 301.

164 Mulberry Bend, the size: Verlyn Klinkenborg, "The Conscience of Place: Where the Other Half Lived," *Mother Jones*, July/August 2001, 55.

164 In the hardest-hit: New York State Assembly, *The Tenement House Problem in New York*, The City of New York, Bureau of Vital Statistics, New York City Department of Health and Mental Hygiene, *Summary of Vital Statistics 2002*.

164 Each year about one hundred: Riis, *How the Other Half Lives*, 188.

164 The suicide rate: "Vital Statistics," *New York Times*, January 1, 1887.

164 "never been other": Riis, *How the Other Half Lives*, 55.

165 Randall's Island: Riis, *How the Other Half Lives*, 255ff.

165 Riis's style was: Mott, *American Journalism*, 430ff.

166 "THE RIVER'S UNKNOWN DEAD": Riis, *The New York World*, May 25, 1883.

167 "SENSATIONAL HAPPENINGS": The headlines and subheadings are from newspapers in Riis's scrapbook. Papers of Jacob A. Riis, Library of Congress.

168 "The readiness of the poor": Riis, *How the Other Half Lives*, 172.

168 "The mothers in their": Riis, "Visiting Tenement-Houses."

168 "In a rear room": Riis, *New York Mercury*, June 14, 1885.

171 the poor as "sinful": This view is reflected in books such as Charles Loring Brace, *The Dangerous Classes of New York and Twenty Years of Work Among Them* (New York: Wynkoop & Hallenbeck, 1872).

172 "LIFE'S STRUGGLE": Riis, *New York Tribune*, July 9, 1881.

172 "A young man": Riis, *New York Tribune*, January 24.

173 "poverty or the fear of": *Mail & Express*, October 9, 1889.

173 "too tired": Riis, *How the Other Half Lives*, 11.

174 Riis's reasons: Riis, *The Making of an American*, 235.

174 According to a legend: Herbert Asbury, *The Gangs of New York* (New York: Alfred A. Knopf, 1927), 206ff.

175 "I have often": Riis, *The Making of an American*, 237.

176 "Whose knife": ibid., 238

176 "I knew even": ibid., 239.

176 "Go back and stay": ibid., 236.

13: THE REFORMERS

179 The 1880s also saw: Burrows and Wallace, *Gotham*, 1065ff.

180 Albon Platt Man: "Memorial of Albon P. Man. An Annual Meeting of the Association of the Bar of the City of New York," January 12, 1892. Richmond Hill Historical Society. Carl Ballenas and Nancy Cataladi: *Richmond Hill: Images of America* (Charleston: Arcadia Publishing, 2002). "For Sixty Years a Lawyer. The Interesting Career of the Late Albon P. Man," *New York Times*, April 1, 1891.

181 "I have to be": Riis, *The Making of an American*, 284.

181 "I came upon Richmond Hill": ibid., 286.

182 She quickly became part: "Interesting Women," *Brooklyn Eagle*, August 4, 1901.

182 The family joined: Raymond C. Hauser and George F. Hagerman, *The Story of Union Congregational Church—Commemorating Sixty Years of Progress and Achievement* (Richmond Hill, NY: Pilgrim Press, 1947), 15.

183 "A new life began": Riis, *The Making of an American*, 242.

183 American views on: Historical overview based on Walter I. Trattner, *From Poor Law to Welfare State* (New York: Free Press, 1974), 1–110.

185 "the great unwashed": Duffy, *A History of Public Health in New York City*, 43.

186 with $155,730 spent: James Trager, *The New York Chronology: The Ultimate Compendium of Events, People, and Anecdotes from the Dutch to the Present* (New York: Harper Resource, 2003), 203.

187 a reaction was inevitable: Burrows and Wallace, *Gotham*, 1071, and McGerr, *A Fierce Discontent: The Rise and Fall of the Progressive Movement in America* (New York: Free Press, 2003), 135ff.

187   Among the less: Richard Hofstader, *The Age of Reform* (New York: Vintage, 1955), 135ff.

187   Henry George was: Burrows and Wallace, *Gotham*, 1031.

189   Though George was not: ibid.

189   His greatest success: Ware, *Jacob A. Riis*, 54.

190   According to *King's Handbook*: King, *King's Handbook of New York City*, 383ff.

190   One reform leader: Burrows and Wallace, *Gotham*, 1031.

191   Vagabonds should not receive: Kim Hopper, "Homelessness," in Jackson, *The Encyclopedia of the City of New York*, 552.

192   By the time Riis: James B. Lane, *Jacob A. Riis and the American City* (Port Washington: Kennikat Press, 1974), 37ff; Burrows and Wallace, *Gotham*, 1158–61.

192   Another reformer whose: For biographical details about Charles Loring Brace, see Stephen O'Connor, *Orphan Trains: The Story of Charles Loring Brace* (Boston: Houghton Mifflin, 2001).

193   A reformer with a less: Robert Guttchen, *Felix Adler* (New York: Twayne, 1973), 17ff.

195   "I sat through": *The Battle with the Slum*, 38–39, and *The Making of an American*, 246.

195   The Health Department tried: Duffy, *A History of Public Health, 1866–1966*.

197   "[I]t has often been said": John Griscom, *Sanitary Conditions of the Laboring Population of New York* (Harper's Brothers, New York, 1845).

199   "In 1881 there was an epidemic": Roger Tracey's unpublished biographical sketch of his friend Jacob Riis. Papers of Jacob A. Riis, Library of Congress.

200   He befriended another: Biographical details about Nagle are drawn from "Dr. John T. Nagle Dead," *New York Times*, July 15, 1919.

14: INTRUDERS

203   "to take pictures": Riis, *The Making of an American*, 267.

204   "It was upon my": ibid., 266.

204   "To watch the picture": ibid., 265.

204   Attempts to photograph: "Using a Gun in Photography," *New York Times*, May 14, 1882.

205   "highly flammable": Michael J. Carlebach, *The Origins of Photojournalism in America* (Washington, D.C.: Smithsonian Institution Press, 1992), 152.

206   Photographer Eadweard Muybridge: ibid., 154ff.

207   A major article in: Maren Stange, *Symbols of Ideal Life: Social Documentary Photography in America, 1890–1950* (Cambridge: Cambridge University Press, 1989), 6.

207   "GUNNING FOR PICTURES": "Gunning for Pictures. Photographs Taken by a Pistol Flash," *New York Times*, October 12, 1887.

208   fashionable detective camera: *Morning Journal*, February 12, 1888.

208   "the intruders": ibid.

209   the amateur photographers already: ibid. and Riis, *The Making of an American*, 273.

210   "FLASHES FROM THE SLUM": *New York Sun*, February 12, 1888.

210   Halftone photomechanical: Carlebach, *The Origins of Photojournalism in America*, 16.

211   It was used for the first time: The photograph entitled A Scene in Shantytown was published on March 4, 1880, and depicted old shacks near Central Park.

211   Skilled handmade woodcut: Carlebach, *The Origins of Photojournalism in America*, 159.

211   "I am flattered by": *Morning Journal*, February 12, 1888.

211   In 1887, an anonymous: Riis saved the one-dollar check and the note from the writer and glued it into his scrapbook. Paper of Jacob A. Riis, Library of Congress (box 12).

212   "real photos": "Caught with the Camera. Amateurs on the Hunt for Picturesque Views," *New York Times*, January 14, 1890.

212 "I am downright sorry": Riis, *The Making of an American*, 265.

213 Every year 4,000 people: Riis, *How the Other Half Lives*, 302.

213 "The very blackness": Riis, *The Making of an American*, 271.

214 "a particularly tattered": Riis, *How the Other Half Lives*, 78.

214 "like rats": illustrated lecture, 1894. Jacob A. Riis Papers, The New York Public Library.

215 Riis could also at times be so clumsy: Riis, *The Making of an American*, 271.

215 "novel photographic views": *New York Herald*, January 27, 1888.

215 called his photos "shocking": "A Police Reporter's Camera," *New Jersey News*, January 27, 1888.

216 "No man quarrels with": quoted in Carlebach, *The Origins of Photojournalism in America*, 1.

217 The spontaneity: Naomi Rosenblum, *A World History of Photography*, 3rd ed. (New York: Abbeville, 1997), 358–59.

15: FLOWER POWER

219 Saturday, March 10: Mary Cable, *The Blizzard of '88* (New York: Atheneum, 1988), 1.

220 "THE REMARKABLE STORM": *Long Island Democrat*, March 13, 1888.

221 On February 28: Newspaper clippings from Riis's scrapbook. Papers of Jacob A. Riis, New York Public Library.

222 "THE OTHER HALF": ibid.

222 "To wit": ibid.

223 "There were three": Riis, "What One Flower Did," *Garden* magazine, December 1897.

223 "The shout": ibid.

223 Two months: Riis, *The Making of an American*, 291.

224 "FLOWERS FOR THE POOR": *New York Tribune*, June 23, 1888.

225 On June 24 more: *New York Tribune*, June 25, 1888.

225 "Wherever we went": Riis, *The Making of an American*, 289.

225 The well-known priest: ibid., 290.

225 "Last Sunday": *New York World*, June 26, 1888.

16: THE MANIFESTO

229 "In a church": Riis, *The Making of an American*, 297.

230 He was also the author: Lane, *Jacob A. Riis and the American City*, 48ff.

230 Thus in spite of: Riis, *The Making of an American*, 297.

230 "find a man who could": ibid.

231 Present in the audience: ibid., 300.

232 "Turn but a dozen": Riis, "How the Other Half Lives: Studies Among the Tenements," *Scribner's* magazine, December 1889.

234 It was from Jeannette Gilder: Gilder to Riis, December 5, 1889. Papers of Jacob A. Riis, Library of Congress.

235 "Are we going to lose you now?": Riis, *The Making of an American*, 303ff.

235 "It was my habit": ibid.

235 "I got up at five o'clock": ibid.

236 Elisabeth became pregnant: Riis to A. T. Schauffler, December 5, 1890. Papers of Jacob A. Riis, Library of Congress.

236 The tenements "generate evil": Riis, *How the Other Half Lives*, 15ff.

236 The reader is taken back: ibid., 20f.

237   "It was the stir and bustle": ibid.
237   "the tenants died": ibid., 10.
238   "Be a little careful, please!": ibid., 28ff.
238   Several of Riis's: For his descriptions of Jews, see ibid., 107 and 110; Italians, 48ff.; Germans, 27; blacks, 155; Chinese, 92 and 102.
238   following the civil rights: Examples of his later critics include Francesco Cordasco, *Jacob Riis Revisited: Poverty and the Slum* (Garden City, NY: Doubleday, 1968), xxi; Lewis Fried and John Fierst, *Jacob A. Riis: A Reference Guide* (Boston: G. K. Hall, 1977), xiii; Cindy Weinstein, "How Many Others are There in the Other Half?" *Nineteenth-Century Contexts*, 24, no. 2 (2002): 195–216.
239   However, it has been lost: See, for example Riis, *How the Other Half Lives*, 104–5 and 109–10. For Riis's positive descriptions of: Italians, ibid., 53; Germans, 27; Chinese, 102.
240   "a story of thousands": ibid., 160.
240   "it is better that I": ibid., 171.
240   "with a husband sick to death": ibid., 173.
240   "One free excursion": ibid., 177.
242   "A great many books come": *Silver Cross*, January 1891.
242   "is a volume": *Epoch*, January 1891.
242   "written a powerful book": *New York Times*, January 4, 1891.
242   "such a study": *The Dial*, April 1891.
242   "His book": *The Critic*, December 27, 1890.

17: BROTHERS

245   In an article Riis: Riis, "Red Tape Extravagance," *Mercury*, April 6, 1884.
245   "When I joined the Police": Theodore Roosevelt to Riis, October 25, 1897. The Theodore Roosevelt Papers, Library of Congress.
247   "He and I looked": Theodore Roosevelt, *An Autobiography* (New York: Da Capo, 1985), 178.
248   " 'Theodore Roosevelt is the man' ": Lincoln Steffens, *The Autobiography of Lincoln Steffens* (New York: Harcourt, Brace and Company, 1931), 257–58.
248   " 'Hello, Jake' ": ibid.
249   One of Roosevelt's first: "Farewell to Williams," *New York Times*, May 28, 1895; Riis, *Theodore Roosevelt: The Citizen*, 130.
249   "It will break you": Riis, *Theodore Roosevelt: The Citizen*, 130.
250   "At 2:00 AM": Riis and Roosevelt's nightly spy mission, "Police Caught Napping. President Theodore Roosevelt Makes an Early Morning Tour," *New York Times*, June 8, 1895; "Roosevelt Out Incognito," *New York World*, June 8, 1895.
251   "It was raining outside": Riis, *The Making of an American*, 259.
253   "Roosevelt wanted to": Riis, *Theodore Roosevelt: The Citizen*, 144.
253   "I used to": Roosevelt, *An Autobiography*, 172.
254   The lawsuits: "Rear Tenements Must Go. Board of Health to Begin Condemnation Proceedings Soon," *New York Times*, June 23, 1896.
255   "Directly or indirectly" Riis, *The Making of an American*, 349.
255   Thousands of New Yorkers: It was Sunday, June 16, 1897. *New York Times*, June 16, 1897. Ware, *Jacob A. Riis*, 159.
255   "Sweet Rosie O'Grady": ibid.

18: THE GOLDEN YEARS

257 "golden years": Riis, *The Making of an American*, 304.

257 Nellie Bly, of the: Burrows and Wallace, *Gotham*, 1152–53.

257 Heading into the: For a good introduction to muckraking, see Lila Weinberg, *The Muckrakers* (New York: Simon & Schuster, 1961).

258 Born into privilege: Biographical sketch of Steffens based on Steffens, *The Autobiography*.

258 "By now": ibid., 169.

259 "I was awed": ibid., 173.

261 the good government movement: Burrows and Wallace, *Gotham*, 1193ff.

261 Riis played a significant: Riis, *The Making of an American*, 344.

263 Settlement houses opened: Allen F. Davis, *Spearheads for Reform: The Social Settlements and the Progressive Movement* (New York: Oxford University Press, 1968), 3ff.

263 "The deadly certainty": Riis to Richard Gilder, January 12, 1897, quoted from Ware, *Jacob A. Riis*, 152.

263 "the Old Chief": Riis, *The Making of an American*, 372.

263 Still, it was not nearly: Riis's income and expenses are listed in his pocket books from the 1890s. Papers of Jacob A. Riis, Library of Congress.

263 Riis supplemented: Ware, *Jacob A. Riis*, 81.

264 Max Fischel, in his mid-twenties: For biographical information on Fischel, see obituary, *New York Times*, March 25, 1939; Steffens, *The Autobiography of Lincoln Steffens*, 203–4.

265 Middle-aged, with graying: Steffens, *The Autobiography of Lincoln Steffens*, 203; see also Roger Tracey's unpublished biographical sketch in the Papers of Jacob A. Riis, Library of Congress.

266 "SOME THINGS WE DRINK": The series of articles in the *Evening Sun* on Croton water sewage ran from August 1 to September 21, 1891. Newspaper clippings, Riis's scrapbook. Papers of Jacob A. Riis, Library of Congress.

266 "It cost millions of": Riis, *The Making of an American*, 230.

266 "Our life is like a romance": Riis to Emma Reinsholm, January 1, 1895. Danish Emigration Archives.

267 In a letter: ibid.

267 "You had better not": Ware, *Jacob A. Riis*, 118.

267 "one pigeon": ibid., 121.

267 "The Yule was": ibid., 119.

268 Riis paid a visit to: ibid., 96, and Susanne Benthien, "Jacob A. Riis og Ribe," *Historisk Samfund for Ribe Amt* 27 (1996–98).

269 Riis's strongest memory: Benthien, "Jacob A. Riis og Ribe."

19: THE MAKING OF AN AMERICAN

272 their bond was reinforced: Kathleen Dalton, *Theodore Roosevelt: A Strenuous Life* (New York: Alfred A. Knopf, 2002), 152ff.

272 "Dear Jake": letter in the Papers of Jacob A. Riis, Library of Congress.

272 "When are you going": Roosevelt to Riis, November 1, 1901. The Theodore Roosevelt Papers, Library of Congress.

272 "I should like to go": Roosevelt to Riis, May 2, 1900. The Theodore Roosevelt Papers, Library of Congress.

272 "I would like": Roosevelt to Riis, March 18, 1902. The Roosevelt Papers, Library of Congress.

273   Riis was flattered: Lane, *Jacob A. Riis and the American City*, 167.

273   Riis never hesitated: ibid., 130, 167, and 174.

273   "Jacob Riis is New York's": The original document is held in the Danish Emigration Archives, Aalborg.

273   "The crowd felt": *Brooklyn Daily Eagle*, September 8, 1903. See also *New York Times*, September 9, 1903.

274   "Dear Jake": Roosevelt to Riis, January 9, 1904. The Theodore Roosevelt Papers, Library of Congress.

274   "Let us send her": J. Owre Riis, Epilogue, *The Making of an American*.

274   so surely it could not: *Nordlyset* (a Danish newspaper in Brooklyn), February 24, 1903.

275   "Dearest Lamb": Jacob-Elisabeth correspondence, Papers of Jacob A. Riis, Library of Congress.

275   "Isn't our style": Lane, *Jacob A. Riis and the American City*, 146.

276   Riis's condition improved: Roger Tracey's unpublished biographical sketch.

276   They received fine: Riis, *The Making of an American*, 309.

276   "Strange to say": ibid., 153ff.

276   Readers from New York to California: Riis to Emma Reinsholm, March 18, 1906. Danish Emigration Archives, Aalborg.

277   The day began with a: *Silver Cross*, April 1901.

277   "Little White House": *Brooklyn Eagle*, March 6, 1901.

278   "Darling John!": Elisabeth to John, March 10, 1905. Papers of Jacob A. Riis, Library of Congress.

278   "O pray for us": J. Owre Riis, Epilogue, *The Making of an American*; Ware, *Jacob A. Riis*, 235.

278   "The lamb is dead": Riis's pocket diary. Papers of Jacob A. Riis, Library of Congress.

278   "Beloved Friend": Roosevelt to Riis, May 18, 1905. The Theodore Roosevelt Papers, Library of Congress.

279   and losing faith: Lane, *Jacob A. Riis and the American City*, 179.

280   "he would have to marry": Roger Tracey's unpublished biographical sketch.

280   "I really did not love": J. Owre Riis, Epilogue, *The Making of an American*.

282   "Mr. Jacob Riis and wife": Benthien, "Jacob A. Riis og Ribe."

283   "I sincerely doubt I will": Riis to Emma Reinsholm, March 5, 1913. Papers of Jacob A. Riis, Library of Congress.

283   In his old age: Riis's life in Barre is based on J. Owre Riis, Epilogue, *The Making of An American*, and Riis, "Our Happy Valley," *The Craftsman*, November 1913.

285   Riis was buried: *New York Times*, May 29, 1914; *Worcester Gazette*, June 5, 1914; Ed Riis to John Riis, May 31, 1914, Papers of Jacob A. Riis, Library of Congress.

EPILOGUE

286   Ten years after: Alland and the discovery of Riis the photographer draws from Alexander Alland Sr., *Jacob A. Riis. Photographer & Citizen* (New York: Aperture, 1974) and Bonnie Yochelsen, *Jacob Riis* (London: Phaidon Press, 2001).

SELECTED BIBLIOGRAPHY

Ackerman, Kenneth D. *Boss Tweed: The Rise and Fall of the Corrupt Pol Who Conceived the Soul of Modern New York*. New York: Carroll & Graf, 2005.

Asbury, Herbert. *Gangs of New York*. New York: Alfred A. Knopf, 1927.

Alland, Alexander. *Jacob A. Riis: Photographer & Citizen*. New York: Aperture, 1974.

Anbinder, Tyler. *Five Points: The 19th-Century New York City Neighborhood That Invented Tap Dance, Stole Elections, and Became the World's Most Notorious Slum*. New York: Free Press, 2001.

Bencard, Mogens. *Ribe i tusind år*. Ribe: Bygd, 1978.

Black, Mary. *Old New York in Early Photographs: 196 Prints, 1853–1901, from the Collection of the New-York Historical Society*. New York: Dover, 1973.

Brace, Charles Loring. *The Dangerous Classes*. New York: Wynkoop & Hallenbeck, 1872.

Brands, H. W. *The Reckless Decade: America in the 1890s*. New York: St. Martin's Press, 1995.

Bremner, Robert H. *From the Depths: The Discovery of Poverty*. New York: New York University Press, 1956.

———. *American Philanthropy*. Chicago: University of Chicago Press, 1960.

Bruce, Robert V. *1877: Year of Violence*, Indianapolis: Bobbs-Merrill Company, 1959.

Burns, Ric, and James Sanders. *New York: An Illustrated History*. New York: Alfred A. Knopf, 1999.

Burrows, Edwin, and Mike Wallace. *Gotham. A History of New York City to 1898*. New York: Oxford University Press, 1999.

Campbell, Helen. *Darkness and Daylight: or, Lights and Shadows of New York Life. A Woman's Pictorial Record of Gospel, Temperance, Mission, and Rescue Work*. Hartford, CT: Hartford Publishing Company, 1897.

Carlebach, Michael. *The Origins of Photojournalism in America*. Washington: Smithsonian Institution Press, 1992.

Cashman, Sean Dennis. *America in the Gilded Age: From the Death of Lincoln to the Rise of Theodore Roosevelt*. New York: New York University Press, 1993.

Cooper, John Milton Jr. *The Warrior and the Priest: Woodrow Wilson and Theodore Roosevelt*. Cambridge: Harvard University Press, 1983.

Crane, Stephen. *Maggie: A Girl of the Streets*. New York: D. Appleton and Company, 1896.

Czitrom, Daniel. *Media and the American Mind: From Morse to McLuhan*. Chapel Hill: University of North Carolina Press, 1982.

Dalton, Kathleen. *Theodore Roosevelt: A Strenuous Life*. New York: Alfred A. Knopf, 2002.

Davis, Allen F. *American Heroine: The Life and Legend of Jane Addams*. New York: Oxford University Press, 1973.

――――. *Spearheads for Reform: The Social Settlements and the Progressive Movement*. New York: Oxford University Press, 1968.

Dickens, Charles. *American Notes*. New York: Harper, 1842.

Duffy, John. *A History of Public Health in New York City, 1866–1966*. New York: Russell Sage Foundation, 1974.

Duncan, Bingham: *Whitelaw Reid: Journalist,. Politician, Diplomat*. Athens: University of Georgia Press, 1975.

Fried, Lewis, and John Fierst. *Jacob A. Riis: A Reference Guide*. Boston: G. K. Hall, 1977.

Friis, Torsten. *Forsvaret af Ribe og togtet mod Tønder 1848*. Ribe: Forlaget Liljebjerget, 1998.

Gandal, Keith. *The Virtues of the Vicious: Jacob Riis, Stephen Crane, and the Spectacle of the Slum*. New York: Oxford University Press, 1997.

George, Henry: *Progress and Poverty*. William Reeves, 1883.

Gilfoyle, Timothy. *City of Eros: New York City, Prostitution, and the Commercialization of Sex, 1790–1920*. New York: W. W. Norton, 1992.

Gordon, John Steele. *The Great Game: The Emergence of Wall Street as a World Power, 1653-2000*. New York: Simon & Schuster, 2000.

Guttchen, Robert. *Felix Adler*. New York: Twayne, 1973.

Hassner, Rune. *Jacob A. Riis. Reporter med kamera i New Yorks slum*. Stockholm: K. Bogtryckeriet P.A. Norstedt & söner, 1970.

Hofstader, Richard. *The Age of Reform*. New York: Vintage, 1955.

Homberger, Eric. *The Historical Atlas of New York City*. New York: Henry Holt and Company, 1994.

Hvidt, Kristian. *Flugten til Amerika eller Drivkræfterne I masseudvandringen fra Danmark, 1868–1914*. København: Gyldendal, 1971.

――――. *Gyldendal og Politikens Danmarkshistorie, 1850–1900*. København: Gyldendal and Politikens Forlag, 1990.

Hunter, Robert. *Poverty*. New York: Macmillan, 1904.

Jackson, Kenneth T., ed. *The Encyclopedia of New York*. New Haven: Yale University Press, 1995.

Jeffers, Paul H. *Commissioner Roosevelt: The Story of Theodore Roosevelt and the New York City Police, 1895*. New York: John Wiley and Sons, 1994.

Jeppesen, Torben Grøngaard. *Danskere i USA 1850–2000—en demografisk, social og kulturgeografisk undersøgelse af de danske immigranter og deres efterkommere*. Odense: Odense Bys Museer, 2005.

Johnson, Marilynn S. *Street Justice: A History of Police Violence in New York City*. Boston: Beacon Press, 2003.

Kaplan, Justin. *Lincoln Steffens: A Biography*. New York: Simon & Schuster, 1974.

Katz, Michael B. *A Social History of Welfare in America: In the Shadow of the Poorhouse*. New York: Basic Books, 1996.

King, Moses. *King's Handbook of New York City, 1892: An Outline History & Description of the American Metropolis*. Boston, 1892.

Kluger, Richard. *The Paper: The Life and Death of the New York Herald*. New York: Alfred A. Knopf, 1986.

Lane, James B. *Jacob A. Riis and the American City*. Port Washington: Kennikat Press, 1974.

Larsen, Birgit Flemming, ed.. *Danish Emigration to the U.S.A.* Aalborg: Danish World Wide Archives, 1992.

———. *On Distant Shores*. Aalborg: Danish World Wide Archives, 1993.

Lubove, Roy. *The Progressives and the Slum: Tenement House Reform in New York City, 1890–1917*. Pittsburgh: University of Pittsbrugh Press, 1962.

Mandelbaum, Seymour. *Boss Tweed's New York*. New York: John Wiley and Sons, 1965.

McCabe, James Jr. *Lights and Shadows of New York Life; or, the Sights and Sensations of the Great City*. Philadelphia, Chicago: National Publishing Company, 1872.

McCullough, David. *The Great Bridge: The Epic Story of the Building of the Brooklyn Bridge*. New York: Simon & Schuster, 1972,

———. *Mornings on Horseback: The Story of an Extraordinary Family, a Vanished Way of Life, and the Unique Child Who Became Theodore Roosevelt*. New York: Simon & Schuster, 1981.

McGerr, Michael. *A Fierce Discontent: The Rise and Fall of the Progressive Movement in America, 1870–1920*. New York: Free Press, 2003.

Meyer, Edith Patterson. *"Not Charity, but Justice": The Story of Jacob A. Riis, the Man Who Battled for a Better America*. New York: The Vanguard Press, 1974

Morris, Edmund. *The Rise of Theodore Roosevelt*. New York: Random House, 1979.

Mott, Frank Luther. *American Journalism: a History of Newspapers in the United States Through 260 Years: 1690 to 1950*. New York: Macmillan, 1950.

Phillips, Kevin. *Wealth and Democracy: A Political History of the American Rich*. New York: Broadway Books, 2002.

Plunz, Richard. *A History of Housing in New York City*. New York: Columbia Univeristy Press, 1990.

Riis, Jacob A. *How the Other Half Lives*. New York: Scribner and Sons, 1890.

———. *Nisby's Christmas*. New York: Scribner and Sons, 1893.

———. *Out of Mulberry Street: Stories of Tenement Life in New York City*. New York: The Century Co., 1898.

———. *The Making of an American*. New York: Macmillan, 1901.

———. *The Battle with the Slum*. New York: Macmillan, 1902.

———. *The Peril and Preservation of the Home*. New York: Young People's Missionary Movement, 1903.

———. *Theodore Roosevelt the Citizen*. New York: Macmillan, 1904.

———. *Is There a Santa Claus?* New York: Macmillan, 1904.

———. *The Old Town*. New York: Macmillan, 1909.

———. *Hero-Tales of the Far-North*. New York: Macmillan, 1910.

Roosevelt, Theodore. *An Autobiography*. New York: Macmillan, 1913.

Sante, Luc. *Low Life*. New York: Farrar, Straus and Giroux, 1991.

Sinclair, Upton. *The Jungle*. New York: Doubleday, Page & Co., 1906.

Sloat, Warren. *A Battle for the Soul of New York: Tammany Hall, Police Corruption, Vice, and Reverend Charles Parkhurst's Crusade Against Them, 1892–1895*. New York: Cooper Square Press, 2002.

Stange, Maren. *Symbols of Ideal Life: Social Documentary Photography in America, 1890–1950*. Cambridge: Cambridge University Press, 1989.

Steffens, Lincoln. *The Autobiography of Lincoln Steffens*. New York: Harcourt, Brace and Company, 1931.

Stilling, Niels Peter, and Anne Lisbeth Olsen. *A New Life: Danish Emigration to North America as Described by the Emigrants Themselves in Letters, 1842–1946*. Aalborg: Danish World Wide Archives, 1994.

Stone, Candace. *Dana and the Sun*. New York: Dodd, Mead, 1938.

Swanberg, W. A.: *Pulitzer*. New York: Scribner, 1967.

Trachtenberg, Alan. *The Incorporation of America: Culture & Society in the Gilded Age*. New York: Hill and Wang, 1982.

Trager, James. *The New York Chronology: The Ultimate Compendium of Events, People, and Anecdotes from the Dutch to the Present*. New York: HarperResource, 2003.

Trattner, Walter I. *From Poor Law to Welfare State: A History of Social Welfare in America*. New York: Free Press, 1974.

Walling, George W. *Recollections of a New York Chief of Police*. New York: Caxton Book Concern, 1887.

Ware, Louise. *Jacob A. Riis; Police Reporter, Reformer, Useful Citizen*. New York, London: D. Appleton-Century, 1938.

Waugh, Joan. *An Unsentimental Reformer: Josephine Shaw Lowell*. Cambridge: Harvard University Press, 1997.

Yochelson, Bonnie. *Jacob Riis*. London: Phaidon Press, 2001.

✦═ ACKNOWLEDGMENTS ═✦

T HIS BIOGRAPHY is by no means the work of just one person; it has taken a village—an entire town, in fact. Jacob Riis's hometown, Ribe, has been wonderfully accommodating; first, while I did my research, and later, by throwing me a party to celebrate the publication of the Danish edition. I have spent days—and sometimes nights—working in the local archives and the library of Ribe (I was given the key to the local archives two summers in a row and allowed to come and go as I pleased); I have time and again discussed Riis's childhood with many dedicated and insightful local historians, and a great number of Ripensers have taken me on tours through this medieval town, which lies in the starkly beautiful marshlands of western Denmark.

There are so many to thank in Ribe that I will simply list them in alphabetical order:

Sanne Andersen, Susanne Benthien, Bente and Torben Bramming, Peter Brun, Bente Brund, Lise Frederiksen, Thorkil Funder, John Garp, Birthe Hald, Esther Hansen, Arne Johansen, Bente Kann, Jakob Kieffer-Olsen, Gitte Klinge, Birte Larsen, Louis Lund, Karen Margrethe Melbye, Klaus Melbye, Mogens Melbye, Søren Mulvad, Inge Mørch, Poul Anker Nielsen, Signe Philip, Hanne Skibdal Poulsen, Else Marie Rasmussen, Preben Rudienggard, Vibeke Thiim Sørensen, Karen Villadsen.

I also owe a lot to the city of New York. For over a decade, I called myself a New Yorker. It is easy to feel at home there. I met many bright and caring people, all of whom offered support while I worked on the book: Amy Azzarito, Mark Anselme, Donald Atrium, Carl Ballenas, Tom Bender, Frank and Joen Boccio, Wink, Fred and Craig Bruning, Brian Chan, Al Clarke, Caleb Crain, Joe DiRaimo, Lawrence Downes, Shelley Emling, Pat and Richard Fernandez, Diana and Jeff Frank, Paul Freedman, Wayne Furman, Kathy Goodrich, Maria and Kevin Graziano, Flemming Heilmann, Yo Yo Johnson, Jim Kindall, Irene Krarup, Don and Maria Kiley, Poul Hans Lange, Pamela Leo, Tom and Liz Mozer, Bill Newlyn, Scott Norvell, Caryl Philips, Pat and Joel Rose, Jonalyn Shuon, Corinne VanHouten, Paul and Carol Vitello, Bonnie Yochelson.

I am inestimably grateful for the help and inspiration provided by Peter Gay, who believed in me even though I was a completely unknown writer; my colleagues at the Cullman Center for Writers and Scholars at the New York Public Library, where the fellowship that I was awarded made it possible for me to focus most of my time on writing and research, and in particular Stacy Schiff, who kept encouraging me even after having read my first unedited and, I am sure, rather dreadful chapter; and my most wonderful and visionary editor, Robert Weil, without whose skill and patience *The Other Half* would never have made it to American bookshelves. It has been a privilege to work with him and his team at Norton. A special thanks to the amazingly skilled Janet Byrne and to the always patient and courteous Lucas Wittmann.

I would also like to give special thanks to Christina Frost Hartwig, who provided tremendous support and help to the translator, and Mary Kalb, for caring and careful proofreading.

I am also indebted to Riis's living relatives, who have shown genuine interest and assisted me significantly in my research: Lela Riis Usry Agnew and Lela's husband, David Agnew, Martha (Mimi) Riis Moore, Jim and John Moore.

Thanks also to the staff of the New York Public Library, who, time and again, retrieved obscure archival material that I thought impossible to track down.

Thanks of course also to these great and encouraging friends: Peter Christensen, Knud Møller, Dan Folke Pedersen, Anita Plesner, Johannes Riis, Lars Ringhof.

Finally, I would like to thank my family: my wife, for kindly offering to translate the book—I know it was not the easiest of favors; my children, for their patience with, and interest in, the project; my parents and parents-in law, for helping out whenever my wife and I needed to absent ourselves to write and translate.

My debt to all mentioned is immense. Thank you!

Ribe, Denmark
March 2008

CREDITS

Page 4: Courtesy of the Museum of the City of New York / The Jacob A. Riis Collection
Page 5: Courtesy of the Museum of the City of New York / The Jacob A. Riis Collection
Page 6: Courtesy of the Museum of the City of New York / The Jacob A. Riis Collection
Page 7: Courtesy of the Museum of the City of New York / The Jacob A. Riis Collection
Page 8: Courtesy of the Museum of the City of New York / The Jacob A. Riis Collection
Page 9: Courtesy of the Museum of the City of New York / The Jacob A. Riis Collection
Page 10: Courtesy of the Museum of the City of New York / The Jacob A. Riis Collection
Page 11: Courtesy of the Museum of the City of New York / The Jacob A. Riis Collection
Page 12: Courtesy of the Museum of the City of New York / The Jacob A. Riis Collection
Page 13: Courtesy of the Museum of the City of New York / The Jacob A. Riis Collection
Page 14: Courtesy of the Museum of the City of New York / The Jacob A. Riis Collection
Page 15: Courtesy of the Museum of the City of New York / The Jacob A. Riis Collection
Page 16: Courtesy of the Museum of the City of New York / The Jacob A. Riis Collection

SECOND INSERT

Page 1: Courtesy of the Museum of the City of New York / The Jacob A. Riis Collection
Page 2: Courtesy of the Museum of the City of New York / The Jacob A. Riis Collection
Page 3: Courtesy of the Museum of the City of New York / The Jacob A. Riis Collection
Page 4: Courtesy of the Museum of the City of New York / The Jacob A. Riis Collection
Page 5: Courtesy of the Museum of the City of New York / The Jacob A. Riis Collection
Page 6: Courtesy of the Museum of the City of New York / The Jacob A. Riis Collection
Page 7: Courtesy of the Museum of the City of New York / The Jacob A. Riis Collection
Page 8: Courtesy of the Museum of the City of New York / The Jacob A. Riis Collection
Page 9: Courtesy of the Museum of the City of New York / The Jacob A. Riis Collection
Page 10: Courtesy of the Museum of the City of New York / The Jacob A. Riis Collection
Page 11: Courtesy of the Museum of the City of New York / The Jacob A. Riis Collection
Page 12: Courtesy of the Museum of the City of New York / The Jacob A. Riis Collection
Page 13: Courtesy of the Museum of the City of New York / The Jacob A. Riis Collection
Page 14: Courtesy of the Museum of the City of New York / The Jacob A. Riis Collection
Page 15: Courtesy of the Museum of the City of New York / The Jacob A. Riis Collection
Page 16: Courtesy of the City of Ribe Archives

✺ INDEX ✺

Bederfen, Otto, 37
Beecher, Henry Ward, 110, 156
Beissenhertz, Elisabeth Titusine von, 37
Bellevue Hospital, 190
Bendtsen, Christine, 41, 42, 90, 106,
    107, 111, 112
Bennett, James Gordon, 133
Berlingske Tidende, 89
"big business," 48
Bine, Aunt, 108, 111
"Black Marias," 145
Blackwell's Island, 165
Blind Man's Alley, 215, 233
Blizzard of 1888 (Great White Hurri-
    cane), 219-20, 221
"bloody summer," 129
Bly, Nellie, 257
Board of Commissioners, 248
Booth, William, 242
Bowery, 174, 262
Brace, Charles Loring, 192-93, 241
Brady, Mathew, 216
Brady's Bend, Pa., 55-56
Broadway, 54
Broadway Tabernacle, 221, 230
Brooklyn, N.Y., 53, 121, 125-28,
    156-58, 220, 231
    cost of living in, 159
    growth of, 124
    Riis's household in, 125-27
Brooklyn Bridge, 124, 179, 232
Brooklyn Daily Eagle, 273, 277
Buffalo, N.Y., 57, 72-73, 75-79,
    129
Buffalo Courier, 79
Buffalo Express, 79
Bukdahl, Jørgen, 13
Bull Moose Party, 284
Bulow, Pastor, 111
Bunker Hill, 65
Bunyan, John, 257-58
Burrows, Edwin, 64
Byrnes, Thomas F., 146-48, 168,
    249-50, 259-60

Camden, N.J., 69
Carnegie, Andrew, 48
"Castle, The," 35-36, 43, 57, 89, 121,
    122, 123, 268
Castle Garden, 52, 54, 55, 63, 155, 156
Central Park, 52, 226
Century Magazine, 222, 232, 234, 261,
    263, 273
charity, charitable organizations, 185,
    189-92, 221, 252, 253, 285
Charity Organization Society (COS),
    190, 191, 192
Cherry Street, 232-33, 234, 237
Chicago, Ill., 91-93
Chicago Tribune, 6
Children of the Poor, The (Riis), 276
Children's Aid Society (CAS), 189,
    192-93, 226
Chinatown, 176, 262
Christensen, C. T., 181
Christian IV, King of Denmark, 35-36
Christian IX, King of Denmark, 6,
    40-41, 42, 282
Church of the Resurrection, 230, 283
Circle of the King's Daughters, The,
    261-62
Civil Service Commission, 248
Civil War, U.S., 47, 48, 99, 128, 134,
    135, 136, 162, 190, 200, 216
Clarenceville, N.Y., 180
Clausen, H. V., 16
Cleveland, Grover, 247
Coit, Stanton, 262
Cold, Mathilde, 16
Columbia Law School, 246
Columbia University, 194
Columbus Park, *see* Mulberry Bend
    Park
Commission for the Advancement of
    the Gospel Among Danes in
    Noth America, 155
Committee of Seventy, 261
Committee on the Elevation of the Poor
    in Their Homes, 189-90

Shanks, William Franklin Gore, 133,
136–37, 139–40, 142, 144, 171,
176, 183
Shaw, Robert Gould, 190
Sheepshead Bay, 139, 144
Silver Cross, 242
Simmons, Ichabod, 110, 156
Sinclair, Upton, 260
slumlords, 196, 197, 240
slums:
child abuse in, 239
culture and commerce in, 174
daily life in, 173–74
description of family life in, 234
despair in, 240
Dickens's description of, 65
diseases in, 67, 164, 234
in hot summer days, 161–62
income levels in, 159
lack of educational opportunities in,
159
New York Times description of, 66–67
organized crime in, 174–75
overcrowding and filth in, 64–65,
163–64, 197–98
portion of city population living in, 4,
8, 234
prostitution in, 239
Riis's exposure to, 4–5, 67, 102,
150–52, 161–76, 195, 204, 235,
238, 250–51, 265
Riis's photographic record of,
209–13, 214
settlement houses in, 262, 263
"slumming stories" written about, 171
suicide rates in, 164
see also tenements
Smith, Alva, 186
social Darwinism, 48, 185
social reform, 5, 183, 189–95, 255, 257,
261–62
Society for Prevention of Cruelty to
Children, 189
Society of Photographers (Berlin), 207

Sønderballe, Denmark, 89
soup kitchens, 191
South Brooklyn News, 102–3, 108, 109,
110, 121, 124, 126, 133, 156,
181, 279
Spanish-American War, 271–72
Splid, Maren, 14
Spuyten Duyvil Creek, 53
Standard Oil, 260
Stanley, Henry Morton, 133–34, 257
State Charities Aid Association (SCAA),
189, 190
Staten Island, N.Y., 53, 155
Steers, Henry, 150
Steffens, Lincoln, 248–49, 255, 258–60,
264
Stewart, Alexander T., 141–42, 145
Støcken, Frederik H. von, 24, 35
Strong, Josiah, 229, 230
Strong, William, 248, 261
Struggle for Self-Government, The (Stef-
fens), 258
*Suicides in New York City During the
11 Years Ending Dec. 31, 1880*
(Nagle), 200
Swedish wars, 14

Tabb, John, 225
Talmage, T. V., 107, 108, 109
Tammany Hall, 137, 189, 261
Tarbell, Ida, 258, 260
Tenderloin, 147, 175
Tenement Club, 261
Tenement-House Committee, *see* Drexel
Committee
tenements:
clean-up efforts in, 195
crime in, 236
daily life in, 173–74
demolition of, 253–54
description of conditions in, 66–67,
150–52, 162, 198, 233, 234
disease epidemics in, 195–96, 236,
237

ABOUT THE AUTHOR

AN ACCLAIMED journalist and historian, Tom Buk-Swienty was a Fellow at the Cullman Center for Scholars and Writers at the New York Public Library, 2002–2003, where he did much of the research for this book. He first published *The Other Half* to great acclaim in his native Denmark, where it became a national bestseller. He divides his time between writing nonfiction books and teaching narrative journalism at the Department for Journalism at the University of Southern Denmark, where he is the department chair for the graduate program at the Journalism School.

For ten years Buk-Swienty was the American bureau chief for the Danish newsweekly *Weekendavisen*. Based at that time in New York, he covered three U. S. presidential elections (1996, 2000, and 2004), crisscrossed the country numerous times, and wrote extensively on the American psyche for a wide Danish audience. His Danish bestseller *AmerikaMaxima* appeared in 1999.

Buk-Swienty is now at work on a biography of the Danish nuclear physicist Niels Bohr. He lives with his family in the town where Jacob Riis was born, Ribe, Denmark.